Hello! 365 Basil Recipes

(Basil Recipes - Volume 1)

Best Basil Cookbook Ever For Beginners

Ms. Ibarra

Ms. Ingredient

Content

Introduction

***

Why I Love Cooking

Hi all,

Welcome to MrandMsCooking.com—a website created by a community of cooking enthusiasts with the goal of providing books for novice cooks featuring the best recipes, at the most affordable prices, and valuable gifts.

Before we go to the recipes in the book "Hello! 365 Basil Recipes", I have an interesting story to share with you the reason for loving cooking.

My mom would always tell me:

Cooking is an edible form of love…

As a young kid, I helped my mom cook. She would always cook any dish I liked. Observing how she cooked motivated me to try cooking. Ten years later, I'm sharing with you my cooking inspiration as well as the reasons why I love it.

1.   Trying something different

Various cuisines of the world use different kinds of ingredients. You can download and share a lot of recipes on the internet. Even so, you can add your own unique twists to recipes and experiment with various versions and styles.

Trying out new recipes and ingredients isn't bad when cooking, as long as you produce something edible…

2.   Enjoyment

Whomever you cook for— family, friends, or even yourself—you'll surely have fun doing it. It's satisfying to see how the combination of various spices, meat, and vegetables yield an awesome flavor. From cutting to cooking them, the whole process is nothing but pure joy.

3.   Receiving wonderful feedback

Don't you get a sense of pride, joy, and accomplishment when people love the dish you've cooked and let you know their thoughts? You'll definitely savor the moment when you hear someone praise your cooking skills.

Each time someone tells me, "This has a great flavor" or "This is insanely delicious!" I get more motivated to become a better cook…

4.   Healthy eating

Rather than consuming processed food, using fresh ingredients for your dishes makes them good for the body. Cook your own meals so that you can add more fresh vegetables and fruits to your diet. Cooking also allows you to discover more about the different nutrients in your meals.

Because you prepare your meals yourself, having digestive problems will be the least of your worries…

5.   Therapeutic activity

Based on my experience, cooking calms the mind. Finding food in the fridge, gathering the ingredients, getting them ready, and assembling everything together to create a yummy dish are more relaxing than just spending idle time on the couch watching TV. Cooking never makes me stressed.

My mother would always tell me: Cooking is an edible way to make your loved ones feel loved…

Keeping Up Your Passion for Cooking

Cooking is not for everyone. But people who are passionate about cooking and their families are fortunate indeed. It spreads happiness around. Do you love cooking? Sustain your passion—it's the best feeling ever!

When combined with love, cooking feeds the soul…

From my unending love for cooking, I'm creating this book series and hoping to share my passion with all of you. With my many experiences of failures, I have created this book series and hopefully it helps you. This Ingredient Recipes Series covers these subjects:

- Cheese Recipes
- Butter Recipes
- Red Wine Recipes
- Cajun Spice Recipes
- Mayonnaise Recipes
- ...

I really appreciate that you have selected "Hello! 365 Basil Recipes" and for reading to the end. I anticipate that this book shall give you the source of strength during the times that you are really exhausted, as well as be your best friend in the comforts of your own home. Please also give me some love by sharing your own exciting cooking time in the comments segment below.

List of Abbreviations

LIST OF ABBREVIATIONS	
tbsp(s).	tablespoon(s)
tsp(s).	teaspoon(s)
c.	cup(s)
oz.	ounce(s)
lb(s).	pound(s)

365 Amazing Basil Recipes

***

1. 20-minute Basil, Chicken & Tomato Rice

"Basil adds flavor to this dish."
Serving: 4 | Prep: 10m | Ready in: 31m

Ingredients

- 2 tbsps. extra virgin olive oil
- 1 lb. chicken tenders, cut into strips
- 1 cup chopped onions
- 1 cup sliced red pepper (1/4-inch x 1 1/2 inch)
- 1 tsp. minced fresh garlic
- 2 cups water
- 1 (14.5 oz.) can diced tomatoes
- 1 cup UNCLE BEN'S® Flavor Infusions Chicken & Herb Rice
- 1/2 cup chiffonade fresh basil leaves
- 1/4 cup shredded Parmesan cheese

Direction

- In a big skillet, heat olive oil on medium-high heat.
- Put in chicken strips; cook 4-6 minutes until just done.
- Add in fresh garlic, red pepper slices and onion.
- Keep cooking 4-5 minutes, mixing occasionally, till vegetables are barely tender.
- Put in rice, tomatoes and water.

- Put cover on pan and keep cooking until mixture just boils.
- Decrease to medium-low heat; continue to cook 10 minutes till liquid is absorbed and rice is tender.
- Take out cover; mix in Parmesan cheese and basil leaves. Chill the leftovers in the fridge.

Nutrition Information

- Calories: 404 calories;
- Total Carbohydrate: 43.1 g
- Cholesterol: 69 mg
- Total Fat: 11.5 g
- Protein: 31.2 g
- Sodium: 768 mg

2. Alaskan Halibut Caprese

"A low carb halibut recipe that is high in flavor!"
Serving: 4 | Prep: 10m | Ready in: 20m

Ingredients

- nonstick cooking spray
- 4 (4 oz.) fillets halibut
- salt and ground black pepper to taste
- 8 oz. fresh mozzarella cheese, sliced
- 8 large whole basil leaves
- 8 tomato slices
- 3 tbsps. balsamic vinegar
- 1 1/2 tbsps. olive oil
- 1/3 cup chopped fresh basil

Direction

- Preheat an oven to 230°C/450°F. Put oven rack 5-in. away from heat source. Use cooking spray to prep a baking sheet.
- On prepped baking sheet, put halibut. Bake for 4-6 minutes till lightly browned. Flip fillets. Use black pepper and salt to season. Keep cooking for 1-2 more minutes till flesh is opaque.

- Put a slice mozzarella cheese, basil leaf, and tomato slice, in that order over every filet; repeat layers.
- Put halibut into oven. Bake for 2 minutes till cheese starts to melt.
- In a bowl, whisk olive oil and balsamic vinegar. Put on halibut portions. Put chopped basil over; serve.

Nutrition Information

- Calories: 330 calories;
- Total Carbohydrate: 5 g
- Cholesterol: 78 mg
- Total Fat: 16.4 g
- Protein: 38.2 g
- Sodium: 418 mg

3. Alaskan Smoked Salmon Dip

"This dip favorite does not need a cruise line or airfare! This appetizer is packed with flaky smoked salmon and has a mayo-and-cream cheese base. Combine roasted tomatoes with McCormick® Chicken Bruschetta Seasoning Mix and lemon juice for a tangy and flavorful dish. You can serve with crackers or baguette."
Serving: 24 | Prep: 10m | Ready in: 35m

Ingredients

- 1 lb. plum (roma) tomatoes, cut into 1/2-inch pieces
- 2 tbsps. vegetable oil
- 1 (1.25 oz.) package McCormick® Chicken Bruschetta Seasoning Mix, divided
- 1 tbsp. lemon juice
- 3/4 cup coarsely chopped smoked salmon
- 1 (8 oz.) package whipped cream cheese
- 1/2 cup mayonnaise
- 2 tbsps. thinly sliced fresh basil

Direction

- Preheat an oven to 425 degrees F. in a large bowl, combine 1/2 package of the Seasoning Mix, oil and tomatoes. Transfer onto a large, shallow, foil-lined baking pan in single layer.

- Roast for about 25 minutes or until browned on top and the tomatoes become soft. Leave to cool.
- In a large bowl, combine lemon juice and cooled tomatoes. Place in the remaining Seasoning Mix, salmon, mayonnaise, and cream cheese. Mix gently until blended well. Stud with basil. You can serve with crackers or chopped baguette.

Nutrition Information

- Calories: 83 calories;
- Total Carbohydrate: 2.4 g
- Cholesterol: 12 mg
- Total Fat: 7.7 g
- Protein: 1.4 g
- Sodium: 220 mg

4. Allergy-friendly Comfort Soup

"This is latex allergen-free, fish free, dairy-free, nut-free, egg-free and gluten-free soup!"
Serving: 10 | Prep: 30m | Ready in: 1h20m

Ingredients

- 2 tbsps. olive oil
- 2 yams, peeled and cubed
- 1 head cauliflower, cut into large florets
- 1 jalapeno pepper, chopped
- 1 (14 oz.) can coconut milk
- 2 cups water
- 2 cups cannellini beans, drained and rinsed
- 1/4 cup chopped fresh basil
- 1 tbsp. soy sauce
- 1 tsp. dry mustard powder
- 1 tsp. ground coriander
- 1 tsp. smoked paprika
- 1/2 tsp. ground ginger
- 1/2 tsp. ground cardamom
- 1/2 tsp. ground turmeric
- 1 bay leaf
- 1 cinnamon stick
- salt and ground black pepper to taste
- 1/4 cup chopped fresh parsley, or to taste

- 1 tsp. soy sauce
- 1/4 cup crumbled goat cheese

Direction

- In a big skillet, heat oil on medium heat. Stir and cook cubes yams in hot oil for 7-10 minutes till fork-tender. Add diced jalapeno pepper and cauliflower to yams. Cook for 10-15 more minutes till cauliflower starts to soften.
- In a stockpot, mix cannellini beans, water and coconut milk on medium high heat. Mix cinnamon stick, bay leaf, turmeric, cardamom, ground ginger, smoked paprika, coriander, mustard powder, 1 tbsp. soy sauce and basil into bean mixture. Season soup with black pepper and salt. Boil soup. Add yam mixture. Lower heat to low. Simmer for 30-45 minutes till cauliflower is tender. Put parsley on top. Drizzle 1 tsp. soy sauce. Sprinkle goat cheese on. Serve.

Nutrition Information

- Calories: 270 calories;
- Total Carbohydrate: 34.9 g
- Cholesterol: 3 mg
- Total Fat: 12.7 g
- Protein: 6.3 g
- Sodium: 278 mg

5. Amatriciana

"A classic Italian recipe. If it's in season, use fresh basil and if not, use fresh flat-leaf parsley."
Serving: 4 | Prep: 15m | Ready in: 35m

Ingredients

- 4 slices bacon, diced
- 1/2 cup chopped onion
- 1 tsp. minced garlic
- 1/4 tsp. crushed red pepper flakes
- 2 (14.5 oz.) cans stewed tomatoes
- 1 lb. linguine pasta, uncooked
- 1 tbsp. chopped fresh basil

- 2 tbsps. grated Parmesan cheese

Direction

- Cook diced bacon in a big saucepan on medium high heat for 5 minutes till crisp; drain all the drippings from the pan except 2 tbsp.
- Add onions; cook for 3 minutes on medium heat. Mix in red pepper flakes and garlic; cook for 30 seconds. Add undrained canned tomatoes; simmer, breaking tomatoes up, for 10 minutes.
- Meanwhile, cook pasta till al dente in a big pot with 4-qt. of boiling salted water; drain.
- Mix basil into sauce; toss with cooked pasta then serve with grated Parmesan cheese.

Nutrition Information

- Calories: 529 calories;
- Total Carbohydrate: 97.6 g
- Cholesterol: 12 mg
- Total Fat: 7.5 g
- Protein: 21.5 g
- Sodium: 702 mg

6. Angel Hair Pasta And Scallops With Margherita® Prosciutto

"Delicious pasta!"
Serving: 4 | Prep: 20m | Ready in: 35m

Ingredients

- 12 oz. angel hair pasta
- 1 1/2 lbs. fresh scallops
- 1 oz. olive oil
- 8 oz. sliced Margherita® Prosciutto or julienned Margherita® Genoa Salami
- 2 garlic cloves, chopped
- 8 oz. sliced grape tomatoes
- 1 lb. sliced crimini mushrooms
- 1 lb. fresh baby spinach
- 8 fluid oz. dry white wine
- 2 tbsps. fresh lemon juice

- salt and pepper to taste
- 4 oz. cold unsalted butter
- 4 oz. fresh basil

Direction

- Follow package instructions to cook pasta. Cover to keep it warm; put aside.
- Heat a 12-in. sauté pan on medium heat, put in 1 oz. of olive oil. Sear scallops 2 minutes per side; take scallops out of pan and cover.
- To the heated pan, add julienned Genoa Salami or sliced Margherita(R) Prosciutto; sauté 2 minutes. Put in mushrooms, tomatoes, and garlic. Sauté 2 more minutes. Pour in lemon juice and wine; cook until decreased by half by deglazing the pan. Put in pepper and salt. Mix in butter until it melts.
- Bring scallops back to the pan and cook until heated through. Put in fresh spinach; cook till spinach is wilted.
- Add cooked pasta to the pan. Stir until pasta is covered well in sauce.
- Use fresh basil to garnish; serve.

Nutrition Information

- Calories: 895 calories;
- Total Carbohydrate: 59.2 g
- Cholesterol: 176 mg
- Total Fat: 40.7 g
- Protein: 63.8 g
- Sodium: 1831 mg

7. Anne's Fabulous Grilled Salmon

"A recipe for grilled salmon prepared in a picnic every year at the Saint Matthew Parish in Seattle, Washington. Goes well with any slice of salmon for grilling but we usually use salmon fillets. You can use king salmon or wild sockeye."

Serving: 6 | Prep: 15m | Ready in: 1h5m

Ingredients

- 1 tbsp. vegetable oil
- 1 tbsp. soy sauce
- 1 tsp. Worcestershire sauce
- 1 lemon, juiced
- 1/2 tsp. grated fresh ginger root
- 2 tbsps. honey
- 1/3 cup chopped fresh basil leaves
- 1 tbsp. finely chopped shallots
- 1 (3 lb.) salmon fillet, with skin

Direction

- Use aluminum foil to form a pan by doubling up the layers of the foil that are big enough to hold the fillet. Transfer foil onto a cookie sheet. Place fillet on top of the foil skin side down. Mix together ginger, oil, basil, soy sauce, shallots, honey, Worcestershire sauce, and lemon juice in a small bowl. Spread on top of salmon and marinate it for 20 minutes while preheating the grill.
- Preheat the grill on medium-low heat. Slide foil containing the salmon off of cookie sheet and over the grill. Close with a lid and then grill fillet for 20 minutes, ten minutes per inch of thickness. The salmon should flake using a fork but should not be very dry. When serving salmon, the skin should stick onto foil and the grill should remain clean. Cut and scoop the fillet off of the skin with a spatula and serve.

Nutrition Information

- Calories: 432 calories;
- Total Carbohydrate: 8.5 g
- Cholesterol: 154 mg

- Total Fat: 21.8 g
- Protein: 48.9 g
- Sodium: 278 mg

8. Antipasto On A Stick

"Make this ahead of time and impress your party with these appetizers!"
Serving: 8 | Prep: 10m | Ready in: 10m

Ingredients

- 8 slices salami, rolled
- 8 (1/2 inch) cubes mozzarella cheese
- 8 pitted black olives
- 4 grape tomatoes, halved
- 4 marinated artichoke hearts, drained and halved
- 8 leaves fresh basil, rolled
- 8 bamboo toothpicks
- 8 tsps. olive oil

Direction

- Insert a toothpick through the salami roll, mozzarella cheese, olive, tomato, artichoke heart, and basil roll, in order. Place the skewers on a plate. Drizzle each with olive oil. Serve.

Nutrition Information

- Calories: 183 calories;
- Total Carbohydrate: 3.4 g
- Cholesterol: 31 mg
- Total Fat: 15.3 g
- Protein: 8.4 g
- Sodium: 696 mg

9. Arrabbiata Sauce

"This sauce is spicy and satisfying. It is amazing with penne pasta."
Serving: 6 | Prep: 15m | Ready in: 35m

Ingredients

- 1 tsp. olive oil
- 1 cup chopped onion
- 4 cloves garlic, minced
- 3/8 cup red wine
- 1 tbsp. white sugar
- 1 tbsp. chopped fresh basil
- 1 tsp. crushed red pepper flakes
- 2 tbsps. tomato paste
- 1 tbsp. lemon juice
- 1/2 tsp. Italian seasoning
- 1/4 tsp. ground black pepper
- 2 (14.5 oz.) cans peeled and diced tomatoes
- 2 tbsps. chopped fresh parsley

Direction

- In a big saucepan or skillet, heat oil over medium heat, and sauté garlic and onion with oil for 5 minutes.
- Stir in tomatoes, black pepper, Italian seasoning, lemon juice, tomato paste, red pepper, basil, sugar, and wine, and then set to boil. Bring down the heat to medium and simmer, uncovered, for 15 minutes.
- Stir in parsley and ladle over your choice of hot cooked pasta.

Nutrition Information

- Calories: 77 calories;
- Total Carbohydrate: 11.8 g
- Cholesterol: 0 mg
- Total Fat: 1 g
- Protein: 1.9 g
- Sodium: 258 mg

10. Artichoke And Roasted Red Pepper Pasta

"You can use whatever pasta you love to make this quick and tasty dish."
Serving: 4 | Prep: 20m | Ready in: 1h5m

Ingredients

- 1 1/2 cups penne pasta
- 1 (14 oz.) can artichoke hearts in water, drained and diced
- 1/2 cup canned roasted red bell pepper, drained and diced
- 1/3 cup diced onion
- 1/3 cup diced mushrooms
- 5 cloves garlic, mashed
- 2 tbsps. chopped fresh basil
- salt and ground black pepper to taste
- 1/2 cup chicken stock
- 1/2 cup reduced-fat Alfredo sauce
- 1/2 cup reduced-fat cottage cheese

Direction

- Heat the oven to 350°F (175°C).
- In a large pot, bring slightly salted water to a boil. In the boiling water, cook penne pasta in 8 minutes, stirring occasionally, until cooked through but still firm to the bite; drain.
- In a food processor, add basil, garlic, mushrooms, onion, roasted red pepper and artichoke hearts; pulse several times until finely chopped.
- Heat a large skillet over the medium heat. In the hot skillet, cook and stir vegetables from food processor for 15 - 20 minutes, until tender. Add black pepper and salt for seasoning.
- In the pan, pour the chicken stock and bring to a boil while using a wooden spoon to scrape the browned food bits off of the pan bottom. Decrease heat to low. Mix the Alfredo sauce into artichoke mixture.
- In the bottom of a casserole dish, spread cottage cheese; spread the Alfredo sauce mixture over the top of the cottage cheese. Put

in penne pasta and stir. Using aluminum foil to cover casserole dish.
- Bake in the oven for 20 - 30 minutes, until bubbly.

Nutrition Information

- Calories: 462 calories;
- Total Carbohydrate: 78 g
- Cholesterol: 20 mg
- Total Fat: 8.1 g
- Protein: 20.9 g
- Sodium: 904 mg

11. Artichoke Jalapeno Hummus Dip

""Refreshing hummus with a kick of spice.""
Serving: 8 | Prep: 10m | Ready in: 10m

Ingredients

- 1 (15 oz.) can chickpeas, drained
- 2 (6 oz.) jars artichoke hearts, drained
- 1/2 cup Greek yogurt
- 1/2 cup fresh basil
- 1/3 cup pickled jalapeno pepper slices
- 1/4 cup olive oil
- 1 lemon, juiced
- 2 tbsps. hemp seeds
- 2 cloves garlic
- 1 tsp. ground paprika
- 1 tsp. ground cayenne pepper
- 1/2 tsp. curry powder

Direction

- Mix curry powder, cayenne pepper, paprika, garlic, hemp seeds, lemon juice, olive oil, jalapeno pepper slices, Greek yogurt, basil, artichoke hearts, and chickpeas in a food processor. Blend it until it is smooth.

Nutrition Information

- Calories: 160 calories;
- Total Carbohydrate: 14.5 g

- Cholesterol: 3 mg
- Total Fat: 9.6 g
- Protein: 5.1 g
- Sodium: 411 mg

12. Arugula Salad With Avocado Citrus Vinaigrette

"Impress your guests with this easy to make but regal recipe. You can serve it with grilled chicken or salmon for a main dish."
Serving: 4 | Prep: 20m | Ready in: 20m

Ingredients

- 1 avocado - peeled, pitted and diced
- 1/4 cup chopped red onion
- 2 tbsps. fresh lime juice
- 2 tbsps. grapefruit juice
- 2 tbsps. rice wine vinegar
- 1/2 tsp. ground black pepper
- 1/2 tsp. sea salt
- 1/4 cup olive oil
- 1 tbsp. honey
- 3 tbsps. chopped cilantro
- 1 leaf fresh mint, chopped
- 1 leaf fresh basil, chopped
- 2 1/2 cups baby arugula leaves
- 2 oz. kalamata olives, pitted and halved
- 2 oz. cherry tomatoes, halved
- 2 tbsps. freshly shaved Parmesan cheese, or to taste

Direction

- In a blender, process sea salt, avocado, black pepper, red onion, rice wine vinegar, lime juice, and grapefruit juice for half a minute until smooth. While blending, pour in olive oil and add basil leaves, honey, mint, and cilantro. Process for a few seconds more until the herbs resemble just tiny flecks.
- In a salad bowl, stir cherry tomatoes, arugula, and Kalamata olives; add shaved Parmesan cheese on top. Pour in vinaigrette over the salad; mix well. Serve.

Nutrition Information

- Calories: 282 calories;
- Total Carbohydrate: 13.7 g
- Cholesterol: 2 mg
- Total Fat: 25.4 g
- Protein: 2.9 g
- Sodium: 501 mg

13. Arugula Salad With Cannellini Beans

"A delicious and quick warm salad."
Serving: 4 | Prep: 15m | Ready in: 23m

Ingredients

- 2 tbsps. olive oil
- 2 cloves garlic, minced
- 1 (14.5 oz.) can diced tomatoes
- 3 tbsps. white wine
- 1 tsp. dried sage
- 1 tsp. dried thyme
- 1 (15 oz.) can cannellini beans, drained and rinsed
- 2 tbsps. chopped fresh basil
- salt and pepper to taste
- 3 cups arugula
- 1/4 cup shaved Parmesan cheese (optional)

Direction

- In a big skillet, heat olive oil on medium heat. Cook garlic in hot oil for 1 minute. Add thyme, sage, wine and tomatoes. Put heat on medium high. Simmer for 2-3 minutes. Mix basil and cannellini beans in. Season with pepper and salt. Keep cooking for 3-4 minutes till beans heat through.
- On a serving platter, put arugula. Over arugula, spoon bean mixture. Put shaved parmesan cheese on top if you want.

Nutrition Information

- Calories: 466 calories;
- Total Carbohydrate: 71.2 g

- Cholesterol: 4 mg
- Total Fat: 9.5 g
- Protein: 23.1 g
- Sodium: 245 mg

14. Asparagus, Potato, And Onion Frittata

"A great lunch dish!"
Serving: 6 | Prep: 15m | Ready in: 45m

Ingredients

- 2 tbsps. olive oil
- 2 potatoes, shredded
- 1/4 cup chopped onion
- 1/2 tsp. salt
- 1/4 tsp. fresh ground black pepper
- 1 lb. asparagus, trimmed and cut into 2-inch pieces
- 1 cup diced ham
- 6 eggs
- 1 tbsp. milk
- 1/2 cup shredded mozzarella cheese
- 1/2 cup shredded white Cheddar cheese
- 1 tbsp. chopped fresh basil

Direction

- Preheat oven to 175°C/350°F then grease 9x13-inch baking dish.
- Heat olive oil in big skillet on medium heat; mix and cook onion and shredded potato in hot oil for 5 minutes till potatoes start to brown. Season with pepper and salt. Add ham and asparagus; cook for 5-7 minutes till asparagus is tender. Put in the prepared baking dish. In small bowl, whisk milk and eggs; evenly put on dish. Scatter white Cheddar and mozzarella cheese over potato mixture.
- In the preheated oven, bake for 20-25 minutes till middle is set. Use basil to garnish; serve.

Nutrition Information

- Calories: 281 calories;
- Total Carbohydrate: 17.7 g
- Cholesterol: 213 mg
- Total Fat: 16.3 g
- Protein: 17.3 g
- Sodium: 639 mg

15. Aunt Eileen's Stuffed Eggplant

"A culinary delight using fresh eggplant from the garden!"
Serving: 4 | Prep: 20m | Ready in: 1h

Ingredients

- 2 (1 lb.) eggplants
- 2 tbsps. olive oil
- 1 medium onion, chopped
- 3 cloves garlic, minced
- 6 sprigs fresh parsley, chopped
- 1 1/2 cups fresh bread crumbs
- 1/2 cup grated Gruyere cheese
- 2 tbsps. chopped black olives
- 1 tbsp. capers
- 1 lemon, juiced
- 1 tsp. chopped fresh basil
- 1/4 tsp. crushed red pepper flakes
- 1 tsp. salt
- pepper to taste
- 12 slices tomato
- 1/4 cup grated Gruyere cheese
- 4 tbsps. olive oil

Direction

- Heat the oven to 350°F (175°C) beforehand. Halve the eggplant, scoop out the pulp, leaving a half inch shell. Finely chop the flesh.
- In a skillet, heat 2 tbsps. olive oil over medium heat. Cook prepared eggplant for about 60 seconds. Stir in parsley, garlic, and onion, and cook until tender. Transfer the mixture into a large bowl, and stir in lemon juice, capers, chopped olives, 1/2 cup Gruyere, and bread crumbs. Sprinkle pepper, salt, pepper flakes

and basil to season. Stuff into the eggplant shells.

- Add overlapping slices of tomato on top of stuffed eggplants. Evenly sprinkle with the rest of 1/4 cup cheese and drizzle with the rest of 4 tbsps. olive oil. Put on baking sheet.
- Bake in prepared oven for half an hour.

Nutrition Information

- Calories: 418 calories;
- Total Carbohydrate: 34.2 g
- Cholesterol: 22 mg
- Total Fat: 28.9 g
- Protein: 12.5 g
- Sodium: 900 mg

16. Authentic Thai Steak Salad

"An original Thai recipe."
Serving: 6 | Prep: 15m | Ready in: 25m

Ingredients

- 1/2 tsp. ground black pepper
- 1/4 tsp. kosher salt
- 1 (1 1/2-lb.) flank steak
- 1/4 cup fresh lime juice
- 2 tbsps. soy sauce
- 1 tbsp. brown sugar
- 1 tbsp. fish sauce
- 2 tsps. minced garlic
- 1 tsp. chile-garlic sauce (such as Sriracha®)
- 2 heads romaine lettuce
- 1/3 cup fresh mint leaves
- 1/3 cup fresh cilantro leaves
- 1/3 cup fresh Thai basil leaves

Direction

- On medium-high heat, preheat an outdoor grill and oil the grate slightly. Drizzle salt and pepper onto flank steak.
- On preheated grill, cook steak till it reaches desired doneness, about 5-6 minutes on each side. An instant-read thermometer inserted

into the middle registers 60 degrees C (140 degrees F).

- In a bowl, mix chile-garlic sauce, garlic, fish sauce, brown sugar, soy sauce and lime juice.
- In a bowl, combine basil, cilantro, mint, and romaine lettuce; scoop roughly 6 tbsp. of lime juice mixture on top of romaine mixture. Coat by tossing.
- Slice steak into strips and add strips to leftover lime juice mixture; let rest for steak to marinate for 1-2 minutes. Put steak over romaine mixture.

Nutrition Information

- Calories: 132 calories;
- Total Carbohydrate: 8 g
- Cholesterol: 27 mg
- Total Fat: 4.5 g
- Protein: 15.7 g
- Sodium: 640 mg

17. Authentic, No Shortcuts, Louisiana Red Beans And Rice

"A Louisiana classic."
Serving: 8 | Prep: 20m | Ready in: 8h20m

Ingredients

- 1 lb. dried red beans, soaked overnight
- 10 cups water
- 1 lb. andouille sausage, sliced into rounds
- 1 large sweet onion, chopped
- 1 green bell pepper, chopped
- 1 jalapeno pepper, seeded and chopped (optional)
- 8 cloves garlic, chopped
- 1 tsp. ground black pepper
- 1 tsp. Creole seasoning, or to taste
- 6 fresh basil leaves, chopped
- 1 ham hock
- 4 cups cooked rice

Direction

- In a slow cooker, put water and beans. Heat a skillet on medium high heat. Brown sausage in skillet; use a slotted spoon to remove sausage from skillet, then put into the slow cooker. Keep drippings. Put garlic, jalapeno pepper, green pepper and onion into the drippings; mix and cook for 5 minutes till tender. Put everything from the skillet into slow cooker.
- Season mixture using creole seasoning and pepper. Add ham hock and fresh basil leaves. Cover; cook till beans are tender for 8 hours on low. Uncover and put heat on high to cook till it has a creamy texture if bean mixture is too watery.

Nutrition Information

- Calories: 556 calories;
- Total Carbohydrate: 61.5 g
- Cholesterol: 50 mg
- Total Fat: 22.3 g
- Protein: 27.2 g
- Sodium: 615 mg

---

18. Avocado Whole Wheat Pasta Salad

"A great vegan food."
Serving: 6 | Prep: 20m | Ready in: 30m

Ingredients

- 1 (12 oz.) box whole wheat rotini pasta
- 3 tbsps. extra-virgin olive oil
- 3 tbsps. white vinegar
- lemon, juiced
- 1 tbsp. honey
- 2 avocados - peeled, pitted, and chopped
- 1 green bell pepper, sliced
- 1 large carrot, cut into matchstick-size pieces
- 6 green onions, sliced
- 1 stalk celery, sliced
- 1 clove garlic, minced
- 2 tsps. chopped fresh basil

- 2 tsps. chopped fresh parsley
- 2 tsps. chopped fresh cilantro
- 1 tsp. lemon zest
- salt and ground black pepper to taste

Direction

- Fill a pot with salted water; heat to a boil. Add rotini and cook at a boil 10 minutes until tender but firm to the bite. Drain. Run under cold water to avoid sticking.
- In a bowl, whisk together honey, lemon juice, vinegar, and olive oil until the dressing is smooth.
- In a bowl, combine cilantro, parsley, basil, garlic, celery, green onions, carrot, green bell pepper, avocados, and pasta. Drizzle over the pasta mixture with dressing; toss to coat. To pasta salad, add pepper, salt, and lemon zest. Serve at room temperature.

Nutrition Information

- Calories: 394 calories;
- Total Carbohydrate: 55.5 g
- Cholesterol: 0 mg
- Total Fat: 17.5 g
- Protein: 10.4 g
- Sodium: 27 mg

---

19. Bacon And Feta Stuffed Chicken Breast

""The title pretty much says it all. This dish is easy to make and very delicious.""
Serving: 8 | Prep: 10m | Ready in: 3h10m

Ingredients

- 8 slices bacon
- 1/2 cup crumbled feta
- 8 skinless, boneless chicken breast halves
- 4 (14.5 oz.) cans diced tomatoes
- 2 tbsps. chopped fresh basil

Direction

- Use a deep large skillet to cook the bacon over medium-high heat for about ten minutes, turning occasionally until evenly browned. Drain bacon slices using paper towel lined plate then let it cool before crumbling the bacon into small pieces.
- Use a small bowl to mix the bacon and feta together.
- Cut the side of the chicken breast 2 to 3 inches lengthwise to make a pocket. Fill the space with the mixture then seal using toothpicks.
- Transfer the chicken in a slow cooker and add in the tomatoes and basil.
- Cook the chicken using the high setting for about 3 hours or until the chicken is no longer pink in the middle.

Nutrition Information

- Calories: 246 calories;
- Total Carbohydrate: 7.2 g
- Cholesterol: 87 mg
- Total Fat: 7.3 g
- Protein: 33.7 g
- Sodium: 711 mg

20. Bacon Avocado Pasta

"This pasta is made of delicious avocado and bacon along with a basil lemon dressing. You can serve it a cold pasta salad or as a hot pasta dish."
Serving: 4 | Prep: 20m | Ready in: 47m

Ingredients

- 1 (8 oz.) package bow-tie pasta
- 6 slices bacon
- 2/3 cup chopped basil
- 3 tbsps. lemon juice
- 2 tbsps. olive oil
- 3 cloves garlic, minced
- 1/4 tsp. ground black pepper
- 1/8 tsp. salt
- 2 avocados, chopped

- 1/2 cup grated Romano cheese

Direction

- Bring to boil lightly salted water in a large pot and add pasta. Cook while stirring frequently for about 12 minutes until they are tender but firm to bite and drain.
- Over medium-high heat, cook bacon in a large skillet while turning frequently for about 10 minutes until browned evenly. Use paper towels to drain and then crumble into small pieces.
- In a small bowl, combine together garlic, basil, pepper, lemon juice, salt and olive oil.
- In a large bowl, mix avocado and bacon pieces. Mix in the basil mixture and pour in pasta. Mix to combine. Top with Romano cheese.

Nutrition Information

- Calories: 400 calories;
- Total Carbohydrate: 43.5 g
- Cholesterol: 31 mg
- Total Fat: 17.9 g
- Protein: 17.7 g
- Sodium: 573 mg

21. Bacon Wrapped Pork Medallions

"The original recipe belongs to my mother, but I have changed it a little bit to make it my own. It's great to enjoy on holidays."
Serving: 4 | Prep: 10m | Ready in: 40m

Ingredients

- 8 slices bacon
- 1 tbsp. garlic powder
- 1 tsp. seasoned salt
- 1 tsp. dried basil
- 1 tsp. dried oregano
- 2 lbs. pork tenderloin
- 2 tbsps. butter

- 2 tbsps. olive oil

Direction

- Turn the oven to 400°F (200°C) to preheat.
- In a big, oven-safe frying pan, cook bacon over medium-high heat for 6-7 minutes until remaining flexible and turning light brown, flipping sometimes. Put the bacon slices on a dish lined with paper towels to strain. Discard the excess bacon fat from the frying pan. In a small bowl, mix together oregano, basil, seasoning salt, and garlic powder. Put aside.
- Wrap bacon strips around the pork tenderloin and use 1-2 toothpicks to keep each bacon strip in place. Between each bacon strip, cut the tenderloin to form the medallions. Coat both sides of the medallions with the seasoning mix by dipping. In the same frying pan, heat oil and butter over medium-high heat to melt. Cook each side of the medallion for 4 minutes.
- Put the frying pan in the preheated oven and bake for 17-20 minutes until the middle of the pork is not pink anymore. An instant-read thermometer should display 145°F (63°C) when you insert it into the middle.

Nutrition Information

- Calories: 417 calories;
- Total Carbohydrate: 2.4 g
- Cholesterol: 133 mg
- Total Fat: 25.5 g
- Protein: 42.3 g
- Sodium: 769 mg

22. Baked Cod In Foil

"Bake cod in the oven with basil, tomatoes and bell pepper."
Serving: 4 | Prep: 25m | Ready in: 45m

Ingredients

- 2 tomatoes, cubed
- 1 red bell pepper, seeded and cubed
- 1 onion, minced

- 2 tbsps. olive oil
- 2 tbsps. chopped fresh basil
- 1 clove garlic, minced
- aluminum foil
- 4 (5 oz.) cod fillets
- lemon, juiced
- salt and ground black pepper to taste

Direction

- Preheat the oven to 200 degrees C (400 degrees F).
- In a bowl, mix garlic and basil, olive oil, onion, bell pepper, and tomatoes well.
- On a working surface, lay 4 aluminum foil sheets and add 1 cod fillet in the middle of each. Scoop tomato mixture equally on top of the 4 fillets. Sprinkle with lemon juice and use pepper and salt to season. Place a second foil sheet over and seal the edges to form a parcel. Repeat with the leftover fillets and tomato mixture.
- Bake in the preheated oven for roughly 20 minutes till cod could be flaked easily using a fork. Take out of the oven and gently unwrap the parcels. Scoop onto warmed plates and serve right away.

Nutrition Information

- Calories: 216 calories;
- Total Carbohydrate: 10.4 g
- Cholesterol: 52 mg
- Total Fat: 8 g
- Protein: 27 g
- Sodium: 146 mg

23. Baked Pasta Primavera

"A great dish for summer."
Serving: 8 | Prep: 25m | Ready in: 45m

Ingredients

- Reynolds Wrap® Pan Lining Paper
- 8 oz. dried fettuccine or linguine pasta

- 1 cup shredded carrots*
- 1 cup fresh or frozen peas
- 1 cup sliced yellow squash
- 1 cup fresh asparagus spears, cut into 1-inch pieces
- 2 tbsps. butter
- 2 tbsps. all-purpose flour
- 1/2 tsp. salt
- 1 cup lowfat milk
- 1/2 cup reduced-sodium chicken broth
- 4 oz. herbed goat cheese
- 1/2 cup cherry tomatoes, halved
- 1/2 cup grated Parmesan cheese, divided
- 1 tbsp. snipped fresh basil
- 1 tbsp. snipped fresh oregano
- 1/4 cup sliced almonds

Direction

- Preheat an oven to 400°F. Line Reynolds wrap Pan Lining Paper on 2-qt. rectangular baking dish, parchment side up; you don't need to grease the dish.
- Follow package directions to cook pasta in Dutch oven; at final 3 minutes of cooking time, add squash, asparagus, peas and/or carrots; drain. Keep 1/4 cup pasta water. Put pasta mixture in Dutch oven. Cover; put aside.
- Melt butter in medium saucepan; whisk salt and flour in. Whisk goat cheese, chicken broth and milk in; mix and cook on medium heat till bubbly and thick. Mix and cook for 1 minute; mix oregano, basil, 1/4 cup parmesan cheese, tomatoes and reserved pasta water in.
- Put milk mixture on pasta mixture; toss to coat. Put pasta mixture in prepped baking dish; sprinkle leftover 1/4 cup parmesan cheese and almonds.
- Bake till sauce is bubbly and mixture just begins to turn golden for 15-20 minutes.

Nutrition Information

- Calories: 269 calories;
- Total Carbohydrate: 30.2 g
- Cholesterol: 26 mg
- Total Fat: 11.5 g
- Protein: 12.5 g

- Sodium: 368 mg

24. Baked Salmon With Basil And Lemon Thyme Crust

"The combination of asparagus and salmon."
Serving: 4 | Prep: 15m | Ready in: 33m

Ingredients

- 1/4 cup olive oil, divided
- 1 1/3 lbs. salmon fillet
- salt and ground black pepper to taste
- 1 lb. fresh asparagus, trimmed
- 2 cloves garlic
- 1/3 cup grated Parmesan cheese
- 1/3 cup chopped fresh basil
- 1 tbsp. lemon juice
- 1 tbsp. fresh lemon thyme
- 1 lemon, zested
- 1/2 tsp. salt
- 1/2 tsp. ground black pepper
- 1 cup fresh bread crumbs

Direction

- Rub over salmon with 1/2 tsp. olive oil and slightly season with pepper and salt. Put salmon in the center of a grill pan.
- In a bowl place asparagus. Drizzle over with 1 1/2 tsp. olive oil and season with pepper and salt. Stir thoroughly and place around the salmon.
- Put garlic cloves in a blender or a food processor and process until crushed. Put in 1/2 tsp. black pepper, 1/2 tsp. salt, lemon zest, lemon thyme, lemon juice, basil and Parmesan cheese; combine well. Put in bread crumbs and the remaining 3 tbsps. oil; pulse until thoroughly blended.
- Place herb mixture atop salmon, forming a crust.
- Choose Auto Cook in a Panasonic Countertop Induction Oven and choose the setting Fish with Vegetables. Arrange grill pan in the oven;

cook 18 minutes till asparagus is tender and salmon flakes easily with a fork.

Nutrition Information

- Calories: 449 calories;
- Total Carbohydrate: 11.7 g
- Cholesterol: 80 mg
- Total Fat: 30.5 g
- Protein: 32.3 g
- Sodium: 583 mg

25. Baked Salmon With Lemony Orzo And Basil-bacon Peas

"Treat your family with this easy to prepare salmon pasta dish with bacon, peas, orzo, lemon, and basil."
Serving: 4 | Prep: 20m | Ready in: 50m

Ingredients

- 1 cup orzo
- 2 tsps. garlic powder
- 5 large basil leaves, thinly sliced, divided
- 2 tsps. sea salt, divided
- 1 (1 1/2 lb.) skin-on, sockeye salmon
- 1/4 cup butter, melted, divided
- 3 slices bacon, chopped
- 1 (16 oz.) package frozen peas
- freshly ground black pepper to taste
- 2 lemons, juiced, divided

Direction

- Preheat oven to 450° Fahrenheit (230 °C). Place a parchment paper or aluminum foil at the bottom of a baking pan.
- Cook orzo in a big pot of lightly salted water for 10 minutes, mixing intermittently, until al dente (firm to bite). Drain.
- In a small bowl, mix half tsp. salt, garlic powder, and four basil leaves.
- Mix garlic powder, 4 leaves basil, and 1/2 tsp. salt together in a small bowl.

- Put the salmon in the prepared pan with its skin-side-down and brush with a tbsp. of butter. Top with the garlic-basil mixture.
- Bake in the 450°F preheated oven for 8 minutes until the salmon is flaky. Take it out of the oven and cool.
- On medium-low heat, cook bacon in a skillet for about 4 minutes until crispy; stir often. Mix in half tsp. of salt, peas, and season with pepper. Cook for 3-4 minutes while stirring until the peas are cooked through.
- In a bowl, combine juice from a 1 lemon, the remaining 1 tsp. of salt, and the remaining 3 tbsps. of butter. Add in the cooked pasta. Mix to coat and season with pepper.
- Evenly distribute the orzo among 4 plates and top each with salmon. Add the peas on the side of the plate and sprinkle the remaining basil. Spread the remaining lemon juice on top.

Nutrition Information

- Calories: 702 calories;
- Total Carbohydrate: 59.7 g
- Cholesterol: 153 mg
- Total Fat: 30.1 g
- Protein: 51.1 g
- Sodium: 1278 mg

26. Baked Snapper With Chilies, Ginger And Basil

"Sea bass and snapper complement Thai flavors really well making them a great choice for this recipe but you may still use any whole fish if you want. Try fresh galangal, if you find one at the market, as an alternative to ginger for a distinct yummy flavor."
Serving: 4 | Prep: 30m | Ready in: 1h

Ingredients

- 1 (1 1/2 lb.) whole red snapper, cleaned and scaled
- 1/2 cup fresh basil leaves
- 2 tbsps. peanut oil
- 2 tbsps. fish sauce

- 2 cloves garlic, minced
- 1 tsp. minced fresh ginger
- 2 red chile peppers, sliced diagonally
- 1 yellow bell pepper, seeded and diced
- 1 tbsp. brown sugar
- 1 tbsp. rice vinegar
- 2 tbsps. water
- 2 tomatoes, seeded and sliced
- 5 leaves basil

Direction

- Preheat the oven to 375°F (190°C). Use an aluminum foil to line a roasting pan.
- Put 1/2 cup of basil leaves inside the incision on the snapper then put it aside. In a big skillet, put in the peanut oil and heat up over high heat setting until smoke are starting to form. Put in the snapper and sear it for a total of about 1 minute on both sides. Put the seared fish in the prepared roasting pan then drizzle it with fish sauce on top. Keep the remaining peanut oil in the skillet aside.
- Put it in the preheated oven and bake for 25-30 minutes until you could flake the fish meat apart with ease using a fork.
- While the fish is baking, let the remaining peanut oil in the skillet heat up over medium heat setting. Mix in the chile peppers, garlic, yellow pepper and ginger and sauté the mixture for about 5 minutes until the peppers are tender. Add in the water, sugar, tomatoes and rice vinegar and give it a mix. Let the mixture simmer over medium-high heat setting until you get the preferred thick consistency of the sauce. Spread the prepared sauce evenly on top of the snapper then top it off with the remaining basil leaves and serve.

Nutrition Information

- Calories: 277 calories;
- Total Carbohydrate: 10.6 g
- Cholesterol: 62 mg
- Total Fat: 9.4 g
- Protein: 36.8 g
- Sodium: 630 mg

27. Baked Tomatoes And Mozzarella

"This recipe may take some time to make, but the delicious result is worth it. It turns the colorless tomato from the store into an amazing vegetable."
Serving: 6 | Prep: 15m | Ready in: 2h45m

Ingredients

- 6 roma (plum) tomatoes, thinly sliced
- 1 tbsp. olive oil
- sea salt and freshly ground black pepper to taste
- 1 (8 oz.) ball of fresh mozzarella cheese, cubed
- 2 tbsps. chopped fresh basil
- 1 clove roasted garlic, mashed into a paste
- 1/4 cup balsamic vinegar
- 2 tbsps. olive oil

Direction

- Turn the oven to 250°F (120°C) to preheat. Oil a baking sheet lightly.
- On the prepared baking sheet, arrange 1 layer of tomato slices. Drizzle 1 tbsp. of olive oil over the tomatoes; lightly sprinkle freshly ground pepper and sea salt over.
- Put the tomatoes in the preheated oven and bake for about 2 hours until they are crunchy around the edges, a bit brown and leathery. Take out of the oven and let it fully cool.
- In a big bowl, mix together roasted garlic, basil, mozzarella cheese and the cooled roasted tomatoes. Use pepper and salt to season to taste. Mix in the leftover 2 tbsps. of olive oil and vinegar, stir thoroughly.

Nutrition Information

- Calories: 186 calories;
- Total Carbohydrate: 5 g
- Cholesterol: 30 mg
- Total Fat: 15 g
- Protein: 7.4 g
- Sodium: 113 mg

28. Banana Squash Soup With Sweet Potato And Green Apple

"For more richness, add coconut milk."
Serving: 6 | Prep: 15m | Ready in: 35m

Ingredients

- 1 tbsp. coconut oil
- 1 tbsp. butter
- 1 white onion, diced
- 3 cloves garlic, chopped
- salt and ground black pepper to taste
- 1 lb. banana squash, cubed
- 1 lb. sweet potatoes, cubed
- 1 green apple, cubed
- 4 cups chicken broth, or as needed
- 1 tbsp. chopped fresh basil
- 1 tbsp. curry powder
- 1 tsp. crushed bay leaf

Direction

- Heat butter and coconut oil together in a big pot/Dutch oven on medium heat; mix and cook garlic and onion in hot butter-oil mixture for 1-2 minutes till slightly soft. Season with black pepper and salt.
- Mix apple, sweet potatoes and squash into the onion mixture; cook for 5 minutes to heat through. Add chicken broth; boil. Add bay leaf, curry powder and basil. Lower the heat; simmer for 15-20 minutes till apples and sweet potatoes are soft. Take off from heat; season with pepper and salt.
- Use a hand blender to puree the soup in the pot till smooth.

Nutrition Information

- Calories: 154 calories;
- Total Carbohydrate: 27.5 g
- Cholesterol: 5 mg
- Total Fat: 4.5 g
- Protein: 2.6 g
- Sodium: 57 mg

29. Bangers And Gnocchi With A Roasted Shallot And Cheese Sauce

""A delicious dish loaded with flavor.""
Serving: 4 | Prep: 10m | Ready in: 45m

Ingredients

- 1 shallot, thinly sliced
- 1 tbsp. olive oil
- 1 1/2 lbs. sweet Italian sausage links
- 1 (16 oz.) package refrigerated gnocchi
- 1/4 cup unsalted butter
- 1/3 cup milk
- 1 (8 oz.) package shredded Italian cheese blend
- 1 tbsp. chopped fresh basil

Direction

- Prepare the oven by preheating to 400°F (200°C).
- In a heavy Dutch oven or pot, toss olive oil and sliced shallot until coated well.
- Arrange sausages on top of shallot mixture.
- Bake for 25-30 minutes in the preheated oven until the sausage is not pink in the center, flipping sausages occasionally to brown evenly. An instant-read thermometer poked into the center should register 160°F (70°C).
- Place sausages onto a platter; reserve, covered.
- In the pot over medium heat where the sausage is cooked, put butter to melt. Mix in milk and bring to a low simmer.
- Slowly whisk in about 3/4 Italian cheese blend until melts; set the rest of the cheese for topping aside. Take the cheese sauce away from the heat, whisking occasionally to keep the sauce smooth.
- Place lightly salted water in a large pot and bring to a rolling boil. Add gnocchi and cook at a boil for about 3 minutes until it floats to the top; drain.

- Serve gnocchi and sausage with cheese sauce on top and dust with basil and reserved cheese.

Nutrition Information

- Calories: 903 calories;
- Total Carbohydrate: 30.2 g
- Cholesterol: 162 mg
- Total Fat: 69.8 g
- Protein: 38.9 g
- Sodium: 1968 mg

30. Banh-mi Style Vietnamese Baguette

"Great sandwiches to serve for your guests and even for yourself! Its' ingredients are delicious, fresh and popular. You can actually find the sandwich which is high in calorie (variation of meat on the mayonnaise) in your local Vietnamese baguette shop but here is a version of a hearty Vegetarian made with portabello mushrooms (if you do not use fish sauce)."
Serving: 2 | Prep: 20m | Ready in: 45m

Ingredients

- 2 portobello mushroom caps, sliced
- 2 tsps. olive oil
- salt and pepper to taste
- 1 carrot, sliced into sticks
- 1 daikon (white) radish, sliced into sticks
- 1 cup rice vinegar
- 1/2 cup fresh lime juice
- 1/2 cup cold water
- 1/2 cup chilled lime juice
- 2 tsps. soy sauce
- 1 tsp. nuoc mam (Vietnamese fish sauce)
- 1/2 tsp. toasted sesame oil
- 2 tbsps. canola oil
- 2 tsps. minced garlic
- 1/3 cup white sugar
- 1/3 cup cold water
- 1 jalapeno pepper, thinly sliced
- 8 sprigs fresh cilantro with stems
- 1 medium cucumber, sliced into thin strips

- 2 sprigs fresh Thai basil
- 2 (7 inch) French bread baguettes, split lengthwise

Direction

- Set the oven to 450°F (230°C) for preheating. Arrange the mushrooms on a baking sheet. Drizzle with a bit of olive oil and spice up with pepper and salt. Roast the mushroom for about 25 minutes inside the prepped oven. Let it cool slightly, and cut into strips.
- Meanwhile, put a water in a saucepan and let it boil. Drop the radish sticks and carrot into the boiling water and remove after a few seconds, and submerge them in an ice water placed in a bowl to prevent the vegetables from cooking. In another bowl, stir a half cup of lime juice, rice vinegar and half cup cold water together. Place the radish and carrot to the vinegar and lime marinade and allow soaking for 15 minutes, much longer if it's convenient.
- Make the sandwich sauce: Combine together 1/3 cup water, the remaining lime juice, fish sauce, 1/3 cup sugar, sesame oil, soy sauce and canola oil, mix in a small bowl,.
- To arrange the sandwiches, drizzle a bit of a sandwich sauce on each half of the French loaves. Put the roasted mushrooms on the bottom half of each roll and drizzle with a little more sauce. Top it off with a couple sticks of carrot and radish (without the marinade), a few slices of jalapeno, basil, cilantro and cucumber. Place the other half of the bread on top to close. Serve.

Nutrition Information

- Calories: 760 calories;
- Total Carbohydrate: 128.4 g
- Cholesterol: 0 mg
- Total Fat: 22.8 g
- Protein: 19.5 g
- Sodium: 1282 mg

31. Barilla® Tomato Basil Mac & Cheese

"This dish has a wonderful twist."
Serving: 8 | Prep: 25m | Ready in: 35m

Ingredients

- 1 (16 oz.) box Barilla® Elbows
- 1 cup reduced sodium chicken or vegetable broth
- 1 cup peeled and shredded sweet potato
- 1 cup Barilla® Tomato & Basil Sauce
- 1/4 tsp. salt
- 1 1/2 cups shredded fontina cheese
- 1/4 cup low-fat milk, plus more as needed
- 2 tbsps. chopped fresh basil

Direction

- Allow 4-6-qt. of water to come to a rolling boil, add Elbows and salt to taste, gently stir.
- Cook pasta following the package instructions, take away from the heat and strain thoroughly.
- In the meantime, boil broth in a small pot and add sweet potato, cook until tender, or about 3-4 minutes, and then take away from the heat,
- Mix salt, Tomato & Basil Sauce, broth and sweet potato together in a blender; put the lid on and process until smooth.
- Allow the blended sauce mixture to come to a low simmer in a very big skillet. Take away from heat, gradually mix in cheese until melted (the mixture may seem curdled). Mix pasta into the skillet with the sauce. Let it sit for 5 minutes. Mix in an enough amount of milk to reach a creamy consistency.
- Put fresh basil on top and enjoy.

Nutrition Information

- Calories: 337 calories;
- Total Carbohydrate: 50.2 g
- Cholesterol: 30 mg
- Total Fat: 9.2 g
- Protein: 14.9 g
- Sodium: 400 mg

32. Basil And Prosciutto-wrapped Halibut

"This recipe is tasty and simple. I had a similar dish at a restaurant and then tried it at home. My cast iron pan made it so easy to recreate."
Serving: 2 | Prep: 5m | Ready in: 16m

Ingredients

- 6 leaves basil
- 2 slices prosciutto
- 2 (4 oz.) fillets halibut
- 1/2 tsp. adobo seasoning
- 1 tbsp. olive oil

Direction

- Start preheating oven to 400 deg F or 200 deg C.
- On every slice of prosciutto lay 3 basil leaves. Use Adobo seasoning to season halibut fillets, put them on one side of prepared prosciutto slices, wrap fish fillets with the basil and prosciutto.
- On medium-high, heat an oven-safe pan. When pan is hot, dump in olive oil and add the wrapped halibut fillets.
- Cook for 4 minutes until prosciutto turns golden brown. Turn over fillets and put the skillet in the heated oven. Bake for 5 minutes until fish is heated through and when touched is firm.

Nutrition Information

- Calories: 240 calories;
- Total Carbohydrate: 0.3 g
- Cholesterol: 49 mg
- Total Fat: 14 g
- Protein: 26.5 g
- Sodium: 340 mg

33. Basil Butter

"It's a delicious basil flavored butter recipe."
Serving: 30 | Prep: 10m | Ready in: 10m

Ingredients

- 4 cloves garlic
- 15 leaves fresh basil
- 1/2 tsp. freshly ground black pepper
- 1 cup butter

Direction

- In the bowl of a food processor, add pepper, basil and garlic, then process until the garlic is chopped into small bits. Put in butter and process just to combine together. Scoop into container and chill until firm.

Nutrition Information

- Calories: 55 calories;
- Total Carbohydrate: 0.2 g
- Cholesterol: 16 mg
- Total Fat: 6.1 g
- Protein: 0.1 g
- Sodium: 44 mg

34. Basil Cheesecake With Strawberry Mousse

"A delicious with the combination of basil cheesecake and strawberry mousse."
Serving: 8 | Prep: 30m | Ready in: 10h33m

Ingredients

- Cheesecake:
- 5 1/3 oz. chocolate cookie wafers
- 2 tbsps. butter, melted
- 1 cup heavy whipping cream
- 1 bunch fresh basil leaves
- 3 (8 oz.) packages cream cheese, softened
- 4 eggs
- 3/4 cup white sugar
- 1 tbsp. all-purpose flour
- 1 tbsp. cornstarch
- Mousse:
- 1 (.25 oz.) package powdered gelatin
- 2 1/2 tbsps. cold water
- 1 1/3 cups strawberries, hulled and sliced
- 1/4 cup white sugar
- 3/4 cup heavy cream
- 2 tbsps. heavy cream

Direction

- Set oven to 165° C (325° F) and start preheating. Line parchment paper on a 9-in. springform tin.
- In a food processor, combine butter and chocolate wafers; process until forming fine crumbs. Evenly press the crumbs onto the bottom of tin. Place crust in the fridge.
- In a food processor, combine basil and 1 cup heavy cream; process until smooth. Put in cornstarch, flour, 3/4 cup sugar, eggs and cream cheese; blend until smooth. Pour over the chilled crust, using a spatula to smooth top.
- Place in the preheated oven and bake 1 hour until the surface is firm except for a small spot in center, this spot will jiggle when the tin is gently shaken. Stop heating and open the oven. Allow cheesecake to stay in the oven 1 hour, until completely cooled.
- Chill cheesecake in the fridge 6 hours until fully set.
- In a small bowl, mix water and gelatin together; allow to stand 3-5 minutes until softened.
- In a blender, put strawberries; blend until frothy and smooth.
- Add 1/3 of the strawberries to a saucepan on medium heat; pour in 1/4 cup sugar. Mix 3 minutes until sugar is dissolved. Take away from heat; mix in gelatin mixture. Stir in the rest of strawberries.
- Use an electric mixer to whip 3/4 cup and 2 tbsps. heavy cream until forming stiff peaks. Fold in strawberry mixture to form mousse.
- Run a knife following edges of the tin to take cheesecake out; put on a serving platter. Use

mousse to cover top and sides. Chill in the fridge 2-3 hours until mousse is set.

Nutrition Information

- Calories: 747 calories;
- Total Carbohydrate: 46.7 g
- Cholesterol: 270 mg
- Total Fat: 58.1 g
- Protein: 13.3 g
- Sodium: 438 mg

35. Basil Chicken Ravioli Carbonara

"Italian-style skillet dinner, ready in 20 minutes, really quick."
Serving: 4 | Prep: 10m | Ready in: 20m

Ingredients

- 1 (9 oz.) package refrigerated four-cheese-filled ravioli
- 1 (14 oz.) package uncooked chicken breast pieces for stir-fry
- 1 (9 oz.) pouch Progresso™ Recipe Starters™ creamy Parmesan basil cooking sauce
- 1/4 cup half-and-half
- 1/4 cup cooked real bacon pieces (from a jar or package)
- Garnishes, if Desired:
- Shredded Asiago or Parmesan cheese (optional)
- Chopped fresh basil leaves or parsley (optional)

Direction

- Cook and drain ravioli following package instruction.
- Heat a tbsp. vegetable oil in 10-inch skillet over medium-high heat. Put in chicken; let it cook for 2 to 4 minutes, flipping from time to time till brown. Mix in half-and-half, cooked ravioli and cooking sauce; lower heat. Without

cover, let simmer for 3 to 5 minutes till sauce is hot.
- Dust with basil, cheese and bacon.

Nutrition Information

- Calories: 402 calories;
- Total Carbohydrate: 23.6 g
- Cholesterol: 104 mg
- Total Fat: 17.8 g
- Protein: 35 g
- Sodium: 651 mg

36. Basil Pecan Pesto

"Pine nuts topped with pecans for a tasty dish."
Serving: 12 | Prep: 15m | Ready in: 15m

Ingredients

- 3 cups fresh basil leaves
- 1 1/2 cups pecans
- 4 cloves garlic
- 1/2 cup shredded Parmesan cheese
- 3/4 cup olive oil
- 1/2 tsp. kosher salt
- 1 pinch ground black pepper to taste

Direction

- In a food processor, combine pepper, salt, olive oil, Parmesan cheese, garlic, pecans and basil until a lightly chunky paste forms.

Nutrition Information

- Calories: 232 calories;
- Total Carbohydrate: 2.7 g
- Cholesterol: 3 mg
- Total Fat: 24.3 g
- Protein: 2.9 g
- Sodium: 132 mg

37. Basil Pesto Bread

"This dish is very simple. It's just Italian bread spread with pesto and has a layer of cheese and tomatoes. Making it may take some time, but the result is worth it. You can freeze it and thaw when enjoy."
Serving: 16 | Prep: 25m | Ready in: 30m

Ingredients

- 3 cups fresh basil leaves
- 1/2 cup olive oil
- 2 cloves garlic, peeled
- 1/4 cup toasted pine nuts
- 1/4 cup grated Parmesan cheese
- 1 (1 lb.) loaf Italian bread
- 3 roma (plum) tomatoes, thinly sliced
- 1 (8 oz.) package mozzarella cheese, sliced

Direction

- Puree garlic, olive oil, and basil leaves in a food processor or a blender. Stir in Parmesan cheese and pine nuts. Keep blending until reaching the wanted consistency.
- Start preheating the broiler.
- Cut Italian bread into slices with the wanted thickness. Spread on each slice with 1 layer of pesto. Put mozzarella cheese and roma (plum) tomatoes on top.
- On a big cookie sheet, put 1 layer of the topped bread slices. Put in the preheated oven and broil until the cheese turns slightly brown and bubbly, about 5 minutes.

Nutrition Information

- Calories: 194 calories;
- Total Carbohydrate: 15.7 g
- Cholesterol: 10 mg
- Total Fat: 11.5 g
- Protein: 7.3 g
- Sodium: 273 mg

38. Basil Shrimp

"If a friend lets you taste something delicious, ask for the recipe. This shrimp recipe is so easy to follow and the taste is fantastic. Make sure to save some for yourself when you serve this because they are gone quick."
Serving: 9 | Prep: 25m | Ready in: 1h30m

Ingredients

- 2 1/2 tbsps. olive oil
- 1/4 cup butter, melted
- 1 1/2 lemons, juiced
- 3 tbsps. Dijon mustard (such as Grey Poupon Country Mustard™)
- 1/2 cup minced fresh basil leaves
- 3 cloves garlic, minced
- salt to taste
- white pepper
- 3 lbs. fresh shrimp, peeled and deveined
- skewers

Direction

- Combine melted butter and olive oil in a nonporous, shallow bowl or dish. Mix in the garlic, basil, lemon juice and mustard then put white pepper and salt to taste. Mix in the shrimps until fully coated. Cover the bowl and keep in the fridge for an hour.
- Set the grill on high heat and preheat. Get each shrimp from the marinade and insert onto skewers. Throw away the marinade.
- Slightly grease the grill grate and put the shrimp skewers on top of the preheated grill. Grill for 4 minutes or until the shrimps become pink in color, turn once to cook both sides.

Nutrition Information

- Calories: 206 calories;
- Total Carbohydrate: 2.4 g
- Cholesterol: 244 mg
- Total Fat: 10.2 g
- Protein: 25 g
- Sodium: 426 mg

39. Basil Vinaigrette

"The key to making this easy-to-prepare dressing a lot more special is by using a good quality olive oil. It pairs well with asparagus and artichoke salad."
Serving: 16 | Prep: 5m | Ready in: 5m

Ingredients

- 1 cup fresh basil leaves
- 1/4 cup roasted garlic
- 2 tbsps. grated Parmesan cheese
- 1/4 cup balsamic vinegar
- 3 cups olive oil
- salt and pepper to taste

Direction

- Use a blender to combine the vinegar, cheese, garlic, and basil together. Add in the oil and blend gently. Season with pepper and salt.

Nutrition Information

- Calories: 367 calories;
- Total Carbohydrate: 1.4 g
- Cholesterol: < 1 mg
- Total Fat: 40.7 g
- Protein: 0.5 g
- Sodium: 12 mg

40. Bean And Kale Ragu

"A fantastic Italian style veggie stew."
Serving: 6 | Prep: 10m | Ready in: 1h25m

Ingredients

- 2 tbsps. olive oil
- 1 onion, chopped
- 1 lb. kale, stems removed and leaves coarsely chopped
- 1 (14 oz.) can diced tomatoes with green chile peppers
- 2 cloves garlic, minced
- 1 1/2 cups water
- 2 bay leaves

- 1/4 tsp. ground cumin
- 1 tsp. onion powder
- 2 (15 oz.) cans canned cannellini beans, drained and rinsed
- 1 tbsp. chopped fresh oregano
- 1 tsp. chopped fresh basil
- salt and ground black pepper to taste

Direction

- In a big deep skillet, heat olive oil on medium high heat. Add kale and onions. Stir and cook for 5-7 minutes till kale wilts and lessens in volume and onion is transparent.
- Lower heat to medium. Mix onion powder, cumin, bay leaves, garlic, water, green chiles and tomatoes into kale mixture. Simmer veggie mixture for 1 hour till kale is soft. Mix cannellini beans in. Keep simmering for 10 minutes till beans heat through. Mix basil and oregano in. To taste, put pepper and salt.

Nutrition Information

- Calories: 206 calories;
- Total Carbohydrate: 31.9 g
- Cholesterol: 0 mg
- Total Fat: 5.7 g
- Protein: 8.7 g
- Sodium: 592 mg

41. Beef Pho

"You can add plum sauce and hot sauce and top it with bean sprouts, lime juice, basil, and cilantro."
Serving: 6 | Prep: 30m | Ready in: 6h30m

Ingredients

- 5 lbs. beef knuckle, with meat
- 2 lbs. beef oxtail
- 1 white (daikon) radish, sliced
- 2 onions, chopped
- 2 oz. whole star anise pods
- 1/2 cinnamon stick
- 2 whole cloves

- 1 tsp. black peppercorns
- 1 slice fresh ginger root
- 1 tbsp. white sugar
- 1 tbsp. salt
- 1 tbsp. fish sauce
- 1 1/2 lbs. dried flat rice noodles
- 1/2 lb. frozen beef sirloin
- TOPPINGS:
- Sriracha hot pepper sauce
- hoisin sauce
- thinly sliced onion
- chopped fresh cilantro
- bean sprouts (mung beans)
- sweet Thai basil
- thinly sliced green onion
- limes, quartered

Direction

- In a very big (9-quart of more) pot, put in beef knuckle. Season using salt then put in 2 gallons of water. Boil then cook for about 2 hours.
- Skim fat off the soup's surface. Add onions, radish, and oxtail. Tie ginger, peppercorns, cloves, cinnamon stick, and anise pods in a spice bag or cheesecloth. Add to soup. Mix in fish sauce, salt, and sugar. Simmer for at least 4 hours or more (the longer it simmer, the better) on medium-low heat. Taste when done cooking, adding salt to your preference. Strain the broth and put back in the pot to simmer. Get rid of bones and spices. Keep beef knuckle meat for another use if you want.
- Boil lightly salted water in a big pot. Soak rice noodles for about 20 minutes in water then cook for about 5 minutes in boiling water until its soft yet not mushy. Cut frozen beef to paper thin slices. It should be able to instantly cook. Put some noodles in every bowl and put several raw beef slices on top. Place boiling broth on beef and noodles into the bowl. Serve with Sriracha sauce and hoisin sauce on the side. Put lime, green onions, basil, bean sprouts, cilantro, and onion on the table to add as toppings.

42. Beet, Greens, And Zucchini Tart

"This tart is golden and puffy. It has a scent of buttery crust and veggies. You can enjoy it at room temperature or warm with a salad. You can prepare it in advance and enjoy later at room temperature."
Serving: 8 | Prep: 20m | Ready in: 2h

Ingredients

- 4 beets (with greens), beets trimmed and greens chopped
- 1 sheet frozen puff pastry, thawed
- 1 tbsp. olive oil
- 1 onion, diced
- 1 large zucchini, diced
- 1 small red jalapeno pepper, minced
- 1/4 cup roughly chopped basil leaves
- 5 eggs, lightly beaten
- 1 1/2 cups milk
- 3/4 tsp. salt, or to taste
- 1/4 tsp. fresh ground black pepper, or to taste

Direction

- Turn the oven to 375°F (190°C) to preheat. Wrap aluminum foil around the beets to form a packet.
- In the oven, put the packet and roast for 20-25 minutes until the beets are tender but remain firm. Take out of the oven and put aside to cool. Increase the oven temperature to 400°F (200°C).
- Rinse chopped beet greens and strain thoroughly.
- Roll puff pastry until it fits the sides and bottom of the 9-in. spring-form pan, trimming as necessary. Use a fork to prink the bottom pastry in several places, line aluminum foil onto the pastry, and put on dried beans or pie weights to cover.
- Bake the pastry for 10 minutes and take out of the oven. Discard the weights and foil. Lower the oven temperature to 325°F (165°C).

- In a big skillet, heat olive oil over medium heat. Add jalapeno, zucchini and diced onion; stir and cook for 5 minutes until the vegetables start to get tender and the onion is opaque. Mix in beet greens until they start to wilt. Take the skillet away from the heat and stir in basil.
- In a bowl, beat together milk and eggs. Use pepper and salt to season.
- Slip off the skins of the beets and slice into slices, about 1/4-in. each.
- On the pastry bottom, evenly arrange the greens-zucchini mixture. Top with beet slices. Gradually pour over the beets with the milk-egg mixture, be careful to not overflow the pastry edge.
- Put in the preheated oven and bake for 40-50 minutes until the tart is firm and puffy. Let it cool before cutting, about 1/2 hour.

Nutrition Information

- Calories: 280 calories;
- Total Carbohydrate: 24 g
- Cholesterol: 106 mg
- Total Fat: 17 g
- Protein: 8.7 g
- Sodium: 388 mg

---

43. Best Chicken Parmesan

"A delicious dish with a crispy crust and zesty marinara sauce."
Serving: 4 | Prep: 30m | Ready in: 50m

Ingredients

- Marinara Sauce:
- 3 tbsps. extra-virgin olive oil
- 1/2 onion, finely chopped
- 4 garlic cloves, minced
- 1 (14 oz.) can Italian crushed tomatoes with basil
- 1/2 cup chicken broth
- 2 tbsps. red wine
- 1/2 tsp. garlic powder
- 1/2 tsp. onion powder
- 1/2 tsp. dried oregano
- 1/2 tsp. Italian seasoning
- 1 pinch crushed red pepper flakes
- salt and ground black pepper to taste
- 1 pinch white sugar
- 3 tbsps. chopped fresh basil leaves
- 1 lb. rigatoni
- 4 boneless, skinless chicken breasts
- Breading:
- 1 cup all-purpose flour
- 1/2 tsp. garlic powder
- 1/4 tsp. salt
- 1/4 tsp. ground black pepper
- 2 eggs
- 3 tbsps. milk
- 1 cup Italian-seasoned bread crumbs
- 1/4 cup grated Parmesan cheese
- 1 tsp. dried oregano
- 1 tsp. Italian seasoning
- 1/2 tsp. garlic powder
- 1/4 tsp. salt
- canola oil for frying
- 3/4 cup shredded mozzarella cheese
- 1/4 cup grated Parmesan cheese

Direction

- Heat a big skillet on medium heat. Pour olive oil in the hot skillet and let it get hot. Put in garlic and onion; mix 2 minutes. Add in crushed tomatoes. Mix in sugar, pepper, salt, red pepper flakes, 1/2 tsp. Italian seasoning, 1/2 tsp. oregano, onion powder, 1/2 tsp. garlic powder, red wine, and chicken broth. Decrease to low heat and simmer 15 minutes, stirring sometimes, till the sauce thickens. Mix in chopped basil during the final minute of cooking.
- During cooking sauce, bring a big pot filled with slightly salted water to a boil. In the boiling water, cook rigatoni 13 minutes, mixing occasionally, until tender but firm to the bite. Drain.
- Set oven to 230° C (450° F) and start preheating. Line parchment paper on a rimmed baking sheet.

- In a resealable plastic bag, place chicken breasts. Use a meat mallet to flatten to 1/4-in. thickness.
- Prepare a breading station with three big mixing bowls: In the first bowl, combine 1/4 tsp. pepper, 1/4 tsp. salt, 1/2 tsp. garlic powder, and flour. In the second bowl, beat eggs and milk together. In the third bowl, combine 1/4 tsp. salt, 1/2 tsp. garlic powder, 1 tsp. Italian seasoning, 1 tsp. oregano, 1/4 cup Parmesan cheese, and bread crumbs.
- Dredge each piece of chicken to the flour mixture; shake to remove excess. Dunk into the egg mixture and then use bread crumbs to coat. Follow the same steps for the rest of chicken. Arrange on a plate.
- In a big cast iron skillet on medium-high heat, heat around 1 inch of canola oil until hot yet not smoking. In batches, add breaded chicken to the skillet and cook on each side for 1-2 minutes until golden brown. Remove chicken to the baking sheet. Top with 1/4 cup Parmesan cheese and mozzarella cheese.
- Place in the preheated oven and bake 5 minutes till cheese is melted and the internal temperature of chicken reaches 74° C (165° F). Serve with rigatoni and marinara sauce.

Nutrition Information

- Calories: 1168 calories;
- Total Carbohydrate: 139.4 g
- Cholesterol: 189 mg
- Total Fat: 38.9 g
- Protein: 63 g
- Sodium: 1528 mg

44. Best Spaghetti Sauce In The World

"You'll love this sauce."
Serving: 4 | Prep: 10m | Ready in: 25m

Ingredients

- 3 tbsps. butter

- 1 tsp. minced garlic
- 16 roma (plum) tomatoes, chopped
- 1/2 cup chicken stock
- 1/3 cup dry vermouth
- 2 tbsps. fresh basil, chopped

Direction

- Melt butter in a big saucepan on low heat. Stir in the garlic then sauté until it becomes slightly golden, 1 to 2 minutes. Stir chopped tomatoes into the pan then mix in chicken stock, using 1 to 2 tbsps. of water to make it thin if necessary. Allow it to cool on medium heat until it becomes bubbly. Mix in Vermouth and cook for another 5 minutes. Just before serving, stir in basil.

Nutrition Information

- Calories: 156 calories;
- Total Carbohydrate: 12.9 g
- Cholesterol: 24 mg
- Total Fat: 9.2 g
- Protein: 2.5 g
- Sodium: 196 mg

45. Best Steak Marinade In Existence

"A family recipe."
Serving: 8 | Prep: 15m | Ready in: 15m

Ingredients

- 1/3 cup soy sauce
- 1/2 cup olive oil
- 1/3 cup fresh lemon juice
- 1/4 cup Worcestershire sauce
- 1 1/2 tbsps. garlic powder
- 3 tbsps. dried basil
- 1 1/2 tbsps. dried parsley flakes
- 1 tsp. ground white pepper
- 1/4 tsp. hot pepper sauce (optional)
- 1 tsp. dried minced garlic (optional)

Direction

- Blend garlic and hot pepper sauce (optional), pepper, parsley, basil, garlic powder, Worcestershire sauce, lemon juice, olive oil and soy sauce for 30 seconds on high speed till well mixed in blender.
- Put marinade over preferred meat; cover. Refrigerate for maximum of 8 hours; cook meat as desired.

Nutrition Information

- Calories: 145 calories;
- Total Carbohydrate: 5.6 g
- Cholesterol: 0 mg
- Total Fat: 13.6 g
- Protein: 1.4 g
- Sodium: 688 mg

46.Bison Red Curry

""Fresh basil, a lot of colourful vegetables and bite-sized bits of sirloin steak are put together to create the delicious bowl of red coconut curry, cooked in an Asian style.""
Serving: 4 | Prep: 10m | Ready in: 30m

Ingredients

- 1 tbsp. vegetable oil
- 1 lb. bison sirloin steak, cut into bite-size pieces
- 1 (14 oz.) can unsweetened coconut milk
- 1/3 cup beef broth
- 1 tbsp. fish sauce
- 1 tbsp. brown sugar
- 3 tbsps. red curry paste
- 1 cup sliced red or yellow bell pepper
- 1 cup sliced carrots
- 1 cup sliced fresh mushrooms
- 1 cup frozen cut green beans
- 1/3 cup chopped fresh basil
- Hot cooked jasmine rice
- Naan (optional)

Direction

- At medium to high heat, warm oil in the big skillet until heated. Insert the bison sirloin steak pieces, cooking for 5 minutes until browned everywhere. Move the steak pieces out of the pan. Insert the brown sugar, fish sauce, broth and coconut milk into the pan, whisking the curry paste in. Boil and leave it boiling lightly for 5 minutes. Add green beans, mushrooms, carrot and bell pepper, stirring. Proceed with boiling lightly until the sauce thickens a little and the vegetables tenderize, about 5-7 minutes. Stir from time to time. Add the bison sirloin steak pieces, stirring until thoroughly heated. Move it away from the heat. Add 1/3 cup of basil, stirring. Put it atop the jasmine rice and serve together with naan, if desired.

Nutrition Information

- Calories: 455 calories;
- Total Carbohydrate: 30.2 g
- Cholesterol: 59 mg
- Total Fat: 33.1 g
- Protein: 30.2 g
- Sodium: 659 mg

47. Bo Nuong Xa

"A traditional Vietnamese dish beef skewers that can be grilled or broiled."
Serving: 6 | Prep: 20m | Ready in: 4h30m

Ingredients

- 2 tsps. white sugar
- 2 tbsps. soy sauce
- 1 tsp. ground black pepper
- 2 cloves garlic, minced
- 2 stalks lemon grass, minced
- 2 tsps. sesame seeds
- 1 1/2 lbs. sirloin tip, thinly sliced
- skewers
- 12 leaves romaine lettuce

- fresh cilantro for garnish
- fresh basil for garnish
- fresh mint for garnish
- thinly sliced green onion for garnish

Direction

- Combine the sesame seeds, lemon grass, garlic, pepper, soy sauce and sugar in a medium bowl. In the dish, put the meat, then mix to coat. Put cover, and chill for 4 hours.
- Preheat the grill for high heat. Get rid of marinade, and onto skewers, thread meat accordion style.
- Grease grill grate with oil and throw away marinade. On the grill, lay skewers. Cook 5 minutes each side. Take off from skewers and serve on lettuce leaves or serve hot on skewers. Top with sliced green onions, basil, mint and cilantro.

Nutrition Information

- Calories: 204 calories;
- Total Carbohydrate: 5.7 g
- Cholesterol: 61 mg
- Total Fat: 11.1 g
- Protein: 20.1 g
- Sodium: 348 mg

48.Bocconcini Salad

"Bocconcini, bite-size balls of fresh mozzarella is the soul of this salad. If possible, prep this dish with mozzarella di bufala, which made from water buffalo's milk. This cheese is creamier and softer than mozzarella that made from cow's milk"
Serving: 4 | Prep: 20m | Ready in: 20m

Ingredients

- 1 lb. bocconcini (bite-size mozzarella balls)
- 8 cherry tomatoes, halved
- 1/2 cup chopped green bell pepper
- 1/2 cup chopped celery
- 1/2 cup Belgian endive leaves

- 1/2 cup coarsely chopped arugula, stems included
- 1 1/2 tbsps. fresh lemon juice
- 3 tbsps. extra virgin olive oil
- 2 tbsps. chopped fresh basil leaves
- salt and freshly ground black pepper

Direction

- Combine arugula, endive, celery, bell pepper, cherry tomatoes and mozzarella in a large salad bowl.
- Add olive oil and lemon juice together, whisk properly then pour over the salad. Toss well in order that all ingredients are well coated with dressing. Move salad to individual serving plates if needed. Sprinkle basil on top of salad; add salt and pepper to season, serve immediately.

Nutrition Information

- Calories: 448 calories;
- Total Carbohydrate: 6.2 g
- Cholesterol: 90 mg
- Total Fat: 35.7 g
- Protein: 25.9 g
- Sodium: 875 mg

49.Bombay Chicken And Rice

"This recipe is so delicious with fruit, seasonings, curry, butter and chicken meat."
Serving: 6 | Prep: 20m | Ready in: 1h20m

Ingredients

- 1 cup uncooked long-grain white rice
- 6 oz. diced dried mixed fruit
- 1/2 cup chopped onion
- 1 1/2 tsps. sugar
- 1 tsp. salt
- 2 cups water
- 1 (3 lb.) chicken, cut into pieces
- 2 tbsps. butter, melted
- 4 tsps. curry powder, divided

- 1/2 tsp. paprika

Direction

- Preheat the oven to 190 degrees C (375 degrees F).
- In the 9x13 in. baking pan, stir the salt, sugar, onion, fruit and rice. Add in the water. Arrange the chicken parts on top of rice mixture. In the small-sized bowl, stir the paprika, curry powder and butter. Brush the butter mixture on top of the chicken pieces. Cover the pan tightly using the aluminum foil.
- Bake in preheated oven till the rice softens and the chicken juices come out clear, for 60 minutes.

Nutrition Information

- Calories: 521 calories;
- Total Carbohydrate: 47.2 g
- Cholesterol: 107 mg
- Total Fat: 21.6 g
- Protein: 34.2 g
- Sodium: 518 mg

50. Boss Pizza Sauce

"This is an excellent pizza sauce that is delicious and easy to make, also good for your health."
Serving: 12 | Prep: 10m | Ready in: 10m

Ingredients

- 1 (15 oz.) can low-sodium tomato sauce
- 1 (6 oz.) can low-sodium tomato paste
- 2 tsps. ground black pepper
- 1 1/2 tsps. dried oregano
- 1/2 tsp. dried basil leaves
- 1/2 tsp. garlic powder
- 1 1/2 tsps. salt
- 1/4 tsp. dried thyme leaves
- 1/4 tsp. dried cilantro
- 1/4 tsp. dried parsley
- 1/4 tsp. onion salt

Direction

- In a bowl, combine together onion salt, parsley, cilantro, thyme, salt, garlic powder, basil, oregano, ground black pepper, tomato paste and tomato sauce until well blended.

Nutrition Information

- Calories: 24 calories;
- Total Carbohydrate: 5.7 g
- Cholesterol: 0 mg
- Total Fat: 0.2 g
- Protein: 1.2 g
- Sodium: 347 mg

51. Braised Lamb Shanks

"This lamb shanks slow cooked recipe is great when served with grilled zucchini and mushroom risotto."
Serving: 4 | Prep: 20m | Ready in: 3h20m

Ingredients

- 2 large white onions, chopped
- 4 lamb shanks
- 2 cups dry red wine
- 1 cup balsamic vinegar
- 1/3 cup olive oil
- 4 cloves garlic, pressed
- 2 lemons, quartered
- 2 (14.5 oz.) cans diced tomatoes
- 1 bunch fresh basil, chopped
- 1 tbsp. kosher salt
- 1 tbsp. cracked black pepper

Direction

- Set the oven to 350°F (175°C) and start preheating.
- Arrange onions in 1 layer in the bottom of a medium roasting pan with a lid or Dutch oven. Top over onions with lamb shanks. Pour the olive oil, balsamic vinegar and wine over the lamb. Put a clove of pressed garlic next to each shank, and 1/4 of a lemon on each side.

Top over everything with tomatoes, season with basil, pepper and salt.

- Cover and transfer into the prepared oven. Cook for 3 hours. Make a nice flavorful gravy with the juices from the pan.

Nutrition Information

- Calories: 572 calories;
- Total Carbohydrate: 34.4 g
- Cholesterol: 86 mg
- Total Fat: 25.2 g
- Protein: 32.5 g
- Sodium: 1851 mg

52. Bratwurst Soup

"A tasty and filling soup dish served with a light salad and crusty bread for cold days."
Serving: 12 | Prep: 20m | Ready in: 1h20m

Ingredients

- 5 fresh bratwurst sausages
- 2 tbsps. olive oil
- 2 onions, chopped
- 4 carrots, sliced
- 4 ribs celery, chopped
- 2 tsps. chopped garlic
- 2 (32 oz.) cartons chicken broth
- 1 (14.5 oz.) can diced tomatoes
- 1 cup chopped fresh basil
- 1/4 cup chopped fresh flat-leaf parsley
- 2 tsps. ground thyme
- 1/2 tsp. cayenne pepper
- 6 potatoes, cut into cubes
- 2 (15 oz.) cans cannellini beans, drained and rinsed
- 12 oz. spinach, coarsely chopped, or more to taste

Direction

- Set an outdoor grill to medium-high heat and start preheating, oil the grate lightly.

- Grill the bratwursts for around 5 minutes on each side until heated thoroughly. Allow to cool. Cut each bratwurst into 1/4-inch pieces.
- In a large pot, heat the olive oil on medium-high. Stir and cook the celery, carrots, and onion in the heated oil for 5-8 minutes until the onions become tender. Add the garlic into the onion mixture and stir, cook for a minute until the garlic releases fragrance.
- Stir the cayenne pepper, thyme, parsley, basil, sliced bratwurst, tomatoes, and chicken broth into the onion mixture. Allow to boil, turn down the heat to low; allow to simmer, covered, for 20 minutes.
- Combine the potatoes into the bratwurst mixture, allow to boil, turn down the heat to low and allow to simmer for 15 minutes until the potatoes are nearly heated through.
- Stir in the spinach and beans; allow to simmer for 5-10 minutes until cooked thoroughly and the potatoes are done.

Nutrition Information

- Calories: 334 calories;
- Total Carbohydrate: 39.6 g
- Cholesterol: 27 mg
- Total Fat: 13.9 g
- Protein: 12.3 g
- Sodium: 1347 mg

53. Briam (Greek Mixed Vegetables In Tomato Sauce)

""Either a hot or cold version of this vegetables dish will satisfy you.""
Serving: 12 | Prep: 30m | Ready in: 1h40m

Ingredients

- 4 tomatoes
- 1/2 cup olive oil
- 2 tbsps. red wine vinegar
- 2 tbsps. white sugar
- 1/3 cup chopped fresh parsley
- 1/3 cup chopped fresh mint

- 1/3 cup chopped fresh basil
- 2 tbsps. fresh oregano
- 1/4 cup capers
- 2 cloves garlic
- salt and ground black pepper to taste
- 2 tbsps. olive oil
- 2 onions, sliced
- 2 potatoes, sliced
- 2 eggplant, sliced
- 3 zucchini, sliced
- 3 green bell peppers, sliced
- 2 cups okra

Direction

- Set the oven at 350°F (175°C) and start preheating. In a food processor's bowl, put garlic, capers, oregano, basil, mint, parsley, sugar, red wine vinegar, 1/2 cup of olive oil and three of the tomatoes; process to form a fresh tomato sauce. Season with black pepper and salt; set aside. Chop the remaining tomatoes and set aside.
- Place a skillet on medium heat and heat 2 tbsps. of olive oil, cook onions while stirring for around 10 minutes till slightly golden.
- Combine together the fresh tomato sauce, the reserved chopped tomato, okra, bell peppers, zucchini, eggplant, potatoes and onions; arrange the mixture on a large baking pan. Mix in a little water if necessary so the sauce just covers the vegetables.
- Bake for around 1 hour in the preheated oven or till all the vegetables turn tender.

Nutrition Information

- Calories: 177 calories;
- Total Carbohydrate: 17.7 g
- Cholesterol: 0 mg
- Total Fat: 11.6 g
- Protein: 2.7 g
- Sodium: 97 mg

54. Brick-oven Pizza (brooklyn Style)

""*Easy to prepare famous authentic brick oven pizza and best complemented by chilled pilsner style big beer.*""
Serving: 16 | Prep: 25m | Ready in: 16h31m

Ingredients

- 1 tsp. active dry yeast
- 1/4 cup warm water
- 1 cup cold water
- 1 tsp. salt
- 3 cups bread flour
- 6 oz. low moisture mozzarella cheese, thinly sliced
- 1/2 cup no salt added canned crushed tomatoes
- 1/4 tsp. freshly ground black pepper
- 1/2 tsp. dried oregano
- 3 tbsps. extra-virgin olive oil
- 6 leaves fresh basil, torn

Direction

- In a big bowl, drizzle yeast on hot water. Proof for five minutes. Mix in cold water and salt then mix in flour one cup at a time. Once the dough forms, take out of the bowl and knead on a surface will flour until it's smooth. Halve the dough and form both pieces to snug balls. Rub olive oil on the dough balls and then place in the refrigerator in a big closed container for a minimum of 16 hours. Allow the dough to rise in the big container then take out of the refrigerator an hour before you use it.
- Heat the oven to 550°F with the pizza stone on the bottom rack. Lightly sprinkle flour on pizza peel.
- Take one dough ball and lightly sprinkle it with flour then stretch carefully until it's around 14 inches in diameter or as large as your pizza stone. Set on floured peel. On the crust, place thin cuts of mozzarella. Drizzle generous amounts of grinded black pepper on it. Sprinkle dried oregano. Garnish with

crushed tomatoes but leave empty spaces. Sprinkle olive oil on top.

- Shake quickly back and forth to assure the dough is will easily release from the peel. Put the tip of the peel in the back of the heated pizza stone. Take off peel and leave pizza on the stone.
- Let it bake in the heated oven for 4-6 minutes until the crust starts to brown. Take pizza out of the oven by slipping the peel underneath the pizza. Drizzle several basil leaves on the pizza. Slice and then serve.

Nutrition Information

- Calories: 145 calories;
- Total Carbohydrate: 19.4 g
- Cholesterol: 7 mg
- Total Fat: 4.7 g
- Protein: 5.8 g
- Sodium: 213 mg

---

55. Browned Butter And Mizithra Cheese Pasta With Chicken, Spinach And Herbs

"It's great for the summer evenings."
Serving: 4 | Prep: 15m | Ready in: 41m

Ingredients

- 1 (16 oz.) package linguine pasta
- cooking spray
- 1 tsp. seasoned salt, or to taste
- 3 skinless, boneless chicken breasts
- 1/4 cup butter
- 1 cup chopped fresh spinach
- 1/4 cup chopped fresh basil
- 3 sprigs fresh thyme, leaves removed
- 1/2 cup grated Mizithra cheese
- 1/4 cup pine nuts
- freshly ground black pepper to taste

Direction

- Boil the lightly salted water in a large pot. Cook the linguine at a boil for 11 mins or until tender yet firm to bite, then drain.
- Lightly spray a grill pan with the cooking spray, then heat over medium heat. Add seasoned salt on both sides of the chicken. Cook for 5 mins each side or until juices run clear and the chicken is no longer pink in the middle. An instant-read thermometer should register at least 165°F (74°C) when inserted into middle. Allow to cool slightly.
- In a small saucepan, melt butter over medium heat. Then bring to a low simmer; cook for 5-10 mins or until the butter is almost done foaming and has caramel fragrance.
- In a large bowl, combine thyme, basil, spinach, chicken and linguine. Top with browned butter. Combine by tossing well. Put in pine nuts and Mizithra cheese and toss again. Decorate with the freshly ground black pepper.

Nutrition Information

- Calories: 701 calories;
- Total Carbohydrate: 100.9 g
- Cholesterol: 90 mg
- Total Fat: 23.1 g
- Protein: 37.2 g
- Sodium: 720 mg

---

56. Bruschetta Chicken

"Tasty chicken."
Serving: 4 | Prep: 10m | Ready in: 33m

Ingredients

- 4 (5 oz.) boneless skinless chicken breasts
- 1/4 cup Mazola® Corn Oil
- 2 tbsps. balsamic vinegar
- 2 garlic cloves, finely minced
- 1 tbsp. Spice Islands® Italian Herb Seasoning
- 1/2 tsp. Spice Islands® Fine Grind Sea Salt

- 1/4 tsp. Spice Islands® Fine Grind Black Pepper
- 2 cups diced plum tomatoes
- 1/4 cup diced red onion
- 1/2 cup shredded Italian blend cheese
- 1/4 cup finely chopped fresh basil

Direction

- In a big resealable plastic freezer bag, place chicken breasts, one at a time. Slightly lb. chicken breasts into an even 3/4-in. thickness. In a small bowl, combine pepper, salt, Italian herb seasoning, garlic, balsamic vinegar, and oil; whisk until blended. Pour 1/2 of the marinade over chicken, then reseal the bag; put aside and marinade for no less than 15 minutes. (You can prepare marinade and chicken in advance. Cover and chill in the fridge overnight.)
- Preheat grill to 350° F or medium heat. Mix the rest of marinade with red onion and diced tomatoes; put aside. Take chicken out of marinade and place on the grill surface; get rid of marinade. Grill chicken until cooked through, about 4-6 minutes for each side. Remove chicken to a serving plate; sprinkle shredded cheese over chicken. Scoop bruschetta mixture atop chicken; sprinkle with basil. Serve immediately.

Nutrition Information

- Calories: 359 calories;
- Total Carbohydrate: 7.6 g
- Cholesterol: 92 mg
- Total Fat: 21.6 g
- Protein: 34 g
- Sodium: 523 mg

57. Bruschetta Salad

"Fantastic salad!"
Serving: 4 | Prep: 15m | Ready in: 30m

Ingredients

- 6 Roma tomatoes, sliced into rounds
- 1/2 lb. mozzarella cheese, cut into bite-size cubes
- 1 cup crushed garlic-flavored bagel chips
- 1/2 cup torn fresh basil leaves
- 1/2 red onion, chopped
- 1/4 cup light olive oil
- 3 tbsps. red wine vinegar
- 2 large cloves garlic, minced
- 1 tbsp. dried basil
- salt and ground black pepper to taste

Direction

- In a bowl, combine black pepper, salt, basil, garlic, red wine vinegar, olive oil, red onion, basil, bagel chips, mozzarella cheese, and tomatoes; toss until evenly mixed. Chill in the fridge 15-30 minutes until chilled.

Nutrition Information

- Calories: 434 calories;
- Total Carbohydrate: 31.1 g
- Cholesterol: 36 mg
- Total Fat: 28.9 g
- Protein: 19 g
- Sodium: 746 mg

58. Bulgur Wheat With Pineapple, Pecans And Basil

"This salad is wonderful for lunch or dinner."
Serving: 4 | Prep: 10m | Ready in: 45m

Ingredients

- 2 cups water
- 1 cup bulgur

- 1 (20 oz.) can DOLE® Pineapple Tidbits or Pineapple Chunks, drained
- 1/2 cup chopped pecans
- 2 tbsps. chopped fresh basil
- 2 tbsps. chopped Italian parsley
- 1 1/2 tsps. olive oil

Direction

- In a big saucepan, combine bulgur and water. Heat to a boil. Lower heat and simmer with cover, about 35-40 minutes till bulgur is tender yet not mushy.
- Transfer to big bowl; allow to cool to room temperature.
- Mix oil, parsley, basil, pecans and pineapple tidbits into bulgur. Serve it at room temperature.

Nutrition Information

- Calories: 300 calories;
- Total Carbohydrate: 46.1 g
- Cholesterol: 0 mg
- Total Fat: 12.1 g
- Protein: 5.6 g
- Sodium: 22 mg

59. Butternut Squash Patties

"Use up your use leftover cooked butternut squash to make this delicious butternut squash patties."
Serving: 6 | Prep: 20m | Ready in: 1h20m

Ingredients

- 1 small butternut squash, halved and seeded
- 1/4 cup pine nuts
- 1 cup cooked rice
- 1/2 cup bread crumbs
- 1/4 cup freshly grated Parmesan cheese
- 3 tbsps. finely chopped fresh basil
- 1 egg
- 1 tbsp. finely chopped ginger root
- 1 clove garlic, finely chopped
- salt and ground black pepper to taste

- 2 tbsps. vegetable oil

Direction

- Set the oven at 190° C (375° F) to preheat.
- Arrange butternut squash in a 9x13-inch baking dish with the cut-side up; use aluminum foil to cover.
- Bake it in the preheated oven until the butternut squash becomes tender, approximately 45 minutes. Let it cool slightly. Scoop the butternut squash flesh and put into a bowl; smash it.
- In a dry, heavy skillet, cook while stirring the pine nuts over medium heat until they are toasted and aromatic, about 3-5 minutes.
- Stir black pepper, salt, garlic, ginger root, egg, basil, Parmesan cheese, bread crumbs, rice and pine nuts into the mashed butternut squash until they are mixed evenly; form into patties.
- In a heavy skillet, heat oil over medium heat; cook the patties in batches until they are browned and crispy, approximately 3-5 minutes on each side.

Nutrition Information

- Calories: 245 calories;
- Total Carbohydrate: 34.8 g
- Cholesterol: 34 mg
- Total Fat: 9.9 g
- Protein: 7.4 g
- Sodium: 136 mg

60. California Italian Wedding Soup

"The only changes on the standard soup recipe are the addition of lemon rind and fresh basil. Everyone will be impressed with this quick and easy soup."
Serving: 6 | Prep: 10m | Ready in: 25m

Ingredients

- 1/2 lb. extra-lean ground beef
- 1 egg, lightly beaten

- 2 tbsps. Italian-seasoned breadcrumbs
- 1 tbsp. grated Parmesan cheese
- 2 tbsps. shredded fresh basil leaves
- 1 tbsp. chopped Italian flat leaf parsley (optional)
- 2 green onions, sliced (optional)
- 5 3/4 cups chicken broth
- 2 cups finely sliced escarole (spinach may be substituted)
- 1 lemon, zested
- 1/2 cup orzo (rice-shaped pasta), uncooked
- grated Parmesan cheese for topping

Direction

- Combine the green onions, parsley, basil, cheese, bread crumbs, egg and meat, then form it into 3/4-in balls.
- In a big pan, pour the broth on high heat. Add in meatballs once boiling. Mix in orzo, lemon zest and escarole; boil once again. Lower the heat to medium. Let it cook for 10 minutes at a slow boil or until the orzo is tender, mixing often. Sprinkle cheese on top, then serve.

Nutrition Information

- Calories: 159 calories;
- Total Carbohydrate: 15.4 g
- Cholesterol: 55 mg
- Total Fat: 5.6 g
- Protein: 11.5 g
- Sodium: 99 mg

61. Cao Lau (vietnamese Noodle Bowl)

"This is traditionally from Hoi An, Vietnam. Use rice noodles that are fresh and almost as thick as linguine."
Serving: 6 | Prep: 20m | Ready in: 1h30m

Ingredients

- 2 tbsps. soy sauce
- 4 cloves garlic, minced, or more to taste
- 2 tsps. Chinese five-spice powder

- 2 tsps. white sugar
- 1 tsp. paprika
- 1/4 tsp. chicken bouillon granules
- 1 1/2 lbs. pork tenderloin, cut into cubes
- 2 tbsps. vegetable oil
- 2 tbsps. water
- 2 lbs. fresh thick Vietnamese-style rice noodles
- 2 cups bean sprouts
- 1 cup torn lettuce leaves
- 1 bunch green onions, chopped
- 1/4 cup fresh basil leaves
- 1/4 cup fresh cilantro leaves
- 1/4 cup crispy chow mein noodles, or more to taste

Direction

- Mix chicken bouillon, paprika, sugar, Chinese 5-spice, garlic, and soy sauce in a ceramic bowl or a big glass. Add the pork cubes then evenly coat by tossing. Use plastic wrap to cover the bowl then marinate for at least an hour in the fridge.
- Take pork out of marinade then shake off the excess. Throw out leftover marinade.
- In a big skillet or wok, heat oil on medium heat. Sauté pork for 4-7 minutes in the hot oil until its brown. Add water then sauté for another 2 minutes until pork is cooked through and water evaporates.
- Boil a big pot of water. Rinse the rice noodles in cold water and break noodles apart gently. Submerge noodles in the boiling water for about 30 seconds until half tender. Put bean sprouts in the noodles and water. Keep cooking for another 30 seconds until tender yet firm to chew. Drain.
- Mix pork mixture and noodles together in a big serving dish. Top with crispy chow mein, cilantro, basil, green onion, and lettuce on the noodles.

Nutrition Information

- Calories: 488 calories;
- Total Carbohydrate: 78.1 g
- Cholesterol: 49 mg
- Total Fat: 8.1 g

- Protein: 23.7 g
- Sodium: 373 mg

62. Caprese Chicken

"Healthy chicken with basil straight from the garden."
Serving: 4 | Prep: 15m | Ready in: 4h30m

Ingredients

- 4 (6 oz.) skinless, boneless chicken breast halves
- 1 cup Italian salad dressing
- 1 tbsp. Italian herb seasoning
- 1 tbsp. chicken seasoning (such as Grill Mates® Montreal Chicken Seasoning)
- 2 tbsps. canola oil
- 4 (1/2 inch thick) slices fresh mozzarella cheese
- 4 (1/2 inch thick) slices tomato
- 4 large fresh basil leaves
- 1 tbsp. balsamic vinegar

Direction

- In a resealable plastic bag, combine chicken seasoning, Italian herb seasoning, Italian salad dressing and chicken breasts. Coat chicken with marinade by kneading the bag several times; squeeze to remove air from the bag. Seal; put into the refrigerator for 4-6 hours.
- Turn on the oven to preheat at 500°F (260°C).
- In an ovenproof skillet or a large cast-iron, pour in canola oil over medium-high heat. Heat oil until a small droplet of water pops in the oil. Take the chicken breasts off the marinade; throw away used marinade. Fry chicken breasts in hot oil while flipping for 2 minutes.
- Put the skillet into the oven to bake for about 12 minutes until the juices run clear and the inside of the chicken is no longer pink. Use tomato slice and a slice of mozzarella cheese to top on each chicken breast.
- Put it back to the oven to bake for 3-5 minutes for the cheese to melt. Remove chicken breasts

to a serving platter; use a drizzle of balsamic vinegar and a basil leaf to top each.

Nutrition Information

- Calories: 583 calories;
- Total Carbohydrate: 10.7 g
- Cholesterol: 132 mg
- Total Fat: 39.5 g
- Protein: 43.9 g
- Sodium: 1279 mg

63. Caprese Couscous Salad

"Israeli couscous is balsamic marinated together with mozzarella and tomato."
Serving: 4 | Prep: 20m | Ready in: 50m

Ingredients

- 2 cups diced tomatoes
- 1 cup diced fresh mozzarella cheese
- 1 small shallot, minced
- 1 clove garlic, minced
- 1 tbsp. chopped fresh basil (optional)
- 2 tsps. balsamic vinegar
- 2 tsps. extra-virgin olive oil
- 1/2 tsp. salt
- 1/2 tsp. ground black pepper
- 1 1/4 cups water
- 1 cup pearl (Israeli) couscous

Direction

- In a large bowl, mix the mozzarella cheese, basil, olive oil, black pepper, tomatoes, shallot, balsamic vinegar, salt, and garlic. Refrigerate the mixture for 20-30 minutes.
- Boil the water in a saucepan. Remove it from the heat. Mix in couscous. Cover the pan and let it stand for 10 minutes. Fluff the mixture with a fork. Let the couscous cool first before tossing the tomato mixture.

Nutrition Information

- Calories: 257 calories;

- Total Carbohydrate: 35 g
- Cholesterol: 18 mg
- Total Fat: 7.3 g
- Protein: 12.7 g
- Sodium: 478 mg

64. Caprese Farro Salad

"This dish is Farro stirred with tomato, mozzarella, basil; or the classic Caprese flavors, and then mixed with balsamic vinaigrette."
Serving: 8 | Prep: 10m | Ready in: 55m

Ingredients

- 1 cup farro, rinsed
- 3 cups Swanson® Chicken Broth
- 1 cup red cherry tomatoes, halved
- 1 cup shredded mozzarella cheese
- 1/2 cup basil chiffonade (thinly sliced fresh basil leaves)
- 1/2 cup slivered almonds
- 1/4 cup thinly sliced red onion
- 3 tbsps. balsamic vinaigrette salad dressing

Direction

- In a saucepan, combine Swanson® Chicken Broth and farro; boil it. Lower the heat to medium-low and simmer for 30 minutes until soft. Strain, let it fully cool.
- Remove the cooled farro to a bowl. Mix in sliced onion, almonds, basil, mozzarella and tomatoes. Add the vinaigrette and stir thoroughly.

Nutrition Information

- Calories: 178 calories;
- Total Carbohydrate: 20.9 g
- Cholesterol: 11 mg
- Total Fat: 8.3 g
- Protein: 8 g
- Sodium: 516 mg

65. Caprese Salad With Chicken

"This tasty salad has grilled chicken and avocado alongside traditional ingredients."
Serving: 4 | Prep: 15m | Ready in: 35m

Ingredients

- Dressing:
- 4 tbsps. balsamic vinegar
- 2 tbsps. olive oil
- 2 tsps. maple syrup
- 1 garlic clove, minced
- 1 tsp. dried basil
- 1 tsp. salt
- Salad:
- 4 boneless chicken thighs
- 5 cups mixed salad greens
- 1 avocado - peeled, pitted, and sliced
- 2 medium tomatoes, chopped
- 4 oz. fresh mozzarella cheese, cubed
- 3 tbsps. fresh basil, thinly sliced (optional)

Direction

- In a bowl, mix salt, dried basil, garlic, brown sugar, olive oil and balsamic vinegar. Add chicken thighs into another bowl and add a quarter cup of dressing on top, saving the leftover dressing for making the salad.
- Preheat an outdoor grill to medium heat and oil the grate a bit.
- Grill chicken above indirect heat for 18-20 minutes while flipping once in a while till juices run out clear. Avoid burning by watching carefully. Put aside for 5 minutes prior to slicing.
- In a bowl, mix basil, mozzarella cheese, tomatoes, avocado and salad greens. Sprinkle with leftover dressing and combine by tossing. Add grilled chicken on top.

Nutrition Information

- Calories: 401 calories;
- Total Carbohydrate: 14.6 g
- Cholesterol: 71 mg
- Total Fat: 28.2 g

- Protein: 24.3 g
- Sodium: 830 mg

66. Caribbean Grilled Crab Cakes

"You can make this dish in a frying pan instead of on a grill. Fresh crabmeat is the best for this dish, any other kinds of meat work great as well."
Serving: 16 | Prep: 20m | Ready in: 1h

Ingredients

- For Crab Cakes:
- 3/4 lb. crabmeat
- 1 cup plain bread crumbs
- 3/4 cup mayonnaise
- 1 egg, beaten
- 2 green onions, minced
- Hot sauce, to taste
- Salt and pepper, to taste
- For Mango Salsa:
- 1 mango, peeled, pitted and diced
- 1 red onion, diced
- 3 tbsps. chopped fresh basil
- 3 tbsps. chopped fresh cilantro
- 1 lime, juiced
- Minced jalapeno, to taste
- Salt and pepper, to taste
- 2 tbsps. vegetable oil

Direction

- Strain the crabmeat. Combine pepper, salt, hot sauce, green onions, egg, mayonnaise, bread crumbs, and crabmeat in a big bowl until well mixed. Form 16 small cakes from the mixture. Chill for 30 minutes.
- In the meantime, mix pepper, salt, jalapeno (if using), lime juice, cilantro, basil, onion, and diced mango together in a small bowl. Chill until ready to use.
- For grilling: start preheating the grill to medium heat and lightly grease a grill basket or a grate with oil. Grill for 8 minutes, flipping 1 time.

- For pan-fry: In a big frying pan, heat 2 tbsps. vegetable oil over medium heat. Cook the crab cake patties for 4 minutes each side until both sides turn golden brown and crunchy.
- Put mango salsa on top of the crab cakes and serve.

Nutrition Information

- Calories: 157 calories;
- Total Carbohydrate: 8.9 g
- Cholesterol: 32 mg
- Total Fat: 10.9 g
- Protein: 6.4 g
- Sodium: 195 mg

67. Catch Of The Day

"Fresh trout always gives the best flavor."
Serving: 1 | Prep: 15m | Ready in: 35m

Ingredients

- 1 trout, cleaned and head removed
- 1 clove garlic, sliced
- 1 lemon, sliced
- 1 sprig fresh basil
- 1 sprig fresh rosemary
- salt and pepper to taste

Direction

- Preheat outdoor grill to medium high heat.
- Line fish cavity with lemon slices and garlic slices. Stuff rosemary and fresh basil inside. Season with pepper and salt. Wrap foil around fish. Put on a wire rack above a campfire or on a grill.
- Cook over direct heat for 15-20 minutes until fish easily flakes with a fork. Discard herbs and lemon from fish. Hold fish up by the spine then comb meat off the bones with a fork. Serve alongside lemon wedges to squeeze on the fish.

Nutrition Information

- Calories: 415 calories;
- Total Carbohydrate: 2.7 g
- Cholesterol: 201 mg
- Total Fat: 11.9 g
- Protein: 70.3 g
- Sodium: 398 mg

68. Cavatapi With Chicken Ragu, Mozzarella And Basil

"This tasty chicken sauce is made with Sargento Shredded Reduced Sodium Mozzarella and fresh basil."
Serving: 4 | Prep: 10m | Ready in: 25m

Ingredients

- 8 oz. cavatapi or penne pasta, uncooked
- 2 tsps. olive oil
- 1/2 cup minced onion
- 2 cloves garlic, minced
- 1 lb. ground chicken
- 1 (24 oz.) jar spicy red pepper pasta sauce
- 1 cup Sargento® Shredded Reduced Sodium Mozzarella Cheese
- 1/2 cup chopped fresh basil or Italian parsley

Direction

- Cook pasta following the package instructions, leave out the salt.
- In the meantime, in a big saucepan, heat oil over medium heat. Add garlic and onion, sauté for 3 minutes. Add chicken, sauté for 5 minutes until the chicken is not pink anymore. Add pasta sauce and simmer for 10 minutes.
- Strain the pasta, remove to 4 shallow bowls. Put basil, cheese and chicken ragu on top.

Nutrition Information

- Calories: 520 calories;
- Total Carbohydrate: 52.9 g
- Cholesterol: 76 mg
- Total Fat: 11.7 g
- Protein: 44.9 g

- Sodium: 690 mg

69. Chateaubriand Con Vino Brodo

"Use the extra sauce for roasted veggies and potatoes."
Serving: 4 | Prep: 15m | Ready in: 1h5m

Ingredients

- 1 lb. beef tenderloin roast, trimmed
- 2 cloves garlic, quartered
- 1/4 cup extra virgin olive oil
- 1 tbsp. lemon or lime juice
- 1 pinch dried oregano
- 1 pinch dried basil
- 1 pinch dried dill
- 1 pinch dried rosemary
- 1 pinch dried thyme
- 2 tbsps. whole multi-colored peppercorns
- 1 cup water
- 2 tbsps. Dijon mustard
- 1 clove chopped fresh garlic
- 1/4 cup butter
- 1 1/2 cups dry red wine

Direction

- Preheat an oven to 190°C/375°F.
- In roast, cut 8 small slits. Put garlic in slits.
- Mix thyme, rosemary, dill, basil, oregano, lemon juice and olive oil in medium bowl. Brush on roast. Press whole peppercorns into roast with a small spoon. Put roast on a rack in a roasting pan; put water into the bottom of the pan.
- In preheated oven, bake 40 minutes for well done or 20 minutes for medium rare. Transfer roast to cutting board; let sit for 5 minutes.
- Put drippings from roast into small saucepan on low heat. Mix butter, chopped garlic and mustard in; cook till butter melts completely. Add wine; reduce by half. Put sauce on sliced roast.

Nutrition Information

- Calories: 647 calories;
- Total Carbohydrate: 7.7 g
- Cholesterol: 111 mg
- Total Fat: 51.8 g
- Protein: 21 g
- Sodium: 330 mg

70. Checca

"Serve this on Italian bread slices."
Serving: 8 | Prep: 15m | Ready in: 2h15m

Ingredients

- 5 tomatoes, seeded and diced
- 1/2 cup chopped fresh basil
- 1/2 cup olive oil
- 4 cloves garlic, minced
- salt to taste
- 2 tbsps. grated Parmesan cheese, or more to taste

Direction

- In a big non-reactive bowl, combine garlic, olive oil, basil and tomatoes; use salt to season.
- Use plastic wrap to cover the bowl; allow mixture to stand at room temperature 2-10 hours, until flavors meld.
- Just before serving, mix Parmesan cheese into tomato mixture.

Nutrition Information

- Calories: 144 calories;
- Total Carbohydrate: 4.2 g
- Cholesterol: 1 mg
- Total Fat: 14.1 g
- Protein: 1.5 g
- Sodium: 24 mg

71. Cheese And Pecan Pasta Salad

"A resistible salad which is a perfect choice to bring to a party."
Serving: 8 | Prep: 45m | Ready in: 55m

Ingredients

- 1 lb. spaghetti
- 2 tbsps. olive oil
- 2 cloves garlic, minced
- 1/4 cup torn fresh basil leaves
- 1 tbsp. chopped fresh oregano
- 1 tsp. salt
- 1 tsp. ground black pepper
- 1/2 cup half-and-half cream
- 1/2 cup olive oil
- 1 green bell pepper, seeded and thinly sliced
- 1 red bell pepper, seeded and thinly sliced
- 1/2 cup chopped fresh parsley
- 2/3 lb. Jarlsberg cheese, cut into matchsticks
- 1/2 cup toasted, chopped pecans
- 1/4 lb. grated Parmesan cheese

Direction

- Boil a large pot of lightly salted water. Put in spaghetti; cook until tender but still firm to bite, 8-10 minutes. Drain and in a large bowl, toss the spaghetti with 2 tbsps. of olive oil; put aside.
- In a bowl, beat 1/2 cup of olive oil, half-and-half, pepper, salt, oregano, basil, and garlic. Toss them with the cooked spaghetti. Put in pecans, Jarlsberg, parsley, and red and green bell peppers. Toss the salad 1 more time to combine, then dust with Parmesan cheese to serve.

Nutrition Information

- Calories: 645 calories;
- Total Carbohydrate: 49 g
- Cholesterol: 52 mg
- Total Fat: 39.4 g
- Protein: 24.6 g
- Sodium: 593 mg

72. Cheese Omelette With Herbs

"My husband love this omelet that I made"
Serving: 2 | Prep: 5m | Ready in: 15m

Ingredients

- 5 eggs
- 4 tbsps. whole milk
- 4 tbsps. sunflower seeds
- 1 tsp. roasted flax seeds
- 1 tsp. dried chervil
- 1/2 tsp. dried Italian herbs
- 1 small clove garlic, minced
- 1/2 tsp. sea salt
- 1 tsp. freshly ground black pepper
- 1 tbsp. olive oil
- 1/4 tsp. dried basil
- 3 slices Gouda cheese
- 4 leaves fresh basil, chopped

Direction

- In a bowl, combine pepper, salt, garlic, Italian herbs, chervil, flax seeds, sunflower seeds milk and eggs, mix with a fork until well blended using a fork.
- In a nonstick skillet, heat olive oil over medium heat. Pour in egg mixture. Cook for about 5 minutes until egg begins to set. Sprinkle with dried basil and arrange sliced Gouda cheese on top. Use a spatula to cut into 2 halves. Fold each omelet in half and flip over. Cook for 1 minute longer. Decorate with fresh basil and serve.

Nutrition Information

- Calories: 508 calories;
- Total Carbohydrate: 9 g
- Cholesterol: 460 mg
- Total Fat: 40.4 g
- Protein: 29.8 g
- Sodium: 954 mg

73. Cheese Stuffed Olives

"A delectable recipe to impress people!""
Serving: 5 | Prep: 45m | Ready in: 45m

Ingredients

- 4 oz. cream cheese, softened
- 1/2 cup goat cheese, softened
- 1/4 cup freshly grated Parmesan cheese
- 8 leaves fresh basil, chopped
- 1 bulb roasted garlic
- salt and pepper to taste
- 2 (8 oz.) jars jumbo or extra large olives

Direction

- In a food processor, arrange pepper, salt, roasted garlic, basil, Parmesan, goat cheese, and cream cheese; pulse until the mixture becomes smooth and combined properly. To fill the olives, spoon the filling into a pastry bag (or a plastic baggie with one corner cut off), or a cookie press.

Nutrition Information

- Calories: 304 calories;
- Total Carbohydrate: 6.3 g
- Cholesterol: 47 mg
- Total Fat: 27.5 g
- Protein: 10.5 g
- Sodium: 2413 mg

74. Cheesy Oven Roasted Fingerling Fries

"A perfect appetizer."
Serving: 4 | Prep: 15m | Ready in: 40m

Ingredients

- 3 lbs. fingerling potatoes, cut in half lengthwise
- 2 tbsps. olive oil
- 2 tbsps. melted butter
- 1 tsp. garlic salt

- 1 cup shredded fontina cheese
- Fresh parsley, torn
- Fresh basil leaves, torn
- Chopped fresh chives
- Kosher salt and cracked black pepper to taste
- Reynolds Wrap® Aluminum Foil

Direction

- Set oven to 425° F and start preheating.
- Toss together freshly cracked black pepper, garlic salt, butter, olive oil and the halved potatoes in a big bowl.
- Tear 4 big sheets of Reynolds Wrap(R) Aluminum Foil to get 16 inches in length for each. Evenly distribute the potato mixture into sheets of foil and bring up sides of foil. Double fold both ends and top to seal packet, leaving space for heat circulation inside. Arrange packets on a baking sheet and remove to the oven; cook 25 minutes.
- Take 1 package out of the oven. To open package, cut along top fold carefully using a sharp knife, letting steam to escape. Open top of foil packet. Check if the fork are tender and potatoes fully cooked; if not, bring back to the oven, for another 5 minutes.
- When cooked, open up packets; sprinkle some herbs and cheese atop each portion. Allow cheese to melt, then serve. Season to taste with pepper and salt.

Nutrition Information

- Calories: 480 calories;
- Total Carbohydrate: 60.3 g
- Cholesterol: 47 mg
- Total Fat: 21.2 g
- Protein: 14 g
- Sodium: 832 mg

75. Cheesy Parmesan Crusted Crescent Rolls

"These crescent rolls are stuffed with mozzarella cheese and brushed with a butter-herb mixture, and they have a Parmesan cheese on top. Once they're baked, they will have a very lovely golden brown color."
Serving: 8 | Prep: 5m | Ready in: 15m

Ingredients

- 1 (8 oz.) package refrigerated butter-flavored crescent rolls
- 3/4 cup shredded Stella® mozzarella cheese
- 2 tbsps. butter, melted
- 1/8 tsp. dried basil
- 1/8 tsp. dried oregano
- Stella® Parmesan cheese, for topping

Direction

- Turn the oven to 400°F (205°C) to preheat. Coat a big cookie sheet with oil and put aside.
- Roll out crescent rolls, and then separate and put Stella shredded mozzarella cheese on top of each roll. Carefully roll the crescents and put on a cookie sheet.
- In a small bowl, combine dried oregano, dried basil, and butter. Brush over the crescent rolls with this mixture and put Stella Parmesan cheese on top.
- Bake at 400°F (205°C) until turning light brown, about 10 minutes.

Nutrition Information

- Calories: 175 calories;
- Total Carbohydrate: 11.5 g
- Cholesterol: 16 mg
- Total Fat: 11.9 g
- Protein: 4.8 g
- Sodium: 340 mg

76. Cheesy-crust Skillet Pizza

""If you love pizza, then you should try this recipe!""
Serving: 2 | Prep: 10m | Ready in: 20m

Ingredients

- 1 1/2 cups shredded part-skim mozzarella cheese
- 5 cherry tomatoes, thinly sliced
- 2 tbsps. torn fresh basil leaves
- 4 small fresh mozzarella balls (bocconcini), thinly sliced

Direction

- Take a 10" nonstick skillet and heat on medium high heat. Drizzle shredded mozzarella cheese in the skillet evenly and cook for 2-3 minutes until it melts.
- Put basil leaves, tomato slices and fresh mozzarella slices on the cheese already melted. Leave space for "crust" to form. Cook for 2-3 minutes until edges are browned and top is bubbly.
- Take skillet away from the heat and use spatula to loosen pizza. Slice pizza on a cutting board. Cool for a minute before cutting.

Nutrition Information

- Calories: 385 calories;
- Total Carbohydrate: 6.4 g
- Cholesterol: 98 mg
- Total Fat: 25.6 g
- Protein: 31 g
- Sodium: 609 mg

77. Chef Gerard's Award Winning Caesar Salad Dressing

""This recipe of my Dad won numerous awards and was published many times in national cooking magazines. It is different from any other Caesar dressing recipe. No other chefs can beat this recipe even if how many times they tried to. Here's a secret, make this recipe 2 days before serving. My dad said that it is better to store it for 2 days inside the refrigerator to allow the flavors to blend.""
Serving: 6 | Prep: 30m | Ready in: 30m

Ingredients

- 1 tbsp. chopped fresh parsley
- 1 tbsp. chopped green onion tops
- 1 tsp. celery salt
- 1 tsp. chopped fresh oregano
- 1 tsp. chopped fresh basil
- 1 tbsp. crushed black peppercorns
- 1 tbsp. paprika
- 2 large garlic cloves, minced
- 2 cups olive oil (such as Bertolli®)
- 3 tbsps. Burgundy wine (optional)
- 1/2 cup wine vinegar
- 1 (8 oz.) can stewed tomatoes, crushed

Direction

- Make a paste by smashing celery salt, parsley, basil, paprika, garlic cloves, black pepper, oregano, and green onions. Place the paste in a mixer together with Burgundy wine, stewed tomatoes, olive oil, and white wine vinegar. Whisk for 5 minutes and store it inside the refrigerator until serving. Make sure to stir the mixture well before serving.

Nutrition Information

- Calories: 662 calories;
- Total Carbohydrate: 4.4 g
- Cholesterol: 0 mg
- Total Fat: 72.3 g
- Protein: 0.8 g
- Sodium: 334 mg

78. Chef John's Green Hummus

"A simple, green, basil-spiked hummus that's great as a spread."
Serving: 6 | Prep: 10m | Ready in: 10m

Ingredients

- 1/3 cup firmly packed fresh basil leaves
- 4 cloves garlic, chopped
- 1 tbsp. lemon juice, or to taste
- 3 tbsps. olive oil, divided
- 1 (15 oz.) can garbanzo beans, drained
- 1 (15 oz.) can white beans, drained
- salt and ground black pepper to taste

Direction

- Boil a big pot of water and add basil. Cook for about 20 seconds without cover, until it turns bright green. Instantly immerse the basil in the ice water until it becomes cold. To remove the extra moisture, squeeze the basil and use a paper towel pat it dry.
- Put basil, garlic, lemon juice, 1 tbsp. olive oil, garbanzo beans, and white beans, salt, and black pepper, respectively, in a blender, covered, and process until it becomes nearly smooth. Put the leftover 2 tbsps. of olive oil and puree until it becomes smooth.

Nutrition Information

- Calories: 200 calories;
- Total Carbohydrate: 26.5 g
- Cholesterol: 0 mg
- Total Fat: 7.5 g
- Protein: 7.7 g
- Sodium: 144 mg

79. Chicken And Herbs In White Wine

"Yummy chicken recipe with herbs and wine. Serve with noodles (add cooked noodles into pan to dip in broth for 15 minutes), or cook gravy (take away chicken and put cornstarch mixed with water) then use with mashed potatoes."
Serving: 6 | Prep: 20m | Ready in: 2h5m

Ingredients

- 2 tbsps. olive oil
- 1 (4 lb.) chicken, cut into pieces
- garlic powder to taste
- 1/2 lb. fresh mushrooms, sliced
- 1 large onion, diced
- 1/2 tsp. dried basil
- 1/2 tsp. dried oregano
- 1/2 tsp. dried rosemary
- 1/2 tsp. dried thyme
- 1 tsp. garlic salt
- 1/4 tsp. black pepper
- 1 tsp. poultry seasoning
- 1 cup dry white wine
- 1 (10.5 oz.) can chicken broth

Direction

- In a large Dutch oven, heat olive oil over medium heat. Drizzle garlic powder over chicken, then brown on both sides. Transfer the chicken to paper towels.
- Spoon off chicken fat, then move the pan back to stove. Mix in onions and mushrooms; cook while sometimes stirring until onions become softened. Transfer to a medium bowl.
- In a different bowl, blend thyme, rosemary, oregano, and basil. Flavor with poultry seasoning, pepper, and garlic salt together. Mix in wine, then add to mushrooms and onion.
- Transfer chicken back to the Dutch oven. Spread broth and mushroom mixture over chicken; cook, covered, over low heat for around 1 and a half hours till meat starts to fall off the bone.

Nutrition Information

- Calories: 750 calories;
- Total Carbohydrate: 5.6 g
- Cholesterol: 228 mg
- Total Fat: 50.4 g
- Protein: 58.1 g
- Sodium: 760 mg

80. Chicken And Sausage With Bowties

"This pasta recipe is a perfectly hearty meal to fill anyone up but won't take up too much time to prepare. You can even customize the dish to your taste, like adding in a different type of meat and adjusting cooking time for each variation."
Serving: 8 | Prep: 15m | Ready in: 1h

Ingredients

- 1 (16 oz.) package uncooked farfalle pasta
- 2 skinless, boneless chicken breasts
- 1 lb. hot Italian turkey sausage, casings removed
- 1 tbsp. olive oil
- 2 cloves garlic, sliced
- 1 (14.5 oz.) can crushed tomatoes
- 1/2 cup red wine
- 2 tbsps. chopped fresh basil
- 1 tsp. dried rosemary

Direction

- Boil a big pot filled with water that's slightly salted, and add the pasta, cook until they become al dente, about 8-10 minutes.
- Wash the chicken breasts, then cut into large bite-size chunks, and also cut the sausages into the big size portions. Combine garlic and oil in a big deep skillet and cook over a medium-low heat long enough to infuse oil with flavor. Remove the garlic from the oil.
- In the same skillet with the infused oil, add the sausage and chicken, gently brown both of them until opaque. Add the wine and

tomatoes, then let boil then simmer for 20 minutes. Season the sauce with pepper, salt, rosemary, and basil to your taste. Add the cooked drained pasta into the skillet, toss to serve.

Nutrition Information

- Calories: 382 calories;
- Total Carbohydrate: 47.6 g
- Cholesterol: 51 mg
- Total Fat: 9.1 g
- Protein: 24 g
- Sodium: 526 mg

81. Chicken Cacciatore II

"Great recipe from a high-end cooking store."
Serving: 8 | Prep: 30m | Ready in: 1h25m

Ingredients

- 2 (3 lb.) whole chickens, each cut into 8 pieces
- salt and ground black pepper to taste
- 1 cup all-purpose flour
- 2 tbsps. olive oil
- 1 yellow onion, chopped
- 1 large green bell pepper, seeded and chopped
- 6 cloves garlic, minced
- 1 lb. white button mushrooms, quartered
- 2 tsps. chopped fresh oregano
- 1 (28 oz.) can whole peeled tomatoes in juice, coarsely chopped
- 2 tbsps. tomato paste
- 3/4 cup white wine
- 1 1/2 cups chicken stock
- 3 tbsps. capers, drained and rinsed
- 2 tbsps. coarsely chopped fresh basil

Direction

- Season black pepper and salt over the chicken pieces.
- Put flour into a shallow bowl. Press each of the chicken pieces into flour then tap off the excess.

- In a large Dutch oven, heat olive oil over medium-heat until it is almost smoking hot.
- Pan-fry the chicken for 3 minutes per side or until it turns golden brown on both sides. Work in batches to avoid overcrowding the skillet. Put the cooked chicken aside.
- Into the Dutch oven, stir garlic, green bell pepper and onion. Cook until tender, stirring occasionally, about 5 minutes.
- Mix in mushroom. Cook 5-8 minutes longer or until their juice releases.
- Stir in chicken stock, white wine, tomato paste, tomatoes and oregano then bring to a boil.
- Put chicken pieces back to sauce. Cover, lower the heat to medium-low, and simmer for 30-40 minutes or until the juices run clear and inside the chicken is no longer pink.
- Mix in the capers. Top with basil then serve.

Nutrition Information

- Calories: 587 calories;
- Total Carbohydrate: 23.8 g
- Cholesterol: 145 mg
- Total Fat: 29.7 g
- Protein: 51 g
- Sodium: 543 mg

82. Chicken In Basil Cream

"Your ordinary fried chicken will taste a lot better with this recipe. The cream sauce enhances the flavor greatly."
Serving: 4 | Prep: 15m | Ready in: 30m

Ingredients

- 1/4 cup milk
- 1/4 cup dried bread crumbs
- 4 skinless, boneless chicken breasts
- 3 tbsps. butter
- 1/2 cup chicken broth
- 1 cup heavy whipping cream
- 1 (4 oz.) jar sliced pimento peppers, drained
- 1/2 cup grated Parmesan cheese
- 1/4 cup chopped fresh basil
- 1/8 tsp. ground black pepper

Direction

- In separate, shallow bowls, put bread crumbs and milk. Heat margarine or butter in a skillet over medium heat. Dip chicken into the milk, then dip into the crumbs to coat. In the margarine or butter, cook both sides of the chicken for 10 minutes until the juices run clear. Take out and keep warm.
- Pour broth into the skillet. Boil over medium heat, and whisk to loosen browned bits from the pan. Mix in pimentos and cream, stir and boil for 1 minute. Lower the heat.
- Add pepper, basil and Parmesan cheese. Whisk the sauce and cook until fully heated. Add the mixture onto the chicken and enjoy.

Nutrition Information

- Calories: 496 calories;
- Total Carbohydrate: 9.2 g
- Cholesterol: 183 mg
- Total Fat: 35.7 g
- Protein: 34.2 g
- Sodium: 373 mg

83. Chicken Italian

"A simple and quick evening meal with browned chicken breasts in a flavorful tomato base with cheese and herbs served alongside spaghetti."
Serving: 4 | Prep: 10m | Ready in: 30m

Ingredients

- 8 oz. uncooked spaghetti
- 1 tbsp. olive oil
- 2 cloves garlic, finely chopped
- 1 (16 oz.) package boneless skinless chicken breast halves
- 1 tsp. dried basil leaves
- 1/4 tsp. red pepper flakes
- 1 (19 oz.) can Progresso® Vegetable Classics hearty tomato soup
- 1/2 cup shredded mozzarella cheese

Direction

- Following the package instructions, cook the spaghetti and drain.
- At the same time, heat the oil in 10-inch skillet on medium-high until it becomes hot. Cook the chicken and garlic in oil until the chicken turns light brown, for 3-4 minutes per side.
- Dust over the chicken with pepper flakes and basil. Add the soup to the chicken; dust with cheese. Put a cover and bring to a simmer for 10 minutes.

Nutrition Information

- Calories: 452 calories;
- Total Carbohydrate: 55.5 g
- Cholesterol: 67 mg
- Total Fat: 9.4 g
- Protein: 34 g
- Sodium: 677 mg

84. Chicken Manicotti Alfredo

"Rich and flavorful Italian pasta."
Serving: 8

Ingredients

- 3 skinless, boneless chicken breast halves
- 1/2 cup distilled white vinegar
- 1 cup olive oil
- 1 clove crushed garlic
- 1 (12 oz.) package manicotti pasta
- 6 tbsps. butter
- 2 cups heavy whipping cream
- 1/4 tsp. ground nutmeg
- 1 tsp. ground black pepper
- 1 1/2 cups grated Parmesan cheese
- 1 tsp. salt
- 1 pint part-skim ricotta cheese
- 1 egg
- 1 tbsp. chopped fresh oregano
- 1 tbsp. chopped fresh marjoram
- 1 tbsp. chopped fresh basil
- 1 cup shredded mozzarella cheese

Direction

- Marinate chicken with garlic, olive oil and vinegar for no less than 30 minutes in a big resealable plastic bag. Sauté in a little olive oil until done. Put aside.
- In a big pot filled with boiling water, cook pasta until al dente. Drain pasta and put aside.
- At the same time, in a small saucepan on medium-high heat, melt margarine or butter. Put in ground black pepper, nutmeg, salt and heavy cream; mix until sauce thickens. Decrease to low heat. Put in grated Parmesan cheese; mix until cheese is melted. Put Alfredo sauce aside.
- In a big bowl, combine basil, marjoram, oregano, egg and ricotta cheese. Blend in the cooked chicken.
- Stuff chicken-ricotta mixture into the cooked manicotti shells. Arrange half of Alfredo sauce to cover the bottom of a 9x13-in. baking dish. Arrange stuffed shells atop sauce. Pour over shells with the leftover sauce. Sprinkle 1 cup shredded mozzarella cheese over top. Use aluminum foil to cover.
- Bake in the oven preheated to 175° C (350° F), about 45 minutes. Allow to sit 10 minutes; serve.

Nutrition Information

- Calories: 813 calories;
- Total Carbohydrate: 37.4 g
- Cholesterol: 197 mg
- Total Fat: 59.8 g
- Protein: 33.3 g
- Sodium: 811 mg

85. Chicken Parmesan

"A yummy chicken parmesan recipe with a twist."
Serving: 4 | Prep: 25m | Ready in: 1h

Ingredients

- 4 skinless, boneless chicken breast halves

- salt and freshly ground black pepper to taste
- 2 eggs
- 1 cup panko bread crumbs, or more as needed
- 1/2 cup grated Parmesan cheese
- 2 tbsps. all-purpose flour, or more if needed
- 1 cup olive oil for frying
- 1/2 cup prepared tomato sauce
- 1/4 cup fresh mozzarella, cut into small cubes
- 1/4 cup chopped fresh basil
- 1/2 cup grated provolone cheese
- 1/4 cup grated Parmesan cheese
- 1 tbsp. olive oil

Direction

- Preheat oven to 230°C/450°F.
- Between 2 heavy plastic sheets/resealable freezer bags, put chicken breasts on a solid level surface. Use smooth side of meat mallet to firmly lb. chicken to 1/2-inch thick. Thoroughly season chicken with pepper and salt.
- In a shallow bowl, beat eggs; put aside.
- In another bowl, mix 1/2 cup of Parmesan cheese and breadcrumbs; put aside.
- Put flour in a strainer/sifter. Sprinkle on chicken breasts, coating both sides evenly.
- In beaten eggs, dip flour-coated chicken breasts; put breast into breadcrumb mixture, pressing crumbs on both sides. Repeat for every breast. Put breaded chicken breasts aside for 15 minutes.
- In a big skillet, heat 1 cup of olive oil on medium high heat till it starts to shimmer. Cook chicken, 2 minutes per side, till golden. Chicken will complete cooking in oven.
- Put chicken in a baking dish; top 1/3 cup of tomato sauce on each breast. Layer every chicken breast with even amounts of provolone cheese, fresh basil and mozzarella cheese. Sprinkle 1-2 tbsps. of Parmesan cheese over; drizzle 1 tbsp. of olive oil.
- In the preheated oven, bake for 15-20 minutes till chicken breasts aren't pink in middle and cheese is bubbly and browned. Ainstant-read thermometer inserted in middle should read at least 74°C/165°F.

Nutrition Information

- Calories: 471 calories;
- Total Carbohydrate: 24.8 g
- Cholesterol: 187 mg
- Total Fat: 24.9 g
- Protein: 42.1 g
- Sodium: 840 mg

86. Chicken Pesto A La Lisa

""*A flavorful pasta dinner that satisfied my entire family.*""
Serving: 6

Ingredients

- 1/2 cup chopped sun-dried tomatoes
- 1 1/2 cups chicken broth
- 6 skinless, boneless chicken breast halves - cut into strips
- 2 cloves garlic, minced
- 1 tbsp. olive oil
- 2 tsps. cornstarch
- 3/4 cup prepared basil pesto
- 1/4 cup toasted pine nuts
- 1/4 cup chopped fresh basil
- 3/4 cup crumbled feta cheese
- 1 (16 oz.) package fusilli pasta
- 2 tbsps. grated Parmesan cheese

Direction

- In chicken broth, soak sun-dried tomatoes.
- Place a large skillet on medium heat; heat oil and garlic; cook in chicken till done.
- Mix a couple of tbsps. of chicken broth and cornstarch. Mix together basil, pine nuts, pesto, sun-dried tomatoes and the remaining chicken broth into the skillet with the chicken. Combine the cornstarch mixture into the sauce; cook till thickened. A few minutes before serving, put in feta.
- Meanwhile, in a large pot of boiling salted water, cook pasta till al dente. Strain. Serve the

pasta with the sauce spooned over; sprinkle Parmesan cheese on top.

Nutrition Information

- Calories: 702 calories;
- Total Carbohydrate: 63.8 g
- Cholesterol: 97 mg
- Total Fat: 26.9 g
- Protein: 49.5 g
- Sodium: 750 mg

---

87. Chicken Pho

"This recipe of chicken pho straight from Vietnam is best paired with sriracha and hoisin sauce."
Serving: 24 | Prep: 30m | Ready in: 2h

Ingredients

- 10 quarts water
- 3 lbs. chicken bones
- 1 whole chicken
- 1 medium onion
- 1 (1 inch) piece ginger
- 1 (32 fluid oz.) container chicken broth
- 1/4 cup rock sugar
- 3 tsps. fish sauce
- 2 cubes pho ga soup seasoning
- 1 1/2 tsps. salt
- 2 (16 oz.) packages rice stick noodles (banh pho)
- 1/2 lb. bean sprouts
- 1 bunch green onion, chopped
- 1 bunch cilantro, chopped
- 6 sprigs Thai basil, or as needed
- 1 lime, cut in wedges

Direction

- Fill a stockpot with water and let it boil. Meanwhile, put the chicken bones under hot water and rinse to remove impurities.
- Put the bones in the pot of boiling water. Lessen the heat and simmer for about an hour until it is beginning to soften, removing any

fat off the surface of the broth. Remove parboiled bones.

- Put the whole chicken into the pot and make it simmer for about 30 to 40 minutes until no visible pink color in the middle. Take the chicken out from broth and set aside, allowing it to cool. An instant-read thermometer poked near the bone should register 165°F (74°C).
- Mix together the ginger and onion in a skillet over medium-high heat. Sauté for about 7 minutes until both turns nicely browned and aromatic. Smash the ginger using the backside of a knife placed into a chopping board. Place the ginger and onion into the broth. Mix with rock sugar, pho ga seasoning, salt, fish sauce and chicken broth.
- Fill a big pot with water and let it boil. Stir in the rice noodles and boil for about 2 to 3 minutes until soft yet firm to the bite. Drain the noodles.
- Peel off the skin of the cooled chicken; get rid of the bones and skin, and set aside the meat.
- Serve the noodles in bowls and put the chicken meat and broth on top. Garnish with Thai basil, bean sprouts, cilantro and green onion. Squeeze a wedge of lime in each bowl.

Nutrition Information

- Calories: 324 calories;
- Total Carbohydrate: 34.1 g
- Cholesterol: 73 mg
- Total Fat: 11.1 g
- Protein: 19.9 g
- Sodium: 520 mg

88. Chile Basil Sesame Chicken

"This dish is chicken breasts marinated in basil, chile peppers, sesame seeds, soy sauce, chicken broth, sesame oils, and olive oil. You can grill the chicken heavily or lightly as you like."
Serving: 2

Ingredients

- 1/2 cup light soy sauce
- 1/2 cup low-sodium, low-fat chicken broth
- 1 tbsp. olive oil
- 1 tsp. sesame oil
- 2 tsps. toasted sesame seeds
- 2 whole dried chile peppers, cut in half
- 1/4 cup chopped fresh basil
- 1 lb. skinless, boneless chicken breasts

Direction

- For the Marinade: Mix basil, chile peppers, sesame seeds, sesame oil, olive oil, chicken broth and soy sauce in a medium-sized nonporous glass bowl or dish. Stir thoroughly and add chicken. Flip to coat, put a cover on the bowl or dish and chill to marinate for a maximum of 1 day.
- Set the grill to high heat to preheat, put the grate 6-in. from the heat source and lightly grease the grate.
- Take the chicken out of the dish, get rid of any remaining marinade. Grill the chicken over high heat until fully cooked and the inside is not pink anymore, or about 7 minutes on each side.

Nutrition Information

- Calories: 389 calories;
- Total Carbohydrate: 6.9 g
- Cholesterol: 132 mg
- Total Fat: 13.6 g
- Protein: 57.1 g
- Sodium: 2370 mg

89. Chilled Zucchini Soup

"If you enjoy gazpacho or any other kind of cold soups, you'll definitely love this."
Serving: 4 | Prep: 10m | Ready in: 2h35m

Ingredients

- 3 tbsps. olive oil, divided
- 1 onion, finely chopped
- 4 fresh tomato, seeded and chopped
- 4 cups water
- 6 sprigs fresh mint, divided
- 3 zucchini, sliced
- 1 tbsp. cornstarch
- 1 tbsp. cold water
- salt and pepper to taste
- 1 tsp. lemon juice, or to taste
- 2 sprigs fresh basil

Direction

- In a large saucepan, heat 2 tbsps. olive oil over medium heat; cook onion until translucent and tender, about 5 minutes. Add tomatoes and cook for 2 minutes more, stirring regularly.
- Into the saucepan, pour water and bring to a boil. Add zucchini and 4 sprigs of mint. Reduce the heat to low; cover and simmer the soup for 15 minutes. Discard the mint.
- Stir cold water and cornstarch together; add to the soup. Raise heat to medium; whisk the cornstarch mixture until soup is thickened. Season with pepper and salt. Remove from heat and put aside to cool down.
- Refrigerate the soup until cold, about 2 hours. Add lemon juice before serving; garnish with the remaining olive oil, leftover mint, and basil.

Nutrition Information

- Calories: 163 calories;
- Total Carbohydrate: 16.3 g
- Cholesterol: 0 mg
- Total Fat: 10.7 g
- Protein: 3.2 g
- Sodium: 65 mg

90. Chuck And Heather's Panang Curry

"Serve this along with cooked rice."
Serving: 4 | Prep: 20m | Ready in: 35m

Ingredients

- 1 lb. beef flank steak
- 2 cups coconut milk, divided
- 3 tbsps. green curry paste
- 4 tsps. Vietnamese hot chile paste (such as sambal oelek)
- 1 tbsp. chopped fresh basil
- 1/2 tsp. white sugar
- 2 cups cooked rice

Direction

- Slice beef against grain into slices, 1/4-inch each.
- Heat a big skillet or wok on medium-high heat; whisk together curry paste and 1/2 cup coconut milk 1-2 minutes until simmering. Mix in 1/4 cup coconut milk; bring curry mixture back to a simmer. Do the same with the rest of coconut milk, with each addition, bring the mixture back to a simmer, about 7-8 minutes altogether.
- Mix beef and chile paste into the curry mixture; simmer 4-5 minutes until beef is lightly pink inside. Mix in sugar and basil; cook 3-5 minutes longer until beef is cooked through and soft. Serve along with cooked rice.

Nutrition Information

- Calories: 477 calories;
- Total Carbohydrate: 30.8 g
- Cholesterol: 36 mg
- Total Fat: 38.9 g
- Protein: 21.8 g
- Sodium: 309 mg

91. Chunky Butternut Squash And Tomato Soup

"A lovely hearty soup."
Serving: 4 | Prep: 15m | Ready in: 1h15m

Ingredients

- 1 tbsp. butter
- 1 tbsp. olive oil
- 1 large onion, chopped
- 4 cups peeled and cubed butternut squash
- 2 cups carrots, chopped
- 2 cups celery, chopped
- 3 cloves garlic, minced
- 2 cups milk
- 1 tbsp. Italian seasoning
- 1 tbsp. cornstarch
- 1 (14.5 oz.) can no-salt-added diced tomatoes
- 1 1/4 cups low-sodium chicken broth
- 1 (8 oz.) can tomato sauce
- 1 1/4 tsps. sea salt
- 3/4 tsp. ground black pepper
- 2 tbsps. chopped fresh basil

Direction

- Heat olive oil and butter in a big pot on medium heat then add onion; mix and cook for 5 minutes till translucent and tender. Add garlic, celery, carrots and butternut squash; mix to combine. Cook for 2 minutes till slightly tender.
- Put Italian seasoning and milk into the pot with butternut squash mixture; mix cornstarch in slowly till mixed. Boil; mix tomato sauce, broth and diced tomatoes in. Boil; lower the heat to low. Simmer for 45 minutes till squash is soft and flavors are combined well. Season with pepper and salt. Put soup into bowls; sprinkle basil on each top.

Nutrition Information

- Calories: 283 calories;
- Total Carbohydrate: 44.4 g
- Cholesterol: 19 mg
- Total Fat: 9.6 g

- Protein: 9.8 g
- Sodium: 1060 mg

92. Coconut Chicken And Taro Root

"Chicken is simmered with coconut milk, taro, ginger and shallots. It goes perfectly with steamed rice."
Serving: 2 | Prep: 15m | Ready in: 58m

Ingredients

- 1 tbsp. cornstarch, or more to taste
- 1 tbsp. water
- 1 1/2 tsps. light soy sauce
- 1 1/2 tsps. white sugar
- 1 tsp. salt
- 2 skinless chicken thighs, cut into small chunks
- oil for deep frying
- 1 taro, peeled and cut into small chunks
- 1 tbsp. vegetable oil
- 2 shallots, chopped
- 2 slices fresh ginger
- water to cover
- 1 (14 oz.) can coconut milk
- 4 leaves basil
- salt to taste
- 1 pinch white sugar, or to taste

Direction

- In a large bowl, combine water and cornstarch together until dissolved. Put in salt, 1 1/2 tsp. of sugar and soy sauce. Stir in chicken; use plastic wrap to cover and place in the fridge for marinating, about 15 minutes.
- In a deep-fat fryer or large saucepan, heat oil. Fry taro for 3 - 5 minutes, until golden brown. Drain on paper towels.
- In a large skillet, heat the remaining 1 tbsp. of oil over high heat. Put in ginger and shallots; cook and stir for 2-3 minutes, until fragrant. Put in chicken; cook and stir for 3-4 minutes, until no longer pink.

- Remove chicken mixture into a large saucepan. Put in fried taro. Pour in water until covering 3/4 of the mixture. Bring it to a boil; decrease heat to medium, cover up and simmer for about 15 minutes, until an instant-read thermometer inserted into the chicken reads at least 165°F (74°C). Mix in basil and coconut milk. Add in sugar and salt for seasoning.

Nutrition Information

- Calories: 766 calories;
- Total Carbohydrate: 22.7 g
- Cholesterol: 68 mg
- Total Fat: 67.2 g
- Protein: 24.9 g
- Sodium: 1471 mg

93. Cod In Tomatoes With Wine

""If you want to fill your stomach but don't want to ruin your diet at the same time, then this quick-and-easy tasty dish is perfect for you! You can pair it with salad, vermicelli noodles or new potatoes.""
Serving: 2 | Prep: 30m | Ready in: 55m

Ingredients

- 6 vine-ripened tomatoes
- 1 tbsp. vegetable oil
- 3/4 onion, finely chopped
- 2 cloves garlic, chopped
- 1 fresh red chile pepper, seeded and chopped
- 1 cup dry white wine, or more as needed
- salt and ground black pepper to taste
- 1/4 cup chopped fresh basil
- 2 tbsps. chopped fresh parsley
- 2 (4 oz.) cod loins
- 8 large uncooked prawns, peeled and deveined

Direction

- In the bottom of each tomato, cut an "X". Let a pot of water boil. Put in the tomatoes and let it cook in boiling water for 2 minutes. Use a slotted spoon to remove the tomatoes from the pot and put it in a bowl with iced water for 1 minute. Remove the skin of the tomatoes from the "X" side up then slice.

- Heat vegetable oil in a skillet over low heat. Sauté garlic and onion for about 2 minutes until fragrant. Put in the tomatoes and chile pepper and let it cook. Stir for 5-8 minutes until the tomatoes has started to reduce. Add in the wine and let it cook for approximately 5 more minutes over medium heat until the wine has reduced a little bit. Mix in the basil, parsley, salt and black pepper.
- Put the cod loins into the tomato mixture then cover the skillet and let it cook for 5 minutes. Flip the cod over on the other side and let it cook for 3-5 minutes until the fish is flaking apart easily using a fork. Mix in the prawns. Cover the skillet again and let it cook for 2-3 minutes until the prawns are opaque on the inside and bright pink in color on the outside. Put in black pepper and salt to taste.

Nutrition Information

- Calories: 429 calories;
- Total Carbohydrate: 32 g
- Cholesterol: 134 mg
- Total Fat: 9.2 g
- Protein: 35.1 g
- Sodium: 203 mg

94. Corn Salad With Creamy Italian Dressing

"This delicious corn salad is a perfect accompaniment to any grilled meat as a side dish for summertime."
Serving: 6 | Prep: 20m | Ready in: 8h35m

Ingredients

- Dressing:
- 1/2 cup mayonnaise
- 1/4 cup red wine vinegar
- 1/4 cup olive oil
- 1 clove garlic, crushed

- 2 tsps. water
- 1/2 tsp. freshly ground black pepper
- 1/2 tsp. white sugar
- 1/4 tsp. salt
- 1/4 tsp. Italian seasoning
- 1 pinch cayenne pepper, or more to taste
- olive oil
- 1 (16 oz.) package frozen sweet corn, thawed
- 1 cup diced roasted red peppers
- salt and ground black pepper to taste
- 5 fresh basil leaves, thinly sliced, or more to taste
- 1 pinch cayenne pepper, or to taste

Direction

- In a bowl, whisk together a pinch of cayenne pepper, Italian seasoning, 1/4 tsp. salt, sugar, 1/2 tsp. black pepper, water, garlic, 1/4 cup olive oil, vinegar and mayonnaise until creamy and thick. Use plastic wrap to cover dressing and chill about 8 hours to overnight.
- In a big skillet, heat 1 tbsp. olive oil on medium heat, then cook and stir corn in the hot oil for 15 minutes, until toasted and lightly golden brown.
- In a bowl, combine red pepper and corn, then drizzle over corn mixture with enough dressing to coat thoroughly. Season with black pepper and salt.
- Stir into the corn mixture with a pinch of cayenne pepper and basil, then toss.

Nutrition Information

- Calories: 314 calories;
- Total Carbohydrate: 19.4 g
- Cholesterol: 7 mg
- Total Fat: 26.6 g
- Protein: 3 g
- Sodium: 333 mg

95. Country Manor Breakfast Tart

"A heavenly dish!"
Serving: 20 | Prep: 1h | Ready in: 1h40m

Ingredients

- 4 cups all-purpose flour
- 1 tbsp. white sugar
- 1 tsp. baking powder
- 2 tsps. salt
- 1 3/4 cups shortening
- 1/2 cup cold water
- 1 egg
- 1 tbsp. vinegar
- 8 slices bacon
- 1 tbsp. butter
- 1/2 cup chopped onion
- 1/3 cup finely diced smoked ham
- 3 cups heavy cream
- 8 eggs, beaten
- 1/4 tsp. salt
- 1/2 tsp. freshly ground black pepper
- 1/4 tsp. nutmeg
- 3 tbsps. finely chopped fresh basil
- 1 tbsp. fresh thyme, minced
- 1 (3 oz.) package cream cheese, diced
- 1/2 cup shredded Cheddar cheese
- 1/2 cup shredded Monterey Jack cheese
- 1 bunch green onions, chopped
- 1/3 cup sliced almonds

Direction

- Mix salt, baking powder, sugar and flour; cut shortening in till it looks like coarse crumbs. Add vinegar, egg and water; mix, don't overwork. Divide pastry to 2 pieces; cover. Chill for half an hour.
- Preheat an oven to 175°C/350°F. Shape each piece to round; roll crust out on lightly floured surface. Fit carefully into 2 10-in. tart pans.
- In preheated oven, blind bake tart shells in golden brown; cool.
- Cook bacon in big deep skillet till evenly brown on medium high heat. Drain and crumble; put aside.

- In butter, sauté onion till translucent. Divide onion, bacon and ham to 2 even portions; sprinkle on bottom of the tart shells.
- Whisk beaten eggs and cream. Add thyme, basil, nutmeg, pepper and salt; mix well. Put egg mixture on bacon mixture. Sprinkle grated Monterey Jack and Cheddar cheeses and cream cheese cubes on each filled tart's top. Sprinkle cheese with green onions then sliced almonds.
- In preheated 175°C/350°F oven, bake for 30-40 minutes. Slightly cool; cut then serve.

Nutrition Information

- Calories: 495 calories;
- Total Carbohydrate: 23 g
- Cholesterol: 131 mg
- Total Fat: 40.8 g
- Protein: 10 g
- Sodium: 493 mg

96. Couscous Caprese

""This dish is stuffed with basil, couscous, and fresh mozzarella. It's so pleasing on the mouth.""
Serving: 4 | Prep: 10m | Ready in: 35m

Ingredients

- 1 cup boiling water
- 1 cup couscous
- 4 tomatoes
- 16 leaves fresh basil
- 8 oz. fresh mozzarella cheese, diced
- 1/4 cup balsamic vinegar, or to taste

Direction

- Set the oven to 350°F (175°C) for preheating. Grease the baking dish lightly.
- Pour boiling water in a bowl with couscous. Use a plastic wrap to cover the bowl. Soak the couscous for 5 minutes until the water is absorbed completely.
- Cut the tops of the tomatoes. Take a very small part of the bottoms, so they'll be stable

upright. Remove and discard tomato innards using the spoon. Arrange the tomatoes into the prepared baking dish.

- Bake the tomatoes inside the preheated oven for 20 minutes until the edges are lightly charred.
- Using the 4 basil leaves, line the inner walls of each of the tomatoes.
- Toss the mozzarella cheese into the couscous. Stuff the couscous mixture into the tomatoes. Drizzle over balsamic vinegar on top of the stuffed tomatoes.

Nutrition Information

- Calories: 292 calories;
- Total Carbohydrate: 32.6 g
- Cholesterol: 36 mg
- Total Fat: 9.4 g
- Protein: 18.8 g
- Sodium: 367 mg

Direction

- Boil a saucepan of water. Take away from heat and mix in the couscous. Put a cover on and let sit for 10 minutes or until the couscous soaks up in the water entirely. Use a fork to fluff it.
- While waiting for the couscous to soak, mix lemon juice, cayenne pepper, cumin, parsley, cilantro, basil, mint, green onion, garlic, cucumber, jalapeno pepper, and feta cheese. Add the prepared couscous and mix thoroughly.

Nutrition Information

- Calories: 210 calories;
- Total Carbohydrate: 38.3 g
- Cholesterol: 11 mg
- Total Fat: 3.3 g
- Protein: 8.1 g
- Sodium: 155 mg

97. Couscous With A Kick!

" "This salad has jalapeno, basil, mint, lemon, and cucumbers. This is how I imagine a tabbouleh from 'Pasta & Co' would be like." "
Serving: 6 | Prep: 20m | Ready in: 30m

Ingredients

- 3 cups water
- 2 cups couscous
- 1/2 cup crumbled feta cheese
- 1 fresh jalapeno pepper, chopped
- 1/2 cucumber, diced
- 1 clove garlic, minced
- 1/2 cup chopped green onion
- 3 tbsps. chopped fresh mint
- 3 tbsps. chopped fresh basil
- 3 tbsps. chopped fresh cilantro
- 1 tbsp. chopped fresh parsley
- 2 tsps. ground cumin
- 2 tsps. cayenne pepper
- 1 lemon, juiced

98. Couscous With Mushrooms And Sun-dried Tomatoes

"Hearty Portobello mushrooms and lively sun-dried tomatoes are mixed with couscous in this satisfying entree."
Serving: 4 | Prep: 30m | Ready in: 45m

Ingredients

- 1 cup dehydrated sun-dried tomatoes
- 1 1/2 cups water
- 1/2 (10 oz.) package couscous
- 1 tsp. olive oil
- 3 cloves garlic, pressed
- 1 bunch green onions, chopped
- 1/3 cup fresh basil leaves
- 1/4 cup fresh cilantro, chopped
- 1/2 lemon, juiced
- salt and pepper to taste
- 4 oz. portobello mushroom caps, sliced

Direction

- Transfer the sun-dried tomatoes into a bowl containing one cup of water. Let it soak for 30 minutes until rehydrated. Drain the tomatoes, save the water, and then chop them.
- Mix the reserved sun-dried tomato water with enough water to yield 1 1/2 cups in a medium saucepan. Heat to a boil. Mix in couscous. Cover the pan, take out from the heat source and let it stand for 5 minutes until the liquid has been absorbed. Carefully fluff with a fork.
- Heat olive oil in a skillet and then mix in the green onions, sun-dried tomatoes, and garlic. Cook while stirring for about 5 minutes until the green onions become tender. Stir in the lemon juice, basil, and cilantro. Season with pepper and salt. Stir in mushrooms and continue to cook for 3 to 5 minutes. Mix with the cooked couscous and serve.

Nutrition Information

- Calories: 178 calories;
- Total Carbohydrate: 36.1 g
- Cholesterol: 0 mg
- Total Fat: 2 g
- Protein: 7.5 g
- Sodium: 300 mg

---

99. Creamy Basil Margherita Spaghetti

"Margherita spaghetti!"
Serving: 6 | Prep: 30m | Ready in: 45m

Ingredients

- 2 tbsps. extra-virgin olive oil
- 1 medium tomato, diced
- 1/2 medium onion, diced
- 1/4 cup green onions, diced
- 6 cloves garlic, minced, or more to taste
- 1 cup chopped fresh basil
- 2 tbsps. butter
- 2 tbsps. all-purpose flour
- 2 cups heavy whipping cream
- salt and freshly ground black pepper to taste
- 1 tbsp. granulated garlic, or more to taste
- 3 pinches ground thyme, or to taste
- 1 lemon wedge
- 1 (8 oz.) package angel hair pasta
- 1/2 cup Parmesan cheese

Direction

- In a medium frying pan on low heat, heat olive oil. Put in garlic, onion, green onions and tomato. Save 2 tbsps. basil and put the remaining into the frying pan. Cook 5 minutes.
- During cooking vegetables, in a saucepan, melt butter. Put in flour and beat 2 minutes. Pour in 1 cup cream; keep beating 1-2 minutes. Put in pepper and salt. Mix in the rest of cream. To the sauce, add a squeeze of lemon juice, thyme, and granulated garlic.
- Taste the salt; if necessary, modify seasonings. Place cooked vegetables into the sauce and combine well. Simmer on low heat during boiling pasta.
- Heat a big pot filled with slightly salted water to a boil. In the boiling water, cook angel hair pasta, mixing occasionally, about 4-5 minutes until tender but firm to the bite; drain.
- In a bowl, combine reserved basil and Parmesan cheese.
- Serve the pasta in a big bowl or plate. Ladle cream sauce over pasta. Sprinkle Parmesan-basil mixture and another squeeze of lemon juice atop.

Nutrition Information

- Calories: 487 calories;
- Total Carbohydrate: 29.7 g
- Cholesterol: 125 mg
- Total Fat: 37.8 g
- Protein: 9.5 g
- Sodium: 265 mg

100. Creamy Cilantro Pesto Sauce

"Easy recipe!"
Serving: 8 | Prep: 10m | Ready in: 10m

Ingredients

- 1 bunch cilantro leaves
- 1/2 cup reduced-fat cream cheese
- 5 artichoke hearts (optional)
- 2 green onions, or more to taste
- 5 leaves fresh basil, or more to taste
- 2 tbsps. chopped jalapeno pepper
- 1/2 lemon, juiced
- 1 dash salt

Direction

- In a blender, blend salt, lemon juice, jalapeno pepper, basil, green onions, artichoke hearts, cream cheese and cilantro leaves until smooth.

Nutrition Information

- Calories: 45 calories;
- Total Carbohydrate: 2.7 g
- Cholesterol: 9 mg
- Total Fat: 2.9 g
- Protein: 2.2 g
- Sodium: 153 mg

101. Creamy Pasta Bake With Cherry Tomatoes And Basil

"Tasty pasta bake."
Serving: 6 | Prep: 15m | Ready in: 46m

Ingredients

- 1 (16 oz.) package penne pasta
- 1 tbsp. olive oil
- 1 onion, finely chopped
- 3 cloves garlic, minced
- 3 (6 oz.) cans tomato sauce
- 2 tbsps. tomato paste
- 3/4 cup heavy whipping cream
- 1/2 cup grated Parmesan cheese
- salt and freshly ground black pepper
- 1 pinch white sugar
- 1 lb. cherry tomatoes, halved
- 1 1/4 cups shredded mozzarella cheese
- 1 small bunch fresh basil, finely chopped

Direction

- Heat a big pot of slightly salted water to a boil. Put in penne and cook 11 minutes, stirring sometimes, until tender but firm to the bite. Drain, saving 1 cup of cooking water.
- During cooking penne, in a big skillet on medium heat, heat olive oil; cook onion 5 minutes until translucent and soft. Put in garlic and cook 30 more seconds. Mix in tomato paste and tomato sauce; cook 5 minutes until lightly decreased. Put in Parmesan cheese and cream; season with sugar, pepper, and salt.
- Set oven to 200° C (400° F) and start preheating. Oil a baking dish.
- Mix some of pasta cooking water into sauce; put in cooked penne. Take away from heat; mix in basil, 1/2 the mozzarella cheese and cherry tomatoes. Transfer the penne mixture to the prepared baking dish; use remaining mozzarella cheese to cover.
- Place in the preheated oven and bake 20 minutes till cheese is melted.

Nutrition Information

- Calories: 532 calories;
- Total Carbohydrate: 67.8 g
- Cholesterol: 62 mg
- Total Fat: 21.2 g
- Protein: 21.4 g
- Sodium: 780 mg

102. Creamy Tomato-basil Pasta With Shrimp

"A combination of fresh tomatoes and chopped basil along with shrimp and pasta, a seriously high-end entrée."
Serving: 4 | Prep: 15m | Ready in: 25m

Ingredients

- 3 cups farfalle (bow tie) pasta, uncooked
- 1/4 cup KRAFT Sun-Dried Tomato Vinaigrette Dressing, divided
- 1 lb. uncooked medium shrimp, peeled and deveined
- 1 cup fat-free reduced-sodium chicken broth
- 1/2 tsp. garlic powder
- 1/2 tsp. black pepper
- 4 oz. PHILADELPHIA Neufchatel Cheese, 1/3 Less Fat than Cream Cheese
- 2 cups grape tomatoes
- 1/2 cup KRAFT Shredded Parmesan Cheese
- 8 fresh basil leaves, cut into strips

Direction

- Cook pasta following packaging instruction. In the meantime, in big skillet on medium heat, heat 2 tbsps. dressing. Put in shrimp; cook and mix for 2 to 3 minutes till shrimp becomes pink. Take off shrimp from skillet with a slotted spoon; put cover to retain warmth. Throw any drippings in skillet.
- Mix in seasonings, broth and leftover dressing to skillet; allow to cook for 2 minutes till heated through. Put in Neufchatel; cook and mix for 2 to 3 minutes till melted. Mix in tomatoes and cook for a minute.
- Drain the pasta. Combine to ingredients in skillet. Mix in half the basil and Parmesan; atop with shrimp and the rest of the basil.

Nutrition Information

- Calories: 286 calories;
- Total Carbohydrate: 26.7 g
- Cholesterol: 184 mg
- Total Fat: 7.7 g
- Protein: 27.6 g

- Sodium: 633 mg

103. Creamy Tomato-basil Soup

"This delectable tomato-basil soup is very simple to prepare. The dish is perfect for An easy lunch when served with grilled cheese or bread."
Serving: 8 | Prep: 10m | Ready in: 55m

Ingredients

- 1/4 cup butter
- 1/4 cup olive oil
- 1 1/2 cups chopped onions
- 3 lbs. tomatoes - cored, peeled, and quartered
- 1/2 cup chopped fresh basil leaves
- salt to taste
- ground black pepper to taste
- 1 quart chicken broth
- 1 cup heavy cream
- 8 sprigs fresh basil for garnish

Direction

- Place a large pot on medium heat; heat in olive oil and butter. Cook in onions while stirring until tender. Stir in chopped basil and tomatoes. Season with pepper and salt. Transfer in chicken broth; turn the heat down to low; keep cooking for 15 minutes.
- Pour the soup into a blender (or an immersible hand blender instead); blend until perfectly smooth.
- Turn back to the pot; bring the mixture to a boil. Turn the heat down to low; slowly stir in heavy cream. Strain through a strainer. Top a sprig of basil on each serving.

Nutrition Information

- Calories: 258 calories;
- Total Carbohydrate: 10.7 g
- Cholesterol: 56 mg
- Total Fat: 23.9 g
- Protein: 2.8 g
- Sodium: 62 mg

104. Creamy White Chicken And Artichoke Lasagna

"A hearty dish taken straight out of the oven for a winter dinner!"
Serving: 12 | Prep: 25m | Ready in: 50m

Ingredients

- 2 cups boneless skinless chicken breast, cooked and shredded
- 1 (14 oz.) can artichoke hearts, chopped
- 1/2 cup chopped sun-dried tomatoes
- 1 (8 oz.) package KRAFT Shredded Mozzarella Cheese with a Touch of PHILADELPHIA, divided
- 1/2 cup KRAFT Grated Parmesan Cheese
- 2 (8 oz.) packages PHILADELPHIA Cream Cheese, softened
- 1 cup milk
- 1/2 tsp. garlic powder
- 1/4 cup basil, chopped
- 12 lasagna noodles, cooked

Direction

- Set the oven to 350°F, and start preheating.
- Mix 1 cup of mozzarella and Parmesan, tomatoes, artichokes and chicken. Use mixer to beat garlic powder, milk and cream cheese until well combined; mix in 2 tbsp. of basil. Stir half with the chicken mixture.
- Spread half of the leftover cream cheese sauce onto the bottom of a 13-in.x9-in. baking dish; cover with three noodles and one-third of the chicken mixture. Repeating layer with noodles and chicken mixture twice. Add mozzarella and remaining cheese sauce on top; cover up.
- Bake in the preheated oven for 25 minutes, or until heated through. Sprinkle the remaining basil on top. Allow to stand for 5 minutes then cut for serving.

Nutrition Information

- Calories: 342 calories;
- Total Carbohydrate: 25 g
- Cholesterol: 79 mg
- Total Fat: 18.9 g
- Protein: 20.1 g
- Sodium: 522 mg

105. Creole Cornbread Stuffing

"This is good for 1 turkey."
Serving: 20 | Prep: 1h | Ready in: 4h

Ingredients

- Cornbread:
- 2 cups unbleached all-purpose flour
- 2 cups stone ground cornmeal
- 2 tbsps. baking powder
- 1 tsp. salt
- 4 tbsps. white sugar
- 5 eggs, beaten
- 6 tbsps. butter, melted
- 3 cups buttermilk
- Stuffing:
- 2 tbsps. salt
- 2 tsps. ground white pepper
- 2 tsps. ground black pepper
- 2 tsps. cayenne pepper
- 2 tsps. onion powder
- 4 tsps. dried oregano
- 2 tsps. dried thyme
- 6 tbsps. chopped fresh basil
- 4 bay leaves
- 1 cup minced onion
- 1 cup chopped green onions
- 1 cup chopped parsley
- 2 cups chopped red bell pepper
- 2 green chile peppers, chopped
- 2 tbsps. minced garlic
- 1 cup butter
- 2 cups chicken broth
- 1 tbsp. hot pepper sauce
- 2 cups evaporated milk
- 7 eggs, beaten

Direction

- Preheat an oven to 190°C/375°F then butter the 13x9-in. pan.
- Combine sugar, 1 tsp. salt, baking powder, cornmeal and flour; mix well.
- Whisk buttermilk, 6 tbsp. melted butter and 5 eggs together. Add wet to dry ingredients; stir just till incorporated. Put in prepped pan.
- In preheated oven, bake for 55 minutes till toothpick comes out clean and top is browned; Let cool completely.
- Making Stuffing: Mix bay leaves, basil, thyme, oregano, onion powder, cayenne pepper, black pepper, white pepper and 2 tbsp. salt in a small bowl.
- Mix garlic, chili peppers, green/red peppers, parsley, green onions and minced onions in another bowl.
- In a big drying pan, melt 1 cup butter. Add spices; cook for several minutes. Add veggies; cook for 5 minutes. Don't let veggies brown. Add Tabasco and stock; cook while stirring for 5 minutes longer. Crumble cornbread into skillet; mix. Discard from heat.
- Whisk evaporated milk and 7 eggs; put into stuffing mixture. Put back on low heat; cook for 2 minutes, stirring. Remove bay leaves. Put stuffing into a bowl; let cool then stuff the turkey.

Nutrition Information

- Calories: 323 calories;
- Total Carbohydrate: 30.3 g
- Cholesterol: 154 mg
- Total Fat: 18.7 g
- Protein: 9.9 g
- Sodium: 1281 mg

106. Cucumber Caprese Salad

"It's a delicious layered-style cucumber Caprese salad that makes for a pretty presentation."
Serving: 6 | Prep: 15m | Ready in: 30m

Ingredients

- 1/2 cup aged balsamic vinegar
- 2 large Roma tomatoes, sliced into 1/4-inch-thick rounds
- 1 large cucumber, peeled and sliced into 1/4-inch-thick rounds
- 1 (8 oz.) package sliced fresh mozzarella cheese
- 1 cup fresh basil leaves
- 1 tbsp. olive oil
- salt and ground black pepper to taste

Direction

- In a small saucepan, bring balsamic vinegar to a boil on medium heat. Boil for 8 minutes, until reduced to 1/4 cup. Take away from the heat and let cool to room temperature.
- On a small serving platter, arrange in an alternating pattern, respectively, tomatoes, cucumber, mozzarella slices and basil leaves until platter is covered. Pour over the salad with olive oil, then season to taste with salt and pepper. Pour over top with 1-2 tbsp. cooled balsamic vinegar and serve promptly.

Nutrition Information

- Calories: 141 calories;
- Total Carbohydrate: 7 g
- Cholesterol: 24 mg
- Total Fat: 8.4 g
- Protein: 9.9 g
- Sodium: 265 mg

107. Dana's Cream Cheese Dip

"Wonderful flavor!"
Serving: 16 | Prep: 10m | Ready in: 10m

Ingredients

- 1/3 cup toasted pine nuts
- 1 cup fresh basil leaves
- 2 cloves garlic
- 2 (8 oz.) packages cream cheese, softened
- 1 tbsp. balsamic vinegar

Direction

- In a food processor, put garlic, basil and pine nuts; pulse until chopped coarsely. In a bowl, mix together balsamic vinegar and cream cheese until thoroughly combined; mix in pine nut mixture.

Nutrition Information

- Calories: 116 calories;
- Total Carbohydrate: 1.5 g
- Cholesterol: 31 mg
- Total Fat: 11.2 g
- Protein: 2.9 g
- Sodium: 83 mg

108. Decadent Mini Meatloaf

""An easy meal for weeknight created special with the inclusion of a special ingredient and a side of Idahoan Signature Russets Mashed Potatoes. Just put a light salad then serve!""
Serving: 6 | Prep: 10m | Ready in: 40m

Ingredients

- 1 1/2 lbs. ground chuck
- 1 egg
- 1 tsp. salt
- 1/2 tsp. freshly ground black pepper
- 1 tsp. garlic powder
- 1 tbsp. extra virgin olive oil
- 1 onion, finely chopped
- 1 cup chopped fresh figs
- 1/2 cup crumbled feta cheese
- 1 tbsp. chopped fresh basil
- 1 (9.74 oz.) package Idahoan Signature™ Russets Mashed Potatoes

Direction

- Prepare the oven by preheating to 350°F (175°C) Prepare a rimmed baking sheet that is lightly oiled.
- In a bowl, combine garlic powder, pepper, salt, egg, and ground chuck. Form into 6 mini meatloaves then transfer to the prepared baking sheet. In a skillet set on medium-high heat, add oil. Stir and cook the onion for 5-7 minutes until tender. Put in figs and heat well.
- Scatter fig mixture on mini loaves. Place fresh basil and crumbled cheese on top. Place in the preheated oven and bake for 30-40 minutes until not pink in the middle. An instant-read thermometer poked into the middle should register 160°F (70°C).
- Ready Idahoan Signature Russets Mashed Potatoes based on the package directions. Present as a side dish to the meatloaf.

Nutrition Information

- Calories: 320 calories;
- Total Carbohydrate: 8 g
- Cholesterol: 111 mg
- Total Fat: 21.4 g
- Protein: 23.1 g
- Sodium: 603 mg

109. Delicious Pizza Sauce Recipe

"Your child can make this sauce."
Serving: 4 | Prep: 10m | Ready in: 20m

Ingredients

- 2 tbsps. olive oil
- 1 (28 oz.) can crushed tomatoes
- 2 leaves basil, chopped
- 3 cloves garlic, chopped

- 1 pinch salt and ground black pepper to taste
- 1 pinch grated Parmesan cheese

Direction

- Heat olive oil in a saucepan then put in the crushed tomatoes; put over low heat. Mix black pepper, salt, garlic and basil into the tomatoes; simmer. Put parmesan cheese into the sauce. Serve.

Nutrition Information

- Calories: 127 calories;
- Total Carbohydrate: 15 g
- Cholesterol: < 1 mg
- Total Fat: 7.4 g
- Protein: 3.5 g
- Sodium: 263 mg

110. Deluxe Pizza Panini

"Your regular sandwich will taste a lot better with Paninis. This recipe will take your boring pizza to a whole new level. If you have any leftovers, you can reheat it for the next day's lunch."
Serving: 4 | Prep: 20m | Ready in: 25m

Ingredients

- 1 tsp. butter
- 2 tbsps. sliced fresh mushrooms
- 1/2 cup tomato sauce
- 4 ciabatta rolls, split
- 2 cloves garlic, minced
- 1 tbsp. dried oregano
- 8 slices hot Genoa salami
- 8 slices roasted ham
- 2 tbsps. diced red onion
- 2 tbsps. chopped roasted red pepper
- 2 tbsps. chopped black olives
- 4 leaves basil, chopped
- 4 slices provolone cheese

Direction

- In a small skillet, melt butter over medium-high heat; add mushrooms and sauté for 5-7 minutes until soft. Take away from heat and cool.
- Turn on a panini press to preheat following the manufacturer's directions.
- Spread the tomato sauce in an even layer over the cut sides of each ciabatta roll. Sprinkle over each roll with equal amounts of oregano and garlic. On each roll, arrange 2 salami slices side by side, put 2 slices ham on top. Distribute basil, olives, red pepper, mushrooms and red onion among 4 sandwiches and evenly spread on top of the meats. Complete by putting provolone cheese on top and sandwiching roll halves around the fillings.
- On the preheated panini press, cook the sandwiches for 5 minutes until the middle is warm, the cheese melts, and the bread has dark brown grill marks.

Nutrition Information

- Calories: 652 calories;
- Total Carbohydrate: 36.9 g
- Cholesterol: 111 mg
- Total Fat: 38.9 g
- Protein: 37.1 g
- Sodium: 2696 mg

111. Easy Panang Curry With Chicken

"A Panang curry that has chicken indicates the diversity of southern Thailand. You can add four tbsps. of Panang curry paste or five tbsps. of pre-made curry paste if busy. Can serve together with steamed jasmine rice."
Serving: 4 | Prep: 15m | Ready in: 35m

Ingredients

- 1 tbsp. vegetable oil
- 1/4 cup Panang curry paste

- 4 cups coconut milk
- 10 oz. boneless chicken breast, cubed
- 2 tbsps. palm sugar
- 2 tbsps. fish sauce
- 6 kaffir lime leaves, torn
- 2 fresh red chile peppers, sliced
- 1 small bunch Thai basil leaves

Direction

- Over medium-low heat, heat oil in a large pot or wok and add curry paste. Cook while stirring for about 5 minutes until fragrant. Add in coconut milk and heat to boil. Place in chicken and then cook for about 5 minutes until nearly cooked through. Mix in lime leaves, fish sauce, and palm sugar. Let simmer for about 5 minutes until the sauce flavors blend.
- Spoon the sauce and chicken into a large bowl. Stud with basil and red chile peppers.

Nutrition Information

- Calories: 597 calories;
- Total Carbohydrate: 17.8 g
- Cholesterol: 37 mg
- Total Fat: 53.2 g
- Protein: 19.4 g
- Sodium: 896 mg

112.Easy Pasta With Tuna And Tomato Sauce

"A delicious version of a tuna pasta dish with tomatoes, anchovies and capers. You can easily double the recipe for more guests."
Serving: 2 | Prep: 15m | Ready in: 30m

Ingredients

- 1/2 (16 oz.) box penne
- 1 (5 oz.) can tuna, packed in olive oil, drained
- 1/4 cup olive oil, divided
- 1/4 cup finely chopped fresh basil
- 1/2 large organic lemon, juiced and zested

- salt and ground black pepper to taste
- 1 oz. canned anchovy fillets, drained
- 2 tsps. capers
- 1 clove garlic, thinly sliced
- 1 (14.5 oz.) can diced tomatoes
- 1/2 bunch fresh parsley, finely chopped

Direction

- In a large pot, bring slightly salted water to a boil. Put in penne and cook, stirring occasionally, about 11 minutes, until tender yet firm to the bite.
- As pasta is cooking, empty tuna into a bowl and use a fork to mash. Combine with pepper, salt, lemon zest, lemon juice, basil and 2 tbsps. of olive oil.
- In a large skillet, heat the remaining 2 tbsps. of olive oil; then fry the anchovies for 3 minutes. Put in garlic and capers; cook, stirring constantly, for another 3 minutes. Put in tomatoes and tuna mixture; let the sauce simmer for about 5 minutes.
- Drain pasta and put into the sauce. Mix well. Mix in parsley then serve.

Nutrition Information

- Calories: 919 calories;
- Total Carbohydrate: 94.4 g
- Cholesterol: 50 mg
- Total Fat: 46.5 g
- Protein: 37.9 g
- Sodium: 1301 mg

113.Easy Tilapia With Wine And Tomatoes

""A very simple Tilapia recipe that can be cooked in a short time. Foil bag is the great solution for grilling the fish fillets.""
Serving: 4 | Prep: 10m | Ready in: 25m

Ingredients

- 4 (4 oz.) fillets tilapia

- salt and pepper to taste
- 4 tbsps. butter
- 3 cloves garlic, pressed
- 4 fresh basil leaves, chopped
- 1 large tomato, chopped
- 1 cup white wine

Direction

- Turn the grill at medium heat for preheating.
- Take a large piece of aluminum foil and put tilapia fillet side by side on it. Marinate each fish fillet with pepper and salt. On top of each fish portion, put 1 tbsp. of butter and sprinkle with tomato, basil, and garlic. Pour wine over the whole thing. Wrap fish by folding the foil up around and keep it in an air-tight packet. Put on a cookie sheet to easily deliver from and too grill.
- Put the packet onto the preheated grill, then cook the fish for about 15 minutes or until it flakes easily using a fork. Carefully open the packet to avoid being burnt by the steam, serve right away.

Nutrition Information

- Calories: 277 calories;
- Total Carbohydrate: 4.2 g
- Cholesterol: 72 mg
- Total Fat: 13.1 g
- Protein: 23.7 g
- Sodium: 159 mg

114. Easy Walnut Basil Pesto

"Simple pesto you can easily make."
Serving: 8 | Prep: 15m | Ready in: 15m

Ingredients

- 1/4 cup walnuts
- 1/4 cup extra-virgin olive oil
- 1 tbsp. lemon juice
- 3 cloves garlic, minced
- 2 cups packed fresh basil

- 1/4 cup grated Parmesan cheese

Direction

- In a food processor, pulse garlic, lemon juice, olive oil and walnuts until walnuts are chopped finely. Add a little basil leaves at a time, pulsing to form a smooth paste. Stir in parmesan cheese.

Nutrition Information

- Calories: 103 calories;
- Total Carbohydrate: 1.4 g
- Cholesterol: 2 mg
- Total Fat: 10.2 g
- Protein: 1.9 g
- Sodium: 39 mg

115. Easy Zucchini-tomato Side Dish

"An easy vegetable dish to serve in main meal together with pasta."
Serving: 2 | Prep: 15m | Ready in: 25m

Ingredients

- 2 tbsps. olive oil
- 1 small onion, chopped
- 1 clove garlic, minced
- 2 small zucchini, cubed
- 1 tsp. tomato paste
- 1 beefsteak tomato, cubed
- 1 tsp. herbes de Provence, or more to taste
- salt and freshly ground black pepper to taste
- 1 pinch white sugar
- 1 tbsp. chopped fresh basil leaves, or to taste

Direction

- In a big skillet, heat olive oil; cook onion for 5 minutes until translucent and soft. Add in garlic, cook 1/2 a minute. Put in zucchini, cook about 3 minutes until soft. Mix in tomato and tomato paste; season with sugar, black pepper, salt, herbs de Provence. Mix in basil; serve.

Nutrition Information

- Calories: 172 calories;
- Total Carbohydrate: 11.7 g
- Cholesterol: 0 mg
- Total Fat: 13.9 g
- Protein: 2.7 g
- Sodium: 118 mg

116. Egg Salad In Squash Boats

"A fun yellow squash recipe."
Serving: 6 | Prep: 15m | Ready in: 20m

Ingredients

- 6 medium yellow squash
- 4 hard-cooked eggs, finely chopped
- 1/4 cup minced celery
- 1/4 cup minced red bell pepper
- 1/4 cup sliced green olives
- 1/4 cup shredded sharp Cheddar cheese
- 2 tbsps. chopped fresh basil
- 1 tbsp. chopped fresh dill weed
- 2 tbsps. mayonnaise
- 1/4 tsp. cayenne pepper
- 1/4 tsp. seasoned salt

Direction

- Boil big pot of water on medium high heat. Lengthwise, halve squash. Remove then discard pulp. In boiling water, blanch squash halves for 30 seconds. In ice water, plunge squash to halt cooking.
- Mix mayonnaise, dill, basil, shredded cheese, sliced green olives, red pepper, celery and chopped eggs in medium bowl. Season with seasoned salt and cayenne; mix well.
- Put egg mixture in squash halves, mounding if needed. Use plastic wrap to cover; refrigerate till thoroughly chilled.

Nutrition Information

- Calories: 151 calories;
- Total Carbohydrate: 9.2 g
- Cholesterol: 148 mg
- Total Fat: 10 g
- Protein: 7.5 g
- Sodium: 284 mg

117. Eggplant Parmesan Bites

"This dish is one of my favorite entrees."
Serving: 24 | Prep: 30m | Ready in: 1h15m

Ingredients

- 1 tbsp. sea salt (such as Diamond Crystal®), divided
- 1 small eggplant, cut into 1/2-inch rounds
- 1 cup Italian-seasoned bread crumbs
- 1 egg
- 1 tsp. olive oil, or more as needed
- 1/2 cup ricotta cheese
- 24 pita chips, or more to taste
- 24 cherry tomatoes, or more to taste
- 24 basil leaves, or more to taste

Direction

- Set oven to 375°F (190°C) and start preheating.
- Sprinkle eggplant rounds with 2 tsps. salt in colander; let drain for a minimum of 30 minutes. Rinse salt off the eggplant.
- Scatter bread crumbs into a shallow bowl. In a separate bowl, beat egg. Dip eggplant into beaten egg, remember to let all excess egg drip off the eggplant; press into bread crumbs until both sides of eggplant slices are evenly coated.
- Place coated eggplant on a baking sheet and drizzle olive oil on top.
- Bake in the preheated oven for about 10 minutes until eggplant turn to a light brown color.
- In a bowl, mix ricotta cheese and remaining 1 tsp. salt together. Spoon ricotta cheese mixture on top of each eggplant.

- Bake eggplant in the oven for 5 to 7 minutes until cheese is heated through.
- On each pita chip, place 1 eggplant; top with basil leaf and a cherry tomato.

Nutrition Information

- Calories: 71 calories;
- Total Carbohydrate: 9.8 g
- Cholesterol: 9 mg
- Total Fat: 2.2 g
- Protein: 2.6 g
- Sodium: 354 mg

118. Eggplant Parmigiana With Margherita® Pepperoni

"This dish is layered with mozzarella cheese, tomato sauce, savory pepperoni, and breaded eggplant."
Serving: 4 | Prep: 20m | Ready in: 50m

Ingredients

- 2 (16 oz.) eggplants
- Olive oil as needed
- 4 eggs
- 4 tbsps. water
- 1/2 cup freshly grated Parmigiano-Reggiano
- 4 1/2 cups seasoned bread crumbs, divided
- 2 cups marinara sauce
- 1 bunch fresh basil leaves, chiffonade
- 1 lb. fresh mozzarella, sliced 1/8-inch thick
- 8 oz. deli-sliced Margherita® pepperoni, sliced thin

Direction

- Cut each eggplant lengthwise into 1/4-1/2-inch thick slices.
- Heat about 1/4-inch deep olive oil in a big skillet for frying.
- Combine water and eggs in a bowl. Combine 4 cups seasoned breadcrumbs and grated Parmigiana-Reggiano cheese on a big plate. Dip the eggplant into the egg mixture, and then the breadcrumb mixture. In the skillet,

put the breaded eggplant slices and fry until turning golden brown, rotating 1 time if needed. Take out of the skillet.
- Turn the oven to 350°F to preheat.
- Arrange 4 largest eggplant slices in an 8x12-in. baking dish, evenly placing apart from each other. Spread over each slice with 1/4 cup of tomato sauce and sprinkle 1 tsp. of basil over. Place over each with 3 slices pepperoni and 1 mozzarella slice and sprinkle 1 tsp. grated Parmigiano over. Arrange the smaller eggplant slices over each disk and continue the same process with the pepperoni, basil tomato sauce and 2 cheeses. Continue to layer until there is no ingredients left.
- Sprinkle over the top of the eggplant dish with the leftover 1/2 cup seasoned bread crumbs, and bake without a cover for 20 minutes until the top is light brown and the cheese melts.

Nutrition Information

- Calories: 1505 calories;
- Total Carbohydrate: 128.4 g
- Cholesterol: 337 mg
- Total Fat: 79.1 g
- Protein: 66.8 g
- Sodium: 4267 mg

119. Eggs Benedict From Galbani®

"A quick eggs benedict brunch made with hollandaise sauce and mozzarella cheese"
Serving: 2 | Prep: 15m | Ready in: 25m

Ingredients

- 1 tbsp. butter
- 2 English muffins, toasted
- 10 fresh basil leaves
- 8 oz. Galbani® Mozzarella Fresca™, sliced
- 2 slices tomato
- 2 poached eggs
- 4 tbsps. prepared hollandaise sauce
- Chopped fresh chives
- Salt and pepper to taste

Direction

- Spread butter all over the muffins, sprinkle fresh basil on top, put in a tomato slice and some Galbani(R) Mozzarella Fresca(TM) slices. Put in the poached eggs.
- Pour some hollandaise over, sprinkle some chives, season with pepper and salt to taste. Serve instantly.

Nutrition Information

- Calories: 873 calories;
- Total Carbohydrate: 39.3 g
- Cholesterol: 326 mg
- Total Fat: 47.9 g
- Protein: 34.2 g
- Sodium: 1357 mg

120. Exotic Salad

"This salad looks pretty and tasty wonderful."
Serving: 4 | Prep: 15m | Ready in: 15m

Ingredients

- 1 (6 oz.) can sliced mushrooms, drained
- 1 (6 oz.) can sliced black olives, drained
- 1 (6 oz.) can artichoke hearts, drained
- 1 (14.25 oz.) can hearts of palm, drained and sliced
- 1 (15 oz.) can baby corn, drained
- DRESSING
- 1/2 cup olive oil
- 1/4 cup fresh lemon juice
- 1 clove garlic, minced
- salt and pepper to taste
- 2 sprigs fresh parsley, chopped
- 4 leaves fresh basil, chopped

Direction

- Mix baby corn, hearts of palm, artichoke hearts, olives and mushrooms together in a big bowl.

- Mix basil, parsley, pepper, salt, garlic, lemon juice and olive oil together in a small bowl. Add onto the vegetables.

Nutrition Information

- Calories: 366 calories;
- Total Carbohydrate: 15.8 g
- Cholesterol: 0 mg
- Total Fat: 34.1 g
- Protein: 3.4 g
- Sodium: 783 mg

121. Fabulous Zucchini Grinders

"Tasty baked sandwiches."
Serving: 4 | Prep: 20m | Ready in: 50m

Ingredients

- Marinara Sauce:
- 1 tbsp. olive oil
- 2 cloves garlic, peeled and coarsely chopped
- 1 pinch crushed red pepper flakes
- 1 tbsp. chopped fresh basil
- 1 tsp. red wine vinegar
- 1 tsp. white sugar
- 1 (14.5 oz.) can diced tomatoes
- salt and pepper to taste
- Grinders:
- 1 tbsp. butter
- 2 medium zucchini, cubed
- 1 pinch red pepper flakes
- salt and pepper to taste
- 1 1/2 cups shredded mozzarella cheese
- 4 (6 inch) French or Italian sandwich rolls, split

Direction

- For marinara sauce: In a saucepan on medium heat, heat olive oil. Put in red pepper flakes, basil, and garlic; cook and mix 1-2 minutes until fragrant. Mix in pepper, salt, vinegar, and sugar. Put in tomatoes with their juices; simmer 15 minutes on low heat. Take away

- from heat. Transfer to a blender or food processor; puree until smooth.
- Set oven to 175° C (350° F) and start preheating.
- In a skillet on medium heat, melt butter. In butter, cook zucchini until lightly tender and browned. Season with pepper, salt, and red pepper flakes.
- Spoon a generous amount of zucchini mixture into each sandwich roll. Add 1/4 cup marinara sauce to each roll to cover zucchini. Place a handful of shredded mozzarella atop. Close rolls; use aluminum foil to wrap each.
- Place in the preheated oven and bake 15 minutes, till cheese is melted, rolls are soft, and bread is heated through.

Nutrition Information

- Calories: 339 calories;
- Total Carbohydrate: 37.3 g
- Cholesterol: 35 mg
- Total Fat: 15.1 g
- Protein: 16.9 g
- Sodium: 729 mg

122. Fennel Apple Salad

"Sweet, savory, refreshing and easy salad that features orange-Dijon dressing, fennel, herbs, orange, and apple. It works great with roasted herb chicken or grilled fish plus any crisp white wine."
Serving: 4 | Prep: 20m | Ready in: 20m

Ingredients

- 1 bulb fennel, thinly sliced
- 1 medium apple, cut into matchsticks
- 1 clementine (Mandarin orange) - peeled, segmented, and segments cut in half
- 1/4 cup pitted kalamata olives, sliced
- 1 cup thinly sliced Swiss chard
- 1/4 cup chopped fresh basil
- 1/4 cup chopped fresh flat-leaf parsley
- 1 lemon, juiced
- 2 tbsps. orange juice

- 1 tbsp. Dijon mustard
- 1/2 tsp. celery seed
- 1/2 tsp. dried oregano
- sea salt to taste
- 1 pinch freshly ground black pepper to taste
- 1/4 cup extra virgin olive oil

Direction

- In a big bowl, mix Swiss chard, fennel, kalamata olives, Clementine segments, and apple together.
- Sprinkle parsley and basil over the fennel salad.
- In a bowl, stir black pepper, lemon juice, salt, orange juice, oregano, celery seed, and Dijon mustard together.
- While whisking hard, gently trickle olive oil in the lemon juice mixture to blend the dressing.
- Toss the dressing with salad to combine.

Nutrition Information

- Calories: 216 calories;
- Total Carbohydrate: 18.1 g
- Cholesterol: 0 mg
- Total Fat: 16.7 g
- Protein: 2 g
- Sodium: 365 mg

123. Feta Cheese With Basil Salad

""A perfect salad recipe for when the garden is in season! So fast to make and add or discard ingredients if desired.""
Serving: 6 | Prep: 15m | Ready in: 30m

Ingredients

- 1/2 cup chopped walnuts
- 1 pint cherry tomatoes, halved
- 1 bunch fresh basil leaves, sliced
- 1 bunch green onions, sliced
- 1 avocado, peeled and diced
- 1 (6 oz.) package crumbled feta cheese with basil and sun-dried tomatoes
- 1/2 cup kalamata olives, pitted and chopped

- 1 red bell pepper, seeded and diced
- garlic salt to taste
- 1 tbsp. balsamic vinegar, or to taste
- 1 tbsp. extra-virgin olive oil, or to taste

Direction

- In a small skillet over medium heat, put the walnuts. Then cook, continuously stirring, until golden brown in color.
- Gently combine red bell pepper, kalamata olives, feta cheese with sun-dried tomatoes and basil, avocado, green onions, basil, tomatoes and walnuts in a bowl. Add garlic salt to season, and trickle with extra-virgin olive oil and balsamic vinegar. Let it sit for about 15 minutes and toss again prior to serving.

Nutrition Information

- Calories: 278 calories;
- Total Carbohydrate: 13.5 g
- Cholesterol: 25 mg
- Total Fat: 23 g
- Protein: 8.1 g
- Sodium: 566 mg

124. Fish Brodetto

"Tasty and flavorful fish stew."
Serving: 8 | Prep: 25m | Ready in: 1h5m

Ingredients

- 1 lb. lobster tail
- 1 lb. sole fillets
- 1 lb. medium shrimp - peeled and deveined
- 3 tbsps. lemon juice
- 1/4 cup olive oil
- 3 cloves garlic, minced
- 1 large onion, sliced
- 1 (15 oz.) can whole tomatoes
- 1 cup balsamic vinegar
- 3 cups red wine
- 2 quarts water

- 2 sprigs fresh basil leaves, torn
- 3 tbsps. chopped fresh parsley
- salt and pepper to taste

Direction

- Cut sole and lobster into 1-in. chunk. Toss them with lemon juice and shrimp; put aside.
- In a big pot on medium heat, heat olive oil. Put in onions and garlic; cook and mix until translucent. Add wine, vinegar and tomatoes; heat to a simmer and cook 10 minutes. Add water. Put in parsley, basil, water and marinated fish; simmer till lobster is cooked through, about 30 minutes. Season with pepper and salt to taste. Serve along with a nice and crusty bread.

Nutrition Information

- Calories: 337 calories;
- Total Carbohydrate: 12.6 g
- Cholesterol: 167 mg
- Total Fat: 9.1 g
- Protein: 33.9 g
- Sodium: 466 mg

125. Flounder Mediterranean

"This dish is flounder baked with white wine, onion, capers, kalamata olives, and fresh tomatoes. It goes very well with green vegetables and rice."
Serving: 4 | Prep: 15m | Ready in: 45m

Ingredients

- 5 roma (plum) tomatoes
- 2 tbsps. extra virgin olive oil
- 1/2 Spanish onion, chopped
- 2 cloves garlic, chopped
- 1 pinch Italian seasoning
- 24 kalamata olives, pitted and chopped
- 1/4 cup white wine
- 1/4 cup capers
- 1 tsp. fresh lemon juice
- 6 leaves fresh basil, chopped

- 3 tbsps. freshly grated Parmesan cheese
- 1 lb. flounder fillets
- 6 leaves fresh basil, torn

Direction

- Turn the oven to 425°F (220°) to preheat.
- Boil water in a saucepan. In a saucepan, plunge tomatoes and immediately transfer to ice water in a medium-sized bowl; strain. Peel and throw away the skins from tomatoes. Cut the tomatoes and put aside.
- In a skillet, heat olive oil over medium heat; sauté onion for 5 minutes until soft. Mix in Italian seasoning, garlic, and tomatoes; cook for 5-7 minutes until the tomatoes are soft. Stir in 1/2 the basil, lemon juice, wine, capers and olives. Lower the heat, mix in Parmesan cheese and cook for 15 minutes until the mixture decreases to a thick sauce.
- In a shallow baking dish, put flounder. Pour over the fillets with the sauce and put the leftover basil leaves on top.
- Bake in the preheated oven until a fork can easily flake the fish, about 12 minutes.

Nutrition Information

- Calories: 282 calories;
- Total Carbohydrate: 8.2 g
- Cholesterol: 63 mg
- Total Fat: 15.4 g
- Protein: 24.4 g
- Sodium: 777 mg

---

126. Four Cheese Macaroni Casserole

"This casserole gets the best flavor that either adults or children want more and more."
Serving: 6 | Prep: 20m | Ready in: 1h

Ingredients

- 3 cups uncooked macaroni

- 1 (28 oz.) can whole peeled tomatoes, drained and chopped
- 1 tsp. Italian seasoning
- 1 tsp. dried oregano
- 1 tsp. basil
- salt and pepper to taste
- 1 1/2 cups grated Cheddar cheese
- 1 1/2 cups shredded mozzarella cheese
- 3/4 cup freshly grated Parmesan cheese
- 1/4 cup crumbled feta cheese

Direction

- Start preheating the oven at 350°F (175°C).
- Boil on high heat a large pot of lightly salted water. Put in macaroni, and cook about 8 to 10 minutes until al dente. Drain, and transfer hot pasta into a casserole dish.
- In the meantime, in a large bowl, blend pepper, salt, basil, oregano, Italian seasoning and tomatoes.
- Combine into the hot pasta with 1/2 cup of Parmesan, 1 cup of mozzarella and 1 cup of Cheddar. Keep stirring until the cheese melts. Mix in herb mixture and tomato. Scatter over the top of the casserole with 1/4 cup of feta, 1/4 cup of Parmesan, 1/2 cup of mozzarella and 1/2 cup of Cheddar.
- Bake in the prepared oven for about 15 to 25 minutes.

Nutrition Information

- Calories: 511 calories;
- Total Carbohydrate: 47 g
- Cholesterol: 75 mg
- Total Fat: 22.8 g
- Protein: 29.7 g
- Sodium: 887 mg

127. Fresh Tomato Pie

"A good way to make use of tomatoes."
Serving: 8

Ingredients

- 1 (9 inch) pie shell
- 7 ripe tomatoes, sliced
- 1 yellow onion
- 3/4 cup mayonnaise
- 1/3 cup shredded mozzarella cheese
- 1/3 cup grated Parmesan cheese
- ground black pepper to taste
- 2 tsps. fresh basil
- 2 tsps. fresh oregano

Direction

- Set oven to 175° C (350° F) and start preheating.
- Bake pastry shell until browned, about 8-10 minutes.
- Slice onion; arrange in the bottom of the pastry shell. Slice tomatoes; place atop onions. Put in black pepper to taste.
- Combine mayonnaise, parmesan and mozzarella together in a medium bowl. Evenly spread this mixture over tomatoes.
- Bake at 175° C (350° F) until golden brown, about 20-25 minutes. When cooked, use fresh herbs to garnish.

Nutrition Information

- Calories: 283 calories;
- Total Carbohydrate: 14.3 g
- Cholesterol: 14 mg
- Total Fat: 23.8 g
- Protein: 4.3 g
- Sodium: 306 mg

128. Fried Rice With Cilantro

"With this fried rice, you can use seafood, bacon, pork, or chicken."
Serving: 4 | Prep: 15m | Ready in: 30m

Ingredients

- 4 tbsps. vegetable oil
- 5 cloves garlic, finely chopped
- 2 green chilies, diced
- 2 cups cubed skinless, boneless chicken breast meat
- 2 cups cooked jasmine rice, chilled
- 1 tbsp. white sugar
- 1 tbsp. fish sauce
- 1 tbsp. soy sauce
- 2 tsps. chopped green onion
- 2 tbsps. chopped fresh basil leaves
- 5 tbsps. chopped fresh cilantro

Direction

- In a big skillet or a wok, heat oil over medium-high heat. Add garlic and fry until golden, then add chicken meat and chili pepper; stir-fry until fully cooked.
- Once the chicken has cooked, add soy sauce, fish sauce, sugar, and rice. Cook over medium heat, lightly toss. Once the mixture is very combined, mix in cilantro, basil and green onions. Cook for another 1 minute, and then enjoy while still hot.

Nutrition Information

- Calories: 634 calories;
- Total Carbohydrate: 84.4 g
- Cholesterol: 68 mg
- Total Fat: 17.3 g
- Protein: 32.8 g
- Sodium: 562 mg

129. Fried Tomato, Onion, And Mushroom Ragout

""This is an updated version of my mom's recipe.""
Serving: 4 | Prep: 15m | Ready in: 40m

Ingredients

- 2 tbsps. olive oil
- 1 cup chopped onion
- 4 tomatoes, cut into wedges
- 2 cups sliced white mushrooms
- 1/4 cup chopped fresh basil
- salt and black pepper to taste

Direction

- Place a large skillet on medium heat; heat the olive oil; cook while stirring the onion for around 5 minutes, till translucent. Include in mushrooms and tomato wedges; simmer while stirring from time to time for around 20 minutes till the mushrooms and tomatoes are cooked through and the sauce becomes reduced and thickened.
- Sprinkle with pepper, salt and basil; stir to combine.

Nutrition Information

- Calories: 106 calories;
- Total Carbohydrate: 9.8 g
- Cholesterol: 0 mg
- Total Fat: 7.2 g
- Protein: 2.7 g
- Sodium: 10 mg

130. Fusion Risotto Vegan

"A delicious and delectable vegan or non-vegan risotto."
Serving: 10 | Prep: 15m | Ready in: 40m

Ingredients

- 3 tbsps. margarine (such as Earth Balance®)
- 3 basil leaves, finely chopped
- 2 bunches fresh chives, finely chopped
- 6 cups vegetable stock, or more if needed
- 1 onion, cubed
- 1 tomato, cubed
- 3 Yukon gold potatoes, cubed
- 2 tbsps. garlic powder
- 2 tbsps. onion powder
- 1 tbsp. cayenne pepper
- 1 tbsp. ground cumin
- 1 tbsp. paprika
- salt and ground black pepper to taste
- 2 cloves garlic, minced
- 1 (16 oz.) can chickpeas (garbanzo beans), drained and rinsed
- 2 cups Arborio rice

Direction

- In a pot, heat the margarine on medium heat; cook and mix for 1 to 2 minutes the chives and basil till aromatic. In another saucepan, heat the vegetable stock on medium-low heat; retain warmth.
- Into the chive mixture, cook and mix black pepper, salt, paprika, cumin, cayenne pepper, onion powder, garlic powder, potatoes, tomato and onion for around 6 minutes till onion is soft. Put in chickpeas and garlic; cook for 1 to 2 minutes till garlic is aromatic. Mix rice into the mixture of chickpea; cook and mix for 2 to 3 minutes till rice is coated and slightly toasted.
- Into the rice mixture, mix the warm vegetable stock, a cup at a time, waiting till broth is absorbed prior to putting in the next cup. Keep mixing rice and putting in vegetable stock for around 20 minutes till rice is completely cooked.

Nutrition Information

- Calories: 358 calories;
- Total Carbohydrate: 69.5 g
- Cholesterol: 0 mg
- Total Fat: 4.9 g
- Protein: 9.1 g
- Sodium: 457 mg

131. Garbanzos With Fennel

"This delightful soup is delicate in texture but rather sweet in flavor. It is possible to use fresh or frozen peas."
Serving: 6 | Prep: 25m | Ready in: 9h30m

Ingredients

- 1 1/2 cups dry garbanzo beans
- 10 cups vegetable stock
- 4 cloves garlic, minced
- 1/2 tsp. crushed red pepper flakes
- 1 tsp. vegetable oil
- 2 lbs. tomatoes, chopped
- 1 cup fresh basil leaves, chopped
- 2 lbs. fresh fennel bulbs, trimmed and chopped
- 2 medium onions, chopped
- 1/2 tsp. salt
- 1 cup fresh shelled green peas

Direction

- In a pot, cover the garbanzo beans with enough water. Soak it for 8 hours or overnight. Drain and rinse.
- Combine the vegetable stock and soaked beans in a large pot. Stir in red pepper flakes and 2 cloves minced garlic. Bring the mixture to a boil. Adjust the heat to low and simmer for 45 minutes or until the beans are tender.
- Put oil in a skillet and heat it over medium heat. Add the basil, remaining garlic, and tomatoes. Cook for 2 minutes or just until the basil has wilted. Remove it from the heat and put it aside.
- Mix the onions and fennel into the pot with garbanzo beans. Season the mixture with salt. Keep cooking the mixture for 15 minutes. Stir in peas, tomatoes, and basil. Keep cooking for 5 minutes until the peas turn tender. Serve while hot.

Nutrition Information

- Calories: 309 calories;
- Total Carbohydrate: 55.2 g
- Cholesterol: 0 mg
- Total Fat: 5.2 g
- Protein: 15.2 g
- Sodium: 755 mg

132. Garlic Bread Spread

"This recipe can be served with all Italian dishes."
Serving: 10 | Prep: 10m | Ready in: 25m

Ingredients

- 1/2 cup butter, softened
- 1/4 cup grated Parmesan cheese
- 2 cloves garlic, minced
- 1/4 tsp. dried marjoram
- 1/4 tsp. dried basil
- 1/4 tsp. fines herbs
- 1/4 tsp. dried oregano
- ground black pepper to taste
- 1/4 tsp. dried parsley, or to taste
- 1 loaf unsliced Italian bread

Direction

- Turn on the oven to 350°F (175°C) to preheat.
- Combine parsley, black pepper, oregano, fines herbs mix, basil, marjoram, garlic, Parmesan cheese and butter in a bowl until combined thoroughly. Cut Italian bread loaf into half lengthwise; use butter mixture to spread generously on each half.
- Put the garlic bread into oven to bake on the top rack for 10-15 minutes until the butter mixture bubbles and melts. Turn on the broiler; broil for another 1-2 minutes until the bread turns golden brown shade as you desired.

Nutrition Information

- Calories: 274 calories;
- Total Carbohydrate: 34 g
- Cholesterol: 26 mg
- Total Fat: 12.1 g
- Protein: 6.8 g
- Sodium: 489 mg

133. Garlic Chicken Linguine

"A household favorite."
Serving: 8 | Prep: 20m | Ready in: 40m

Ingredients

- 1 (16 oz.) package linguine pasta
- 1/4 cup olive oil
- 1/4 cup chopped garlic
- 6 tomatoes, skinned and chopped, or more to taste
- 4 cups chopped cooked chicken
- 10 slices prosciutto, cut into small pieces, or more to taste
- 1/4 cup chopped fresh basil, or to taste
- 1/4 cup grated Romano cheese

Direction

- Boil a big pot of lightly salted water; cook linguine at a boil for 11 minutes till tender yet firm to chew. Drain; put in a serving bowl.
- Mix and cook garlic and olive oil in a saucepan on medium heat for 3 minutes till fragrant. Add tomatoes; cover. Simmer for 7-10 minutes till tomatoes cook down into a sauce.
- Mix basil, prosciutto and chicken into tomato sauce; mix and cook for 3 minutes till chicken heats through. Put sauce on pasta; put Romano cheese on top.

Nutrition Information

- Calories: 497 calories;
- Total Carbohydrate: 46.7 g
- Cholesterol: 72 mg
- Total Fat: 20.2 g
- Protein: 32.6 g
- Sodium: 445 mg

134. Garlic, Basil, And Bacon Deviled Eggs

""This will be the best deviled eggs you've ever tried!""
Serving: 24 | Prep: 15m | Ready in: 1h10m

Ingredients

- 12 eggs
- 2 large cloves garlic, pressed
- 5 slices bacon
- 1/2 cup finely chopped fresh basil
- 1/3 cup mayonnaise
- 1/4 tsp. crushed red pepper flakes
- salt and pepper to taste
- 1/4 tsp. paprika for garnish

Direction

- In a saucepan, lay eggs in a single layer and add water till eggs get covered by 1 inch. Cover the saucepan and bring to a boil over high heat. Remove from the heat and allow the eggs to stand for 15 minutes in the hot water. Strain. Run cold water over eggs for cooling down. When eggs cool, peel eggs. Halve lengthways and remove the yolks to a bowl. Use a fork to mash the yolks and pressed garlic together.
- In a deep and large skillet, cook the bacon for about 10 minutes over medium-high heat till turns browned evenly. Place on a plate lined with paper towel to drain; chop when bacon cools down. Mix into the mashed egg yolks. Stir into the mixture with pepper, salt, red pepper flakes, mayonnaise, and basil till mixed well. Fill the mixture in egg white halves; use a bit of paprika to dredge over each of stuffed eggs.

Nutrition Information

- Calories: 69 calories;
- Total Carbohydrate: 0.5 g
- Cholesterol: 96 mg
- Total Fat: 5.7 g
- Protein: 3.9 g
- Sodium: 136 mg

135. Garlic-cheese Flat Bread

"I use frozen pizza dough for this flat-bread foundation. Best served with salad or soup."
Serving: 12 | Prep: 10m | Ready in: 25m

Ingredients

- 1 (13.8 oz.) package refrigerated pizza crust
- 1/4 cup butter, melted
- 6 cloves garlic, minced
- 1 tbsp. minced fresh basil
- 1 cup shredded Cheddar cheese
- 1/2 cup grated Romano cheese
- 1/4 cup grated Parmesan cheese

Direction

- Set oven at 205°C (400°F) and start preheating. Use cooking spray to coat a 10x15-inch baking tray lightly.
- Press the dough against the prepared tray. In a small bowl, mix the basil, garlic and butter together; drizzle the mixture on top of the dough. Dredge Parmesan cheese, Romano cheese and Cheddar cheese over.
- Put the tray in the preheated oven and bake for 10 to 12 minutes until it gets crisp. Divide into squares and serve while still warm.

Nutrition Information

- Calories: 186 calories;
- Total Carbohydrate: 16.3 g
- Cholesterol: 27 mg
- Total Fat: 9.9 g
- Protein: 7.6 g
- Sodium: 388 mg

136. Glasser's Greek Marlin

"Marlin steaks cooked in garlic butter sauce and topped with basil and tomato topping."
Serving: 4 | Prep: 10m | Ready in: 35m

Ingredients

- 1/2 cup butter, divided
- 2 tsps. minced garlic, divided
- 3 tomatoes, cubed
- 4 oz. fresh basil, chopped
- 2 tbsps. fresh lime juice
- 2 (6 oz.) swordfish steaks

Direction

- Set an oven to preheat to 175°C (350°F).
- In a medium pot, put 1 tsp. garlic and 1/4 cup butter on medium-low heat. Stir in the lime juice, basil and tomatoes once the butter is melted. Lower the heat to low just before the mixture boils.
- Melt the leftover butter in a small pot and stir in the leftover garlic.
- In a baking pan, lay out the swordfish and drizzle it with the garlic and butter mixture from the small pot.
- Let the fish bake in the preheated oven for 7 minutes. Flip the fish and keep on baking for 7 minutes or until it flakes easily using a fork. To serve, scoop the tomato mixture on top of the fish, then top it with the leftover garlic and butter sauce from the baking pan.

Nutrition Information

- Calories: 332 calories;
- Total Carbohydrate: 5.6 g
- Cholesterol: 93 mg
- Total Fat: 26.7 g
- Protein: 18.6 g
- Sodium: 237 mg

137. Gluten-free Kentucky Fried Chicken™-style Coating

"A yummy baked or deep-fried chicken coating recipe!"
Serving: 10 | Prep: 5m | Ready in: 5m

Ingredients

- 1 cup corn flour
- 2 tbsps. paprika
- 4 tsps. monosodium glutamate (MSG) (optional)
- 1 tbsp. salt
- 1 tbsp. garlic powder
- 1 tbsp. dry mustard
- 1 1/2 tsps. celery salt
- 1 1/2 tsps. ground black pepper
- 1/2 tsp. ground ginger
- 1/8 tsp. ground thyme
- 1/8 tsp. dried basil
- 1/8 tsp. dried oregano

Direction

- In a jar, mix the dry mustard, basil, paprika, pepper, oregano, corn flour, garlic powder, celery salt, thyme, dry mustard, ginger, salt and monosodium glutamate together. Put on the lid and shake well until everything is well-combined.

Nutrition Information

- Calories: 65 calories;
- Total Carbohydrate: 12.3 g
- Cholesterol: 0 mg
- Total Fat: 0.7 g
- Protein: 1.4 g
- Sodium: 1120 mg

138. Gluten-free Portobello Pizza

"Top mushrooms with your favorite pizza topping or chopped garlic to make this gluten-free pizza.""
Serving: 4 | Prep: 10m | Ready in: 30m

Ingredients

- cooking spray
- 4 large portobello mushroom cups, gills removed
- 3 tbsps. extra-virgin olive oil
- 1 pinch salt and ground black pepper to taste
- 2 cups sliced fresh mozzarella cheese, divided
- 1/2 cup sliced cherry tomatoes
- 1/2 cup chopped fresh basil

Direction

- Turn oven to 375°F (190°C) to preheat. Line a baking sheet with aluminum foil and apply cooking spray all over the foil.
- Place mushrooms on the baking sheet with top-side down. Drizzle olive oil over mushrooms and sprinkle with pepper and salt to season. Add 3/4 of the mozzarella cheese and layer evenly over mushrooms and place basil and tomatoes on top. Top with the remainder of mozzarella cheese.
- Bake for 20 to 25 minutes in the preheated oven until cheese melts and mushrooms has softened.

Nutrition Information

- Calories: 269 calories;
- Total Carbohydrate: 2.5 g
- Cholesterol: 47 mg
- Total Fat: 23.2 g
- Protein: 11.1 g
- Sodium: 127 mg

139. Gnocchi In Fontina Sauce

"An easy and quick white cheese sauce."
Serving: 4 | Prep: 10m | Ready in: 20m

Ingredients

- 1 lb. refrigerated gnocchi
- 6 tbsps. unsalted butter
- 2 tbsps. chopped shallots
- 8 oz. Italian fontina cheese, cubed
- 1/3 cup heavy cream
- 3 tbsps. freshly grated Parmesan cheese
- 1 tbsp. chopped fresh basil

Direction

- Boil a big pot of slightly salted water. Put gnocchi, and allow to cook for 5 minutes till soft. Let drain, and reserve.
- Meanwhile, prepare the sauce, as you desire gnocchi to finish first. In a saucepan, liquify the butter over medium heat. Put shallots, and allow to cook for several minutes, till soft. Mix in cream, and heat to nearly a boil. Slowly add in parmesan and fontina cheeses, prevent from boiling. Mix till smooth, then take off from the heat quickly, or the sauce will clump.
- Into serving dishes, put the gnocchi, and scoop sauce on top of each. Jazz up with chopped fresh basil.

Nutrition Information

- Calories: 624 calories;
- Total Carbohydrate: 22.5 g
- Cholesterol: 163 mg
- Total Fat: 51.3 g
- Protein: 19.6 g
- Sodium: 607 mg

140. Gnocchi Primavera

"Fantastic dish for any meal."
Serving: 4 | Prep: 10m | Ready in: 30m

Ingredients

- 1/2 cup freshly grated Parmesan cheese, divided
- 1 tsp. olive oil
- 2 tbsps. pine nuts
- 1 (16 oz.) package potato gnocchi
- 2 tbsps. olive oil, divided
- 1 zucchini, chopped
- 12 fresh mushrooms, cleaned and stems trimmed
- 12 grape tomatoes
- 10 torn fresh basil leaves

Direction

- Spray cooking spray on a nonstick skillet; arrange over medium-low heat. Add Parmesan cheese to the skillet, 2 tbsps. per time. Cook 1 minute until cheese browns at edges, and starts to bubble and melts into thin circle. Flip the crisp; brown the other side 30 seconds. Transfer the crisp to a plate; let cool. Follow the same manner to make other 3 cheese crisps.
- In a skillet on medium heat, heat 1 tsp. olive oil. Cook and stir pine nuts 3 minutes until fragrant and slightly toasted. Take pine nuts out of the skillet; put aside.
- Follow package instructions to cook gnocchi; transfer into a colander placed in the sink to drain.
- Place 1 tbsp. of olive oil in a big skillet on high heat; stir and cook zucchini 2 minutes until just seared. Take zucchini out of the pan. Decrease to medium heat. In the same pan, stir and cook mushrooms 5 minutes till they start to release juices yet are still firm. Drain juices. Bring zucchini back to the pan; put in remaining 1 tbsp. olive oil, drained gnocchi, toasted pine nuts, torn basil leaves and tomatoes; mix a few times to blend; heat through.

- Distribute gnocchi into 4 plates; top each with Parmesan cheese crisp; serve.

Nutrition Information

- Calories: 327 calories;
- Total Carbohydrate: 26.2 g
- Cholesterol: 30 mg
- Total Fat: 21.3 g
- Protein: 10.2 g
- Sodium: 249 mg

141. Gnocchi With Cherry Tomato Sauce

"This fresh, sweet and spicy sauce adds flavor to potato gnocchi."
Serving: 4 | Prep: 30m | Ready in: 50m

Ingredients

- 1 tbsp. olive oil
- 1 large red onion, finely chopped
- 1 clove garlic, minced
- 1/2 minced red chile pepper
- 2 pints cherry tomatoes, quartered
- 1 1/2 cups canned crushed tomatoes
- 1 cup chopped fresh basil
- 2/3 cup kalamata olives, sliced
- 1 (16 oz.) package fresh gnocchi
- 1/4 cup grated Parmesan cheese

Direction

- In a big saucepan on medium heat, heat olive oil. Mix in chile pepper, garlic, and onion; cook 5 minutes till onion is translucent and softened. Rise to medium-high heat, mix in cherry tomatoes. Cook 5 minutes till tomatoes start to form a sauce and their original form is lost. Mix in crushed tomatoes and heat to a simmer. Decrease to medium-low heat and cook 10 minutes.
- During simmering sauce, heat a big pot of slightly salted water to a boil on high heat. Put in fresh gnocchi; cook for 2-3 minutes till

gnocchi float to the surface. Strain gnocchi out gently; place strained gnocchi in a serving dish.
- Mix olives and basil into the simmering sauce; cook 1 minute. Pour the sauce over drained gnocchi; sprinkle Parmesan cheese over top, then serve.

Nutrition Information

- Calories: 358 calories;
- Total Carbohydrate: 40.4 g
- Cholesterol: 26 mg
- Total Fat: 19.5 g
- Protein: 8.8 g
- Sodium: 665 mg

142. Gnocchi With Sweet Basil Pesto And Garlic Butter Shrimp

"A garlicky, buttery shrimp and pesto on top of gnocchi."
Serving: 2 | Prep: 15m | Ready in: 25m

Ingredients

- 1 bunch fresh sweet basil, stemmed
- 5 tbsps. grated Parmesan cheese, divided
- 4 tbsps. pine nuts
- 2 tbsps. olive oil
- 2 cloves garlic
- 1/2 tbsp. salt
- 1/2 tbsp. ground black pepper
- 3 tbsps. butter
- 2 cloves garlic, minced
- 1/4 lb. raw shrimp
- 1 (12 oz.) package potato gnocchi

Direction

- In a blender, mix pepper, salt, whole garlic cloves, olive oil, pine nuts, 4 tbsps. of the Parmesan cheese and basil; puree till pesto turns smooth.
- In a frying pan, melt butter over medium heat. Put in the minced garlic; cook for half a minute

to a minute till aromatic. Put in the shrimp; cook and mix for 2 to 3 minutes till opaque. Take off the heat and retain warmth.

- Boil a big pot of slightly salted water. In boiling water, let gnocchi cook for 2 to 4 minutes till they rise to surface. Drain. Stir pesto into gnocchi and serve along with shrimp. Jazz up with the rest of the Parmesan cheese.

Nutrition Information

- Calories: 732 calories;
- Total Carbohydrate: 37.1 g
- Cholesterol: 174 mg
- Total Fat: 55.8 g
- Protein: 24.5 g
- Sodium: 2288 mg

143. Gnudi (ricotta Gnocchi)

"Potato-basil gnocchi."
Serving: 4 | Prep: 30m | Ready in: 45m

Ingredients

- 1 lb. fresh basil, stems removed
- 1 cup ricotta cheese
- 3/4 cup all-purpose flour, divided
- 1/2 cup freshly grated Parmigiano-Reggiano
- 2 egg yolks, lightly beaten
- 1/4 tsp. freshly grated nutmeg
- 2 tsps. freshly ground white pepper
- 2 tsps. sea salt, or more to taste
- 1/2 lemon, juiced (optional)

Direction

- Boil a big pot of salted water. Put in the basil and cook without a cover for approximately a minute till just wilted. To end cooking process, soak in ice water for a few minutes. Drain. Squeeze into very dry and chop finely.
- In a big bowl, stir nutmeg, egg yolks, the Parmigiano-Reggiano cheese, half a cup of flour and ricotta cheese. Put in the salt, white

pepper and basil; stir till gnudi mixture is well-incorporated.

- With the leftover a quarter cup of flour, sprinkle your hands and shape gnudi mixture into small balls.
- Boil a big pot with salted water. Put in the lemon juice. Working in batches, let gnudi boil for 3 to 4 minutes till they rise to the water surface. Allow to drain.

Nutrition Information

- Calories: 270 calories;
- Total Carbohydrate: 25.7 g
- Cholesterol: 130 mg
- Total Fat: 11 g
- Protein: 18.3 g
- Sodium: 1119 mg

144. Goat Cheese And Asparagus Quinoa

"Replace your usual quinoa breakfast with this recipe. It's perfect for people that do not like sweets for breakfast."
Serving: 1 | Prep: 10m | Ready in: 30m

Ingredients

- 1/2 cup water
- 1/4 cup quinoa, rinsed and drained
- 1/4 tsp. ground sage
- 1 fresh basil leaf
- 3 asparagus spears, chopped
- 1 tbsp. crumbled goat cheese
- 1 tsp. chia seeds

Direction

- In a saucepan, combine sage, quinoa, basil leaf and water; stir and boil water. Cover saucepan with lid, lessen heat to low. For 15 minutes, cook mixture until water is absorbed and quinoa is tender.
- Remove and discard basil leaf from quinoa mixture. Add into quinoa mixture, asparagus, chia seeds and goat cheese; mix and replace lid

on saucepan. For 5 minutes, steam mixture until goat cheese melts and asparagus is slightly softened.

Nutrition Information

- Calories: 205 calories;
- Total Carbohydrate: 30.5 g
- Cholesterol: 6 mg
- Total Fat: 5.5 g
- Protein: 9 g
- Sodium: 44 mg

145. Goat Cheese Stuffed Lamb Burgers

"Craving some Greek flavored hamburgers? Try this now! Creamy and tasty burgers with your favorite herbs! You surely can't resist this meal."
Serving: 6 | Prep: 25m | Ready in: 40m

Ingredients

- 1 tsp. olive oil
- 1/2 cup diced onion
- 2 lbs. ground lamb
- 1 egg
- 1 cup bread crumbs
- 1 clove garlic, minced
- 4 1/2 tsps. salt
- 1 tbsp. ground black pepper
- 4 oz. soft goat cheese
- 1 tbsp. extra-virgin olive oil
- 1 tbsp. chopped fresh basil leaves
- 1 tbsp. chopped fresh oregano

Direction

- On medium heat, place a small skillet and cook 1 tsp. olive oil. Toss in onions; stir and cook for 5 minutes until opaque and soft.
- Knead carefully the lamb, bread crumbs, salt, softened onions, egg, garlic, and pepper together. Split the mixture in 6 pieces and mold in balls. Keep in the refrigerator with cover until needed.

- Combine the basil, oregano, goat cheese, and extra-virgin olive oil until well blended. For 5 minutes chill with cover.
- Set an outdoor grill to medium-high heat; preheat.
- Doing one side of the meat at one time, create a hollow in middle of the ball using your thumb. Add in a heaping tbsp. of goat cheese mixture to fill the hollow. Carefully pull to form meat patty around cheese filling to create a burger patty. Do again with each lamb mixture ball.
- Place patties on preheated grill, 8 minutes a side until color at the center is not pink and cooked through.

Nutrition Information

- Calories: 484 calories;
- Total Carbohydrate: 15.8 g
- Cholesterol: 147 mg
- Total Fat: 31 g
- Protein: 33.7 g
- Sodium: 2071 mg

146. Grandma's Old Italian Spaghetti Sauce With Meatballs

"This sauce is a true classic from Italy that takes quite some time to prepare, but ultimately worth it."
Serving: 12 | Prep: 1h30m | Ready in: 8h

Ingredients

- 2 tbsps. olive oil
- 3 whole garlic cloves, peeled
- 2 pig's feet
- 1 lb. pork neck bones
- 2 (6 oz.) cans tomato paste
- 1 1/2 cups water
- 2 (28 oz.) cans tomato puree
- 1 tbsp. white sugar
- 1 tsp. black pepper
- 3/4 tsp. baking soda
- 1 (16 oz.) loaf fresh Italian bread, torn into 2-inch pieces

- 1 cup water
- 6 eggs, beaten
- 1 lb. ground pork
- 1 lb. ground veal
- 1 lb. ground beef
- 1 tbsp. olive oil
- 1 clove garlic, minced
- 2 tbsps. chopped fresh basil
- salt and pepper to taste
- 6 hard-boiled eggs, peeled (optional)

Direction

- Over medium heat, use a large saucepan to heat 2 tbsps. of olive oil and fry the garlic cloves for about 5 to 8 minutes until they turn fragrant and brown. Take the garlic cloves out of the pan and set them aside for later use. Put the pork neck bones and pig's feet in the saucepan; fry, turning this occasionally, for 15 minutes or until bones and the meat have turned brown.
- Take the garlic cloves you set aside and stir them into the saucepan with the meat. Add 1 1/2 cups of water and tomato paste and mix well. Let this boil, then add the puree of tomato. Lower the heat to low and leave it to simmer for about 3 hours, making sure you stir frequently from the bottom to prevent burning, until the mixture thickens and the pig's feet are tender. Add the baking soda, pepper, and sugar and stir well. Keep simmering while you make the meatballs.
- To prepare the meatballs, take the torn bread and soak it in a bowl with a cup of water. When it has soaked through, squeeze out the excess water and put all the bread in a large bowl with 6 beaten eggs, ground beef, ground veal, and ground pork, and mix thoroughly. This should be able to make 24 meatballs that are 2 and 1/2 inches in diameter.
- To cook the meatballs, heat a tbsp. of olive oil in a large skillet over medium heat. Mix in the minced garlic and the fresh basil that is chopped. Let them cook for a minute then add the meatballs. Add the pepper and salt according to taste and fry them on all sides for

15 minutes, making sure that they are all evenly brown. If necessary, working in batches might be better.
- Put the fried meatballs together with the basil, garlic, and oil from the skillet into the sauce, stirring this gently so you don't make them crumble. Then add the whole hard-boiled eggs and allow them to simmer for 1 1/2 hours more, until the meatballs are cooked, the sauce is thickened and the flavors are combined.

Nutrition Information

- Calories: 599 calories;
- Total Carbohydrate: 38 g
- Cholesterol: 319 mg
- Total Fat: 29.4 g
- Protein: 46.2 g
- Sodium: 1437 mg

147. Grandpa's Garden Chicken Soup

"This is a chicken veggie soup that is cooked with fresh garden vegetarian.""
Serving: 12 | Prep: 30m | Ready in: 2h

Ingredients

- 1 whole chicken, quartered
- water, to cover
- 1/2 large onion, chopped
- 1 stalk celery with leaves, cut into chunks
- 3 cubes chicken bouillon
- 1/4 cup chopped fresh basil
- 1/4 cup chopped fresh parsley
- 1 tbsp. chopped garlic
- 1 pinch salt and ground black pepper to taste
- 2 Yukon Gold potatoes, diced
- 2 kohlrabi bulbs, peeled and diced
- 2 carrots, sliced
- 1 large turnip, diced
- 1/2 medium head cabbage, chopped
- 2 ears sweet corn, cut from cob
- 4 oz. fresh green beans, trimmed

- 1 tomato, chopped

Direction

- In a large stockpot, place chicken pieces and pour water enough to cover the chicken entirely. Add pepper, salt, garlic, parsley, basil, bouillon cubes, celery, and onion; bring the mixture in the pot to a simmer over medium-high heat. Simmer for about 1 hour until chicken is tender and thoroughly cooked.
- Take out celery chunks, and discard. Transfer cooked chicken to a cutting board and allow to cool. Tear as much chicken meat as possible from the bones and chop coarsely. Add chicken back to the stock.
- Stir turnip, carrots, kohlrabi, and potatoes into the soup; cook for about 20 minutes until vegetables are softened. Add tomato, green beans, corn, and cabbage; cook for 7 to 10 more minutes until green beans have softened.

Nutrition Information

- Calories: 209 calories;
- Total Carbohydrate: 15.5 g
- Cholesterol: 50 mg
- Total Fat: 8.5 g
- Protein: 18.6 g
- Sodium: 376 mg

148. Green Bean And Potato Salad

"Potatoes and green beans served in balsamic vinaigrette and Dijon mustard will add a twist on this potato salad."
Serving: 10 | Prep: 15m | Ready in: 45m

Ingredients

- 1 1/2 lbs. red potatoes
- 3/4 lb. fresh green beans, trimmed and snapped
- 1/4 cup chopped fresh basil
- 1 small red onion, chopped
- salt and pepper to taste
- 1/4 cup balsamic vinegar
- 2 tbsps. Dijon mustard

- 2 tbsps. fresh lemon juice
- 1 clove garlic, minced
- 1 dash Worcestershire sauce
- 1/2 cup extra virgin olive oil

Direction

- In a big pot filled with about 1 in. of water, place the potatoes; boil and cook till potatoes are tender, for about 15 minutes. After the first 10 minutes, add in the green beans to steam. Drain the potatoes, let cool and slice into quarters. Move into a big bowl then toss with pepper, salt, red onion and fresh basil. Put aside.
- Whisk together olive oil, Worcestershire sauce, garlic, lemon juice, mustard and balsamic vinegar in a medium bowl. Spread over the salad then stir till coated. Add pepper and salt to taste if desired.

Nutrition Information

- Calories: 176 calories;
- Total Carbohydrate: 17.3 g
- Cholesterol: 0 mg
- Total Fat: 11.3 g
- Protein: 1.9 g
- Sodium: 97 mg

149. Grilled Fennel

"Serve hot for side dish or cold then serve it as a salad."
Serving: 4 | Prep: 15m | Ready in: 25m

Ingredients

- 2 fennel bulbs
- 2 tbsps. olive oil, divided
- 1/2 tsp. ground black pepper
- 1/4 tsp. salt
- 1 tbsp. chopped fresh basil
- 1 tbsp. chopped fresh parsley
- 1 lemon, juiced
- 1 tsp. lemon zest
- 1/2 tsp. freshly ground black pepper

- 1 pinch dried thyme
- 2 tbsps. grated Parmesan cheese

Direction

- Preheat outdoor grill to high heat; oil grate lightly.
- From bottom of every fennel bulb, use vegetable peeler/paring knife to slice a very thin layer. Leave core in place to keep bulb intact. Remove the fennel stalks; keep fronds. Vertically, slice bulbs to 1/4-in. slices. Brush 1 tbsp. olive oil on slices. Sprinkle salt and ground black pepper on each side.
- Grill fennel sides for 5 minutes per side or till charred. Put on serving platter.
- In a bowl, whisk leftover fennel fronds, thyme, freshly ground black pepper, lemon zest, lemon juice, parsley, basil and leftover 1 tbsp. olive oil. Sprinkle parmesan cheese. Drizzle lemon mixture on fennel.

Nutrition Information

- Calories: 109 calories;
- Total Carbohydrate: 9.3 g
- Cholesterol: 2 mg
- Total Fat: 7.7 g
- Protein: 2.5 g
- Sodium: 245 mg

150. Grilled Garlic And Herb Shrimp

"A great recipe from my dad."
Serving: 4 | Prep: 10m | Ready in: 2h15m

Ingredients

- 2 tsps. ground paprika
- 2 tbsps. fresh minced garlic
- 2 tsps. Italian seasoning blend
- 2 tbsps. fresh lemon juice
- 1/4 cup olive oil
- 1/2 tsp. ground black pepper
- 2 tsps. dried basil leaves

- 2 tbsps. brown sugar, packed
- 2 lbs. large shrimp (21-25 per lb.), peeled and deveined

Direction

- Whisk brown sugar, basil, pepper, olive oil, lemon juice, Italian seasoning, garlic and paprika till blended thoroughly in a bowl. Mix in shrimp; toss to coat evenly with marinade. Cover; refrigerate, turning once, for 2 hours minimum.
- Preheat the outdoor grill to medium high heat; oil grill grate lightly and put it 4-in. from the heat source.
- Take shrimp from marinade and drain excess; throw marinade away.
- Put shrimp onto preheated grill; cook, flipping once, for 5-6 minutes till opaque in center. Serve right away.

Nutrition Information

- Calories: 336 calories;
- Total Carbohydrate: 10.2 g
- Cholesterol: 346 mg
- Total Fat: 15.7 g
- Protein: 37.8 g
- Sodium: 401 mg

151. Grilled Lamb With Tomato-basil Marinade

"A simple aromatic grilled lamb that will surely bring an unexpected guest to your Tuscany evening. Indulge!"
Serving: 8 | Prep: 15m | Ready in: 4h23m

Ingredients

- 1 (6 oz.) can tomato paste
- 2/3 cup red wine
- 1 1/2 tbsps. olive oil
- 6 cloves garlic, minced
- 12 leaves fresh basil, cut into ribbons and chopped
- 8 1-inch-thick loin lamb chops

- sea salt and cracked black pepper to taste

Direction

- Preparation for marinade: In a small bowl combine olive oil, basil, garlic, red wine, and tomato paste.
- In a ceramic or glass container put lamb, brush the marinade on both sides thoroughly. Use a plastic wrap to cover and keep in the refrigerator, 4 or more hours.
- Prepare the outdoor grill by lightly oiling the grate and preheat at 475°F (245°C).
- Wipe off most of the marinade, leaving an only light coating on the lamb. Season with pepper and salt.
- For 4-5 minutes a side, grill until lamb becomes firm, color is reddish-pink, and juicy at middle. Insert a meat thermometer at the center and it must not be lower than 130°F (54°C).

Nutrition Information

- Calories: 237 calories;
- Total Carbohydrate: 5.2 g
- Cholesterol: 56 mg
- Total Fat: 15.6 g
- Protein: 15.2 g
- Sodium: 251 mg

152. Grilled Prosciutto And Peach Flatbread Pizza

"This dish has basil, prosciutto, sweet peaches, and ricotta on top. Drizzle honey balsamic reduction over it and your dish have completed."
Serving: 4 | Prep: 15m | Ready in: 44m

Ingredients

- 1 cup balsamic vinegar
- 1/4 cup honey
- 1/2 tsp. lemon juice
- 1/4 tsp. black pepper
- 2 naan bread

- 4 oz. ricotta cheese
- 2 fresh peaches, sliced
- 1 (3 oz.) package prosciutto, torn into pieces
- 3 tbsps. thinly sliced fresh basil

Direction

- In a small saucepan, mix together pepper, lemon juice, honey and balsamic vinegar. Boil balsamic vinegar on high, lower the heat to low. Simmer for 15 minutes until the mixture has decreased to 1/3 cup.
- Set an outdoor grill to medium-high heat to preheat and lightly grease the grate.
- Grill naan for 2-3 minutes until forming char marks. Spread over the charred side with the ricotta cheese. Put prosciutto and peaches on top. Sprinkle basil over. Drizzle balsamic reduction over.
- Put the flatbreads back to the grill. Put cover on the grill and grill for 7 minutes until the flatbread starts to char on the bottom and the cheese melts.

Nutrition Information

- Calories: 355 calories;
- Total Carbohydrate: 53.4 g
- Cholesterol: 33 mg
- Total Fat: 10.7 g
- Protein: 12.8 g
- Sodium: 625 mg

153. Grilled Shrimp Over Zucchini Noodles

"This one is good substitute for pasta."
Serving: 5 | Prep: 10m | Ready in: 15m

Ingredients

- Lemon Basil Dressing:
- 2 cups thinly sliced fresh basil
- 9 tbsps. olive oil, divided
- 1/3 cup toasted sliced almonds, divided
- 1 tbsp. red wine vinegar

- 1 shallot, coarsely chopped
- 2 cloves garlic, coarsely chopped
- 1 lemon, zested
- 1/4 tsp. red pepper flakes
- 1 lb. shrimp, peeled and deveined
- 5 zucchini
- kosher salt and freshly ground black pepper to taste

Direction

- In a blender, process vinegar, red pepper flakes, 1/4 cup almonds, lemon zest, 1/2 cup olive oil, garlic, basil, and shallot until the dressing is smooth.
- In a frying pan, put 1 tbsp. olive oil and heat on medium-high; sauté shrimp 2-4 minutes or until pink and heated through. Take pan away from heat and in a bowl mix shrimp in 2 tbsps. dressing.
- To make spaghetti-size noodle shapes, put a zucchini through a spiralizer. Add to frying pan; stir and cook zucchini noodles until tender on medium heat, 1-2 minutes. Add in 2 tbsps. lemon basil dressing and mix to coat. Take pan away from heat.
- Transfer shrimp onto the top of the zucchini noodles; use black pepper and salt to season. Put remaining almonds on top.

Nutrition Information

- Calories: 356 calories;
- Total Carbohydrate: 8.1 g
- Cholesterol: 138 mg
- Total Fat: 28.6 g
- Protein: 18.4 g
- Sodium: 253 mg

154. Ham And Fresh Basil Pinwheels

"Tortilla rolls, sliced into mini-sandwiches."
Serving: 24 | Prep: 25m | Ready in: 2h30m

Ingredients

- 6 (10 inch) flour tortillas
- 1 (8 oz.) package cream cheese, softened
- 12 slices ham
- 4 oz. fresh basil
- 1 cup sun-dried tomatoes
- 12 leaves red leaf lettuce - rinsed

Direction

- Scatter cream cheese lightly on every tortilla. Along the center of every tortilla, place 2 slices of ham. Put 1 fresh basil layer, then 1 tomatoes layer. Avoid putting ingredients very near to edges of tortilla. Put the lettuce; use sufficient leaf lettuce to cover along the middle of every tortilla, with some frilly leaf edge overhanging.
- Beginning at an end, securely roll up every tortilla. In 4 equally spaced spots of tortilla roll, stick toothpicks. Put tortilla rolls in dish, place cover, and refrigerate to chill for 2 hours.
- Cut every roll into 4 equally sized sandwiches, and serve right away.

Nutrition Information

- Calories: 124 calories;
- Total Carbohydrate: 12.4 g
- Cholesterol: 19 mg
- Total Fat: 4.8 g
- Protein: 5.2 g
- Sodium: 351 mg

155. Happy Shrimp

"You can enjoy this shrimp dish with angel hair pasta or crusty bread."
Serving: 4 | Prep: 20m | Ready in: 40m

Ingredients

- 1/4 cup butter
- 1 1/2 tsps. minced garlic
- 1 lb. peeled and deveined medium shrimp
- 1/4 cup chopped green onions
- 1/4 cup dry white wine
- 1/3 cup heavy cream
- 2 tbsps. chopped fresh basil
- 2 roma (plum) tomatoes, chopped
- 1 pinch cayenne pepper, or to taste
- salt and pepper to taste

Direction

- In a big skillet, melt butter over medium-high heat. Mix in green onions, garlic and shrimp. Stir and cook for 5 minutes until the outside of the shrimp is pink and the middle is not translucent anymore. Put the shrimp aside, and add cayenne pepper, basil, tomatoes, cream and wine. Simmer, and then lower the heat to medium-low, and simmer for 10 minutes until the sauce coats the back of a spoon.
- Return the shrimp to the sauce and mix, and use pepper and salt to season to taste. Thoroughly heat and enjoy.

Nutrition Information

- Calories: 280 calories;
- Total Carbohydrate: 3.1 g
- Cholesterol: 230 mg
- Total Fat: 19.9 g
- Protein: 19.5 g
- Sodium: 330 mg

156. Hearty Fettuccini Bolognese Sauce

"A recipe that keeps very well."
Serving: 6 | Prep: 40m | Ready in: 2h40m

Ingredients

- 1/4 cup extra virgin olive oil
- 2 onions, chopped
- 2 cups chopped celery
- 1 cup chopped carrots
- 2 cloves garlic, chopped
- 1/2 lb. ground veal
- 1/2 lb. chopped pork
- 3/4 lb. mild Italian sausage
- 6 oz. pancetta bacon, diced
- 2 (14.5 oz.) cans whole peeled tomatoes, with liquid
- 1 (14.5 oz.) can chicken broth
- 1/2 cup whole milk
- 5 tsps. chopped Italian flat leaf parsley
- 5 tbsps. chopped fresh basil
- 5 tsps. chopped fresh thyme
- salt and pepper to taste
- 1 lb. fettuccini pasta
- 1 cup grated Parmesan cheese

Direction

- Heat oil in big heavy pot on medium heat; sauté garlic, carrots, celery and onions for 10 minutes till tender. Put heat on high. Add pancetta, sausage, pork and veal; cook till meats brown evenly.
- Mix thyme, basil, parsley, milk, chicken broth and tomatoes in; lower heat to medium low. Simmer for 2 1/2 hours, with no cover; occasionally mix, breaking tomatoes with spoon as you mix. Season to taste with pepper and salt.
- Boil big pot with lightly salted water. Add fettuccini till al dente for 8-10 minutes; drain.
- Serve fettuccini with parmesan cheese and sauce on top.

Nutrition Information

- Calories: 834 calories;
- Total Carbohydrate: 70.8 g
- Cholesterol: 100 mg
- Total Fat: 43.4 g
- Protein: 41.5 g
- Sodium: 1188 mg

157. Hearty Veggie Lasagna

""This new family favorite hearty lasagna is made with 3 varieties of cheese with heaps of veggies, tons of sauce, pasta and the addition of the great northern beans.""
Serving: 6 | Prep: 15m | Ready in: 1h

Ingredients

- 1 (16 oz.) container Borden® Fat Free Cottage Cheese
- 1 (10 oz.) package frozen chopped spinach, thawed
- 2 eggs, lightly beaten
- 8 oz. Borden® Mozzarella Shreds
- 1 cup Borden® Finely Shredded Parmesan Natural Shreds, divided
- 1/2 tsp. salt
- 1/2 tsp. black pepper
- 2 tbsps. olive oil
- 1 1/4 cups chopped onion
- 1 (15 oz.) can Great Northern or pinto beans, rinsed and drained
- 3 cloves garlic, minced
- 1 tsp. chopped fresh oregano
- 1 tsp. chopped fresh basil
- 1/2 tsp. chopped fresh thyme
- 4 cups tomato pasta sauce
- 1 (8 oz.) package lasagna noodles, either oven-ready or cooked per package directions, drained

Direction

- Let oven warm to 375°F. Using non-stick cooking oil, spray a 13x9 inches pan.

- Strain cottage cheese for 15 minutes to eliminate excess liquid then put aside. Using a strainer, press melted spinach with a spoon or paper towels to discard excess water then put aside.
- In a medium-sized bowl, mix cottage eggs, eggs, mozzarella, black pepper, 1/4 cup parmesan and salt then put aside.
- On medium heat, warm olive oil in a big non-stick skillet. Sauté onions until it becomes soft. Sauté beans, oregano, garlic, thyme, basil and drained spinach for 5 minutes. Combine pasta sauce in the mixture for a few minutes longer by stirring.
- Even out on the bottom of the baking dish 1/3 of the pasta sauce mixture. On top of it, place layer of noodles, half of the cottage mixture and the other 1/3 of the pasta sauce. Replicate layer. Do this for the last third of the pasta sauce mixture. Make sure that all of the noodles are covered with sauce by pressing down the top of the lasagna. Place aluminum foil to cover and let it bake for 15 minutes. Take off the foil covering and top leftover 3/4 cup of parmesan cheese. Let it bake until lasagna is completely baked and fizzy for 15 minutes or more.

Nutrition Information

- Calories: 597 calories;
- Total Carbohydrate: 61.8 g
- Cholesterol: 105 mg
- Total Fat: 22.6 g
- Protein: 38.5 g
- Sodium: 1765 mg

158. Herb Bread For Bread Machine

"Enjoy this bread while warm with a soup on the side or toasted with cream cheese on it!"
Serving: 8 | Prep: 10m | Ready in: 3h10m

Ingredients

- 1 cup warm water
- 1 egg, beaten
- 1 tsp. salt
- 2 tbsps. white sugar
- 2 tbsps. extra-virgin olive oil
- 2 tsps. dried rosemary leaves, crushed
- 1 tsp. dried oregano
- 1 tsp. dried basil
- 3 cups all-purpose flour
- 2 tbsps. all-purpose flour
- 2 tsps. bread machine yeast

Direction

- In the bread machine pan, put in warm water then followed by the egg, salt, white sugar, olive oil, rosemary, oregano, basil, flour and bread machine yeast, place the ingredients one by one.
- Let the bread bake on Large Loaf setting in Light Crust option; press the Start button to run the machine.

Nutrition Information

- Calories: 234 calories;
- Total Carbohydrate: 41.2 g
- Cholesterol: 23 mg
- Total Fat: 4.6 g
- Protein: 6.3 g
- Sodium: 302 mg

159. Herb Garlic Oil

"A versatile garlic oil that can be used as a dipping sauce for almost every dish.""
Serving: 4 | Prep: 5m | Ready in: 8h6m

Ingredients

- 1/2 cup olive oil
- 1 clove garlic, roughly chopped
- 1/4 cup extra-virgin olive oil (optional)
- 1/2 tsp. basil
- 1/2 tsp. oregano

Direction

- Heat a skillet on medium-low heat. Pour olive oil slowly into the skillet, sliding skillet away from the burner if oil starts to splatter. Put in garlic, then cook for approximately 60 seconds until sizzling but now browned. Turn the heat off, leave the skillet on burner. Mix in oregano, basil and extra-virgin olive oil. Pour into a container and keep in the refrigerator for 8 hours to overnight, until flavors combined.

Nutrition Information

- Calories: 367 calories;
- Total Carbohydrate: 0.5 g
- Cholesterol: 0 mg
- Total Fat: 41 g
- Protein: 0.1 g
- Sodium: < 1 mg

160. Herbal Shrimp Delight With Beer Sauce

"Fresh greens and herbs topped with tiger shrimp!"
Serving: 6 | Prep: 30m | Ready in: 45m

Ingredients

- 1 cup chopped fresh basil
- 1 cup chopped fresh oregano
- 1 cup chopped fresh parsley
- 1 cup chopped fresh spinach

- 1 cup chopped romaine lettuce
- 5 tbsps. olive oil, divided
- 1 tsp. white wine
- 2 tbsps. all-purpose flour
- 1/4 cup cold water
- 1 small onion, chopped
- 1 green onion, chopped
- 5 cloves garlic, peeled and minced
- 1 tomato, diced
- 1 cup Mexican beer
- 1 tbsp. fresh lime juice
- 1 lb. jumbo shrimp, peeled and deveined
- salt and pepper to taste
- 2 tbsps. freshly grated Parmesan cheese
- freshly ground black pepper to taste

Direction

- Toss together white wine, 3 tbsps. olive oil, romaine lettuce, spinach, parsley, oregano and basil in a medium bowl.
- Blend the water and flour into a paste in a small bowl.
- In a medium saucepan over medium high heat, heat a tbsp. olive oil, sauté for 5 minutes the garlic, green onion and onion, till soft. Add in tomato. Lower heat to low, mix in the water and flour. Cook, mix till thickened. Add in the lime juice and beer, add with pepper and salt to season, let simmer while shrimp cooks.
- In a separate medium saucepan, heat the rest of the olive oil. Sauté shrimp till opaque, 3 minutes per side.
- Take shrimp off heat, and nicely slice while warm. Serve on top of greens mixture and herb, sprinkle beer sauce. Top with freshly ground black pepper and Parmesan.

Nutrition Information

- Calories: 248 calories;
- Total Carbohydrate: 10.4 g
- Cholesterol: 116 mg
- Total Fat: 13.6 g
- Protein: 18.2 g
- Sodium: 153 mg

161. Homemade Italian Red Sauce

"Italian variation of a good sauce that is perfect with any pasta and meatballs!"
Serving: 12 | Prep: 10m | Ready in: 2h20m

Ingredients

- 1/2 cup olive oil
- 1 large onion, minced
- 3 cloves garlic, minced
- 4 cups water
- 2 (32 oz.) cans crushed diced tomatoes
- 1 (16 oz.) can tomato paste
- 1/4 cup chopped fresh basil
- 1 tsp. baking soda
- 1 tsp. white sugar
- salt and ground black pepper to taste

Direction

- Over medium-high heat, heat olive oil in a big saucepan. In this same pan, sauté the garlic and onion for about 5 to 7 minutes in the hot oil until onion becomes translucent.
- After sautéing, lower the heat to a medium-low setting. In the same saucepan, throw sugar, baking soda, basil, tomato paste, crushed tomatoes, and water. Mix well and let the mixture simmer and cook for 2 hours until the consistency of the sauce becomes thick.

Nutrition Information

- Calories: 149 calories;
- Total Carbohydrate: 13.9 g
- Cholesterol: 0 mg
- Total Fat: 9.2 g
- Protein: 3.1 g
- Sodium: 644 mg

162. Homemade Pesto

"This pesto is fresh and tasty."
Serving: 6 | Prep: 15m | Ready in: 15m

Ingredients

- 4 cups packed fresh basil leaves
- 1/4 cup Italian parsley
- 2 cloves garlic, peeled and lightly crushed
- 1 cup pine nuts
- 1 1/2 cups shredded Parmigiano-Reggiano cheese
- 1 tbsp. fresh lemon juice
- 1/2 cup extra-virgin olive oil, or more as needed
- salt and ground black pepper to taste

Direction

- Put garlic, Italian parsley and basil in a food processor, pulse several times to blend, then process 30 seconds till basil is chopped finely. Put in pine nuts and process 30 seconds longer until finely chopped. Add Parmigiano-Reggiano cheese to the mixture and process until finely ground.
- As the machine is running, mix in lemon juice and gradually drizzle olive oil into the pesto until incorporated and the pesto is nicely combined. Stop the machine; season pesto with black pepper and salt to taste.

Nutrition Information

- Calories: 389 calories;
- Total Carbohydrate: 5.4 g
- Cholesterol: 14 mg
- Total Fat: 35.8 g
- Protein: 14.1 g
- Sodium: 343 mg

163. Honey Bean Salad

""A salad dish that even people who don't enjoy beans can appreciate. I needed food that had antibacterial properties and high antioxidants after an x-ray, and this was what I came up with. This wonderful tasting dish is my personal favorite!""
Serving: 6 | Prep: 10m | Ready in: 10m

Ingredients

- 2 (15 oz.) cans kidney beans
- 1 tbsp. honey
- 2 tbsps. apple cider vinegar
- 1/2 tsp. ground black pepper
- 1 tsp. dried basil
- 1 tsp. dried sage
- 2 cloves garlic, minced
- 1/8 tsp. hot pepper sauce (such as Tabasco®), or to taste
- 2 tbsps. olive oil, or to taste

Direction

- In a mixing bowl, add the beans and combine with olive oil, hot pepper sauce, garlic, sage, basil, black pepper, vinegar and honey. Before serving, mix the contents thoroughly until everything is equally coated. Enjoy!

Nutrition Information

- Calories: 173 calories;
- Total Carbohydrate: 25.1 g
- Cholesterol: 0 mg
- Total Fat: 5.1 g
- Protein: 7.7 g
- Sodium: 303 mg

164. Hoy Lai Pad Nam Prik Pow (clams With Chili Paste And Basil)

"I adore making this dish. It's so simple and quick to prepare. I always received compliments from my guests whenever I serve this one on our simple get together."
Serving: 6 | Prep: 10m | Ready in: 20m

Ingredients

- 5 tbsps. vegetable oil
- 5 cloves garlic, minced
- 2 lbs. small clams, thoroughly cleaned
- 3 tbsps. Nam Prik Pao (roasted chile paste)
- 3 tbsps. fish sauce (optional)
- 3 Chee Fah chiles (mild red chiles)
- 1 tbsp. white sugar
- 1 cup Bai Kraprao (holy basil leaves), or to taste

Direction

- In a hot wok or large heavy-bottomed pan, heat the oil over high heat for 1 minute. Stir in garlic and cook for 1 minute just until golden brown. Add the chili paste and clams, and mix until the clams are well-coated.
- Mix in sugar, fish sauce, and chiles. Cook the clams for 5-10 minutes, stirring constantly until the clams have opened.
- Stir in basil and cook for 1 minute until wilted.

Nutrition Information

- Calories: 318 calories;
- Total Carbohydrate: 15.6 g
- Cholesterol: 79 mg
- Total Fat: 13.8 g
- Protein: 31.4 g
- Sodium: 747 mg

165. Infused Olive Oil

"An easy to prepare olive oil mixture."
Serving: 16 | Prep: 5m | Ready in: 1h5m

Ingredients

- 2 cups olive oil
- 1 tsp. coarsely ground black pepper
- 1 tbsp. chopped fresh basil
- 1/2 tsp. coarse sea salt
- 1 pinch crushed red pepper

Direction

- Combine the red pepper, coarse sea salt, basil, coarsely ground black pepper and olive oil in a medium bowl. Put on cover and chill the mixture in the fridge. Let it sit for about an hour prior to serving.

Nutrition Information

- Calories: 239 calories;
- Total Carbohydrate: 0.1 g
- Cholesterol: 0 mg
- Total Fat: 27 g
- Protein: 0 g
- Sodium: 56 mg

166. Insalata Caprese With Avocado

"This salad is really better a hundred times that the original version with just a small change-up."
Serving: 8 | Prep: 15m | Ready in: 15m

Ingredients

- 2 avocados - peeled, pitted, and cubed
- 1 1/2 tbsps. lemon juice
- 4 large tomatoes, cubed
- 1 lb. fresh mozzarella cheese, cubed
- 1/3 cup basil leaves, thinly sliced
- 3 1/2 tbsps. extra-virgin olive oil
- 1 pinch fine sea salt to taste

Direction

- In a big bowl, mix together lemon juice and avocados, then toss to coat. Put in basil, mozzarella and tomato, then toss again. Trickle with olive oil and season with salt.

Nutrition Information

- Calories: 295 calories;
- Total Carbohydrate: 9.7 g
- Cholesterol: 36 mg
- Total Fat: 22.5 g
- Protein: 15.6 g
- Sodium: 399 mg

167. Instant Pot® Chicken Pesto

"Chicken pesto to serve over pasta."
Serving: 12 | Prep: 15m | Ready in: 1h21m

Ingredients

- 1/2 cup pine nuts
- 2 cloves garlic
- 1 bunch fresh basil, stems removed
- 3 tbsps. olive oil, or to taste, divided
- 2 tbsps. grated Parmesan cheese
- salt and ground black pepper to taste
- 1 whole chicken
- 1 cup milk
- 1/2 cup sun-dried tomatoes
- 1 (16 oz.) package penne pasta

Direction

- In a dry saucepan on medium heat, toast garlic cloves and pine nuts. Remove to a food processor; put in pepper, salt, Parmesan cheese, 2 tbsps. olive oil and basil; process until blended.
- Turn on and choose the Sauté function in a multi-cooker (as an Instant Pot(R)). Put in the rest of olive oil to coat the bottom of the pot.
- Season both sides of chicken with pepper and salt; arrange in the pot with breast side down. Cook 5-7 minutes until browned. Flip; keep

browning 5 minutes. Turn off the Sauté function and rub over the chicken with some pesto. Stir in sun-dried tomatoes, milk, and the rest of pesto.
- Close lid and lock. Choose high pressure following manufacturer's instructions and set the timer for 25 minutes. Let pressure build 10-15 minutes. Allow to rest 5-10 minutes. Carefully release pressure 5 minutes with the quick-release method as in manufacturer's instructions. Unlock and take out lid.
- Remove chicken to a separate dish; split all meat from bone. Get rid of skin and bones. Chop meat into bite-size pieces; bring back in with the sauce; mix to combine. Season with pepper and salt.
- Heat a big pot of slightly salted water to a boil. Put in penne and cook 11 minutes, stirring sometimes, until tender but firm to the bite; drain. Place pasta into chicken and sauce; mix to combine.

Nutrition Information

- Calories: 357 calories;
- Total Carbohydrate: 30.6 g
- Cholesterol: 52 mg
- Total Fat: 15.9 g
- Protein: 23.6 g
- Sodium: 126 mg

168. Instant Pot® Quick And Easy Spaghetti Sauce

"Top your pasta dish with this homemade spaghetti sauce made with your Instant Pot®. The fresh tomatoes give the sauce it's full and flavorful taste."
Serving: 6 | Prep: 10m | Ready in: 1h5m

Ingredients

- 2 tbsps. olive oil
- 2 yellow onions, chopped
- 2 cloves garlic, minced
- 1 carrot, chopped
- 1 celery stalk, chopped

- 3 lbs. plum tomatoes
- 1 tsp. dried oregano
- 1 tsp. Italian seasoning
- 1 tsp. sea salt
- 1 tsp. dried basil
- 1/2 tsp. ground black pepper

Direction

- Power on the multi-functional pressure cooker (like Instant Pot®), choose Sauté function. Pour olive oil and heat; toss in garlic and onions. Cook for about 5 minutes until tender and translucent. Stir in tomatoes, carrot and celery and cook for another 4 minutes or until cooked through. Sprinkle with Italian seasoning, salt, basil, oregano and pepper, to taste. Seal the cover and, following manufacturer's directions, program to high pressure and set timer for 25 minutes. Let pressure build for 10-15 minutes.
- Using the natural-release method based on manufacturer's directions, carefully release pressure for 10-40 minutes then unseal and remove cover. Use an immersion blender for blending to achieve desired consistency.

Nutrition Information

- Calories: 125 calories;
- Total Carbohydrate: 18.8 g
- Cholesterol: 0 mg
- Total Fat: 5.2 g
- Protein: 3.4 g
- Sodium: 351 mg

169. Instant Pot® Vegan Spaghetti Squash With Pesto

"A quick vegan main dish. You can make this paleo, dairy-free and gluten-free."
Serving: 4 | Prep: 10m | Ready in: 40m

Ingredients

- Spaghetti squash:

- 1 (3 lb.) spaghetti squash, halved and seeded
- 1 cup vegetable broth
- 1 sprig chopped fresh rosemary
- 1/2 tsp. salt
- Pesto:
- 2 cups fresh basil leaves
- 2/3 cup olive oil
- 1/4 cup pine nuts
- 2 tbsps. nutritional yeast
- 2 cloves garlic
- 1/2 tsp. salt
- 1/4 tsp. ground black pepper

Direction

- In multi-functional pressure cooker like Instant Pot, mix 1/2 tsp. salt, rosemary, vegetable broth and spaghetti squash; close lid. Lock. Following manufacturer's instructions, choose high pressure. Put timer on 7 minutes; let pressure build for 10-15 minutes.
- Carefully use quick release method following manufacturer's instruction to release pressure for 5 minutes. Unlock lid; remove. Remove spaghetti squash; cool for 5-10 minutes till easy to handle. Use a fork to scrape squash insides to spaghetti strands.
- In food processor bowl, pulse pepper, 1/2 tsp. salt, garlic, nutritional yeast, pine nuts, olive oil and basil leaves till smooth. Serve over spaghetti squash.

Nutrition Information

- Calories: 500 calories;
- Total Carbohydrate: 28.4 g
- Cholesterol: 0 mg
- Total Fat: 42.7 g
- Protein: 7.2 g
- Sodium: 758 mg

170. Italian Baked Eggplant With Parmesan (parmigiana Di Melanzane)

"Choose ripe seedless eggplant and let them sit with salt for 1 hour to eliminate the bitterness."
Serving: 8 | Prep: 30m | Ready in: 3h5m

Ingredients

- 3 lbs. large eggplants, sliced lengthwise into 1/4-inch slices
- 2 tbsps. coarse salt, or as needed
- 5 cups vegetable oil for frying
- 2 tbsps. flour for dredging
- Tomato Sauce:
- 2 tbsps. extra-virgin olive oil
- 1/2 onion, finely chopped
- 3 cloves garlic, halved
- 3 (15 oz.) cans tomato puree
- 8 leaves fresh basil leaves, halved
- salt to taste
- 1 1/2 (16 oz.) packages fresh mozzarella cheese, sliced
- 2 1/2 cups freshly grated Parmesan cheese

Direction

- Arrange the eggplant slices in a single layer into a colander that is set on a plate. Sprinkle the eggplant with coarse salt. Cover the slices with another layer of eggplant slices, and then sprinkle them with salt. Repeat another layer for the remaining eggplant. Top the eggplant with a plate and add weight to press some pressure into the eggplant slices. Allow them to stand at room temperature for 1 hour.
- Wash the eggplant slices under the cold running water, washing off all the excess salt. Use paper towels to pat all sides of the eggplant until dry.
- Put oil in a deep skillet and heat it over medium-high. Dip the slices of eggplant in flour, making sure both sides are coated. Working in batches, add slices of eggplant into the hot oil and deep fry each side for 2-3 minutes until golden. Let them drain on paper towels.
- Put olive oil in a large pot and heat it over medium heat. Cook the onion and garlic for 5 minutes until translucent and soft. Pour in tomato puree, salt, and four basil leaves. Cook and often stir for 20 minutes until the sauce begins to thicken. Remove the sauce from the heat, discarding the garlic. Mix in the remaining four basil leaves.
- Set the oven to 350°F or 175°C for preheating.
- Pour 1 layer of tomato sauce all over the bottom of a baking dish. Arrange a single layer of eggplant slices on top of the tomato sauce, covering the sauce. Spread the top with more sauce, Parmesan cheese, and mozzarella slices. Make more layers, making sure you have a total of 3-5. The layers should finish with tomato sauce and Parmesan cheese that is grated.
- Bake it inside the preheated oven for 30-40 minutes until bubbling and heated through. Remove it from the oven. Before serving, allow it to stand for 20 minutes.

Nutrition Information

- Calories: 592 calories;
- Total Carbohydrate: 30.6 g
- Cholesterol: 76 mg
- Total Fat: 38.5 g
- Protein: 35.1 g
- Sodium: 3313 mg

171. Italian Cheesesteak Sandwich

"Sandwiches with an Italian twist."
Serving: 4 | Prep: 15m | Ready in: 30m

Ingredients

- 1 tbsp. butter
- 1 medium onion, thinly sliced
- 1 cup sliced fresh mushrooms
- 1 green bell pepper, thinly sliced
- 1 pinch salt

- 1 clove garlic, minced
- 1/2 lb. very thinly sliced or shaved steak
- 1 (24 oz.) jar RAGÚ® Old World Style® Traditional Sauce
- 1 tsp. dried Italian seasoning
- 1/2 tsp. crushed red pepper flakes
- 4 Italian bread rolls
- 1 clove garlic
- 1 tbsp. extra-virgin olive oil
- 1/3 lb. provolone or fresh mozzarella cheese, sliced
- 1/2 cup fresh basil leaves, torn

Direction

- In a big skillet, melt butter on medium heat. Add a pinch of salt, green peppers, mushrooms and onions; sauté for 2-3 minutes till veggies start to soften. Add minced garlic; cook for 1 minute.
- Push vegetables to 1 side of skillet; add sliced meat in open area. Sauté for 2-3 minutes till not pink.
- Heat Ragu Old World Style Traditional Sauce, crushed red pepper and Italian seasoning in another saucepan on medium heat.
- Put oven rack 6-inches away from heat source; preheat oven's broiler.
- Lengthwise, slice rolls. Put on a baking sheet, opened. Toast under broiler on low heat for 30 seconds; watch carefully to not burn. Take out of oven; rub cut side of whole garlic clove on toasted roll sides. Lightly brush with olive oil.
- Fold the cheese slices in meat and pepper/onion mix; mix till cheese starts to melt. Divide to toasted roll bottoms. Put a generous spoonful of Ragu sauce on top; save the rest for dipping if you want.
- Sprinkle fresh basil on; immediately serve.

Nutrition Information

- Calories: 608 calories;
- Total Carbohydrate: 57.7 g
- Cholesterol: 64 mg
- Total Fat: 28.5 g
- Protein: 29.7 g
- Sodium: 1450 mg

172. Italian Layered Salad With Bison Pepperoni

"This dish is the combination of crisp and colorful green layers, pepperoni seasoning with chopped bison sausage and a creamy basil dressing. This dinner side salad can also be a perfect lunch."
Serving: 8 | Prep: 20m | Ready in: 20m

Ingredients

- 6 cups shredded romaine lettuce
- 1 cup cherry or grape tomatoes, halved
- 1 cup chopped yellow bell pepper
- 1 cup chopped fennel bulb
- 1 1/2 cups cubed fresh mozzarella cheese
- 1 (8 oz.) package bison sausage with pepperoni seasoning
- Basil-Sour Cream Dressing:
- 2/3 cup mayonnaise
- 2/3 cup sour cream
- 1/4 cup milk
- 1/4 cup chopped fresh basil
- 1/2 tsp. salt
- 1/4 tsp. black pepper

Direction

- Line the bottom of a 3-qt clear bowl with 3 cups of romaine. Make layers in the order: tomatoes, bell peppers, fennel, the leftover 3 cups of romaine, the mozzarella cheese, and bison pepperoni. Spread over the salad with Basil-Sour Cream Dressing. Chill, tightly covered up to 24 hours to serve or immediately serve.
- Basil-Sour Cream Dressing
- In a medium bowl, combine black pepper, salt, basil, milk, sour cream and mayonnaise.

Nutrition Information

- Calories: 331 calories;
- Total Carbohydrate: 6.6 g
- Cholesterol: 45 mg
- Total Fat: 28.4 g

- Protein: 18.3 g
- Sodium: 800 mg

173. Italian Marinated Eggplant Antipasto

" "This is a delectable eggplant dish, thinly sliced, lightly fried then marinated for at least 8 hours or overnight in garlic, fresh herbs, olive oil and white wine vinegar mixture. It's a dish definitely worth waiting for! This would make a savory part of an antipasto platter." "
Serving: 4 | Prep: 10m | Ready in: 8h50m

Ingredients

- 4 small eggplant, thinly sliced
- salt and freshly ground black pepper to taste
- 3 tbsps. extra-virgin olive oil, divided, or more if needed
- 1/2 bunch fresh parsley, chopped
- 1/2 bunch fresh basil, chopped
- 6 leaves fresh sage, chopped
- 3 cloves garlic, minced
- 5 tbsps. white wine vinegar

Direction

- Add flavor to the eggplant slices by drizzling it with salt then place it on a plate in a layer. Use another plate and set it as a weight on top of the eggplant slices, set aside and leave it for 30 minutes.
- Wash off the eggplant and pat them dry using paper towels. In a large skillet, heat 1 tbsp. of olive oil over medium heat and cook the eggplant in batches, about 2 minutes per side, or until it has turned slightly browned. If needed, add more olive oil then drain the eggplant on paper towels.
- Put the eggplant slices that you've sautéed into a shallow dish in a layer. Drizzle it over with parsley, sage, basil, garlic, pepper, and salt then with the remaining 1 tbsp. olive oil and white wine vinegar, dribble it on the eggplant slices.

- Cover the dish and leave it to marinate for 8 hours or overnight in the refrigerator.

Nutrition Information

- Calories: 182 calories;
- Total Carbohydrate: 21 g
- Cholesterol: 0 mg
- Total Fat: 10.9 g
- Protein: 4.2 g
- Sodium: 53 mg

174. Italian Vegetable Fusilli With Basil Mint Pesto

"This dish is made with fusilli pasta, pesto, and green vegetables. It's very delicious."
Serving: 4 | Prep: 15m | Ready in: 37m

Ingredients

- 2 tbsps. pine nuts
- 3 cups fresh basil leaves
- 1 cup fresh parsley
- 1 cup mint leaves
- 2 cloves garlic clove, smashed
- 1 1/4 cups olive oil, divided
- 1/4 cup freshly grated Parmigiano-Reggiano cheese
- sea salt and freshly ground black pepper to taste
- 1 (16 oz.) package fusilli pasta (such as De Cecco®)
- 1 lb. asparagus, cut into 1/2-inch pieces
- 1 (5 oz.) bag baby spinach leaves

Direction

- In a skillet, put pine nuts over medium heat. Toast for 2 minutes until turning golden. Remove to a plate and let it cool.
- In a mini chopper or a food processor, mix together garlic, mint, parsley, basil and pine nuts; pulse till finely chopped. Add Parmigiano-Reggiano cheese and 1 cup olive

oil, pulse to blend. Use pepper and salt to season the pesto.

- Boil lightly salted water in a big pot. In the boiling water, cook fusilli for 8 minutes until firm to the bite, tossing sometimes. Strain, saving 1 cup of the cooking water. Clean the pot by wiping it.
- In the pot, heat the leftover 1/4 cup olive oil over high heat. Put in asparagus, use pepper and salt to season. Cook for 4 minutes until browned in spots and crisp-tender. Mix in spinach and cook for 3 minutes until just wilted. Add fusilli and pesto, stir thoroughly to coat. If the pesto seems dry, mix in the saved cooking water.

Nutrition Information

- Calories: 1092 calories;
- Total Carbohydrate: 90.6 g
- Cholesterol: 4 mg
- Total Fat: 74.3 g
- Protein: 23.1 g
- Sodium: 204 mg

175. Jalapeno Pesto

"It's a spicy and tasty take on your typical Italian pesto."
Serving: 14 | Prep: 10m | Ready in: 10m

Ingredients

- 1/4 cup walnuts
- 2 cloves garlic
- 2 cups packed fresh basil leaves
- 3/4 cup shredded Parmagiano-Reggiano cheese
- 1 jalapeno pepper, stem removed
- 2/3 cup olive oil
- salt and ground black pepper to taste

Direction

- In a food processor, pulse garlic and walnuts until chopped finely. Put in jalapeno pepper, Parmigiano-Reggiano cheese and basil, then process until blended. Stream oil into basil

mixture while food processor is running until gets smooth consistency. Season with black pepper and salt.

Nutrition Information

- Calories: 126 calories;
- Total Carbohydrate: 0.8 g
- Cholesterol: 4 mg
- Total Fat: 13 g
- Protein: 2.2 g
- Sodium: 66 mg

176. Jamie's Minestrone

"A bowl of minestrone with rich vegetables."
Serving: 8 | Prep: 35m | Ready in: 1h25m

Ingredients

- 3 tbsps. olive oil
- 3 cloves garlic, chopped
- 2 onions, chopped
- 2 cups chopped celery
- 5 carrots, sliced
- 2 cups chicken broth
- 2 cups water
- 4 cups tomato sauce
- 1/2 cup red wine (optional)
- 1 cup canned kidney beans, drained
- 1 (15 oz.) can green beans
- 2 cups baby spinach, rinsed
- 3 zucchinis, quartered and sliced
- 1 tbsp. chopped fresh oregano
- 2 tbsps. chopped fresh basil
- salt and pepper to taste
- 1/2 cup seashell pasta
- 2 tbsps. grated Parmesan cheese for topping
- 1 tbsp. olive oil

Direction

- Heat the olive oil in a big stock pot over moderately-low heat and sauté the garlic for 2 to 3 minutes. Put in the onion and sauté for 4 to 5 minutes. Put in the carrots and celery, sauté for 1 to 2 minutes.

- Put in the tomato sauce, water and chicken broth; boil, mixing often. If wished put red wine at this stage. Turn the heat down to low and put in pepper, salt, basil, oregano, zucchini, spinach leaves, green beans and kidney beans. Simmer for 30 to 40 minutes, the longer the better.
- Pour water in a medium saucepan and boil. Put in the macaroni and cook till soft. Drain the water and reserve.
- In separate serving bowls, put 2 tbsps. of cooked pasta when soup is heated through and pasta is cooked. Scoop the soup over pasta and scatter Parmesan cheese over top. Sprinkle with olive oil, serve.

Nutrition Information

- Calories: 227 calories;
- Total Carbohydrate: 30 g
- Cholesterol: 1 mg
- Total Fat: 8.3 g
- Protein: 8.6 g
- Sodium: 1142 mg

177. Jeff's Fish Stew

"Serve this along with crusty bread."
Serving: 6 | Prep: 30m | Ready in: 1h24m

Ingredients

- 1/4 cup olive oil
- 1 onion, diced
- 1 green bell pepper, diced
- 2 stalks celery, chopped
- 1 carrot, diced
- 3 cloves garlic, crushed and minced
- 1/2 tsp. dried oregano
- 5 leaves fresh basil, chopped
- salt and ground black pepper to taste
- 2 (15 oz.) cans chicken broth, or more to taste
- 1 (28 oz.) can crushed tomatoes
- 1/2 cup dry white wine

- 1 1/2 lbs. swordfish, cut into bite-sized pieces
- 2 (6.5 oz.) cans whole baby clams, undrained
- 1 tbsp. cornstarch, or as needed

Direction

- In a big pot on medium heat, heat olive oil. Put in carrot, celery, green bell pepper and onion; stir and cook 5 minutes until softened. Put in garlic; stir and cook 1 minute until fragrant. Season with pepper, salt, basil, and oregano.
- Transfer chicken broth to the pot; simmer 20 minutes till carrot and celery are soft. Add white wine and crushed tomatoes; simmer 10 minutes till flavors blend.
- Mix swordfish into the pot and cook 10 minutes until easily flaked with a fork. Add clams with juices and simmer 5 minutes until heated through. Mix in cornstarch, about 3-5 minutes until the stew thickens.

Nutrition Information

- Calories: 407 calories;
- Total Carbohydrate: 21 g
- Cholesterol: 88 mg
- Total Fat: 15.5 g
- Protein: 41.6 g
- Sodium: 1054 mg

178. Jersey Fresh Stewed Tomatoes

"It's an ideal side dish to serve with ham or fish using garden-fresh tomatoes, peppers, celery and onions."
Serving: 8 | Prep: 20m | Ready in: 40m

Ingredients

- 6 large tomatoes - peeled, cored, and chopped
- 3/4 cup chopped green bell pepper
- 1/2 cup chopped sweet onion
- 1/2 cup chopped celery
- 1 tsp. white sugar
- 1/2 tsp. salt
- 1/4 tsp. dried oregano
- 1/4 tsp. dried basil

- 1/8 tsp. black pepper
- 1 tbsp. water
- 1 1/2 tsps. cornstarch

Direction

- In a big skillet, mix together celery, onion, green bell pepper and tomatoes on moderate heat, then cook and stir for about 10 minutes until aromatic. Lower heat and cook for 5 minutes longer, until onion and green bell pepper are softened. Stir in pepper, basil, oregano, salt and sugar.
- In a small bowl, whisk together cornstarch and water, then stir into the skillet. Simmer tomato mixture for about 5 minutes, until thickened.

Nutrition Information

- Calories: 37 calories;
- Total Carbohydrate: 8.2 g
- Cholesterol: 0 mg
- Total Fat: 0.3 g
- Protein: 1.5 g
- Sodium: 159 mg

179. Jimmy Dean Sausage Crostini

"Fresh basil, sweet red pepper, mozzarella cheese and sausage on top of toasted sliced French bread makes this tasty dish"
Serving: 30

Ingredients

- 1 (16 oz.) package Regular Flavor Jimmy Dean Pork Sausage, cooked, crumbled and drained
- 1 medium yellow onion, finely chopped
- 1 1/2 cups shredded mozzarella cheese
- 1 (8 oz.) package cream cheese, softened
- 2/3 cup sweet red pepper, finely chopped
- 1/3 cup fresh basil, finely chopped
- 2 (12 oz.) loaves French bread, sliced 3/4 inch thick
- 4 tbsps. olive oil or melted butter
- 1 1/2 tsps. finely chopped rosemary (optional)
- 3/8 tsp. cayenne pepper (optional)

Direction

- Set the oven to 375°F and start preheating. Combine basil, red pepper, cream cheese, mozzarella, onion and cooked sausage and optional ingredients if wanted in a large bowl; mix thoroughly.
- Arrange sliced bread on a baking sheet, glaze the tops with olive oil or butter and bake until bread is toasted lightly. Remove from oven and spoon sausage mixture on top of each slice.
- Return to oven and bake for 7 to 10 minutes or until the topping becomes hot. Serve while warm.

180. Johnsonville® Italian Sausage Stuffing

"A tasty meal."
Serving: 14 | Prep: 25m | Ready in: 1h35m

Ingredients

- 1 (19.76 oz.) package Johnsonville Mild Italian Sausage Links, casings removed*
- 1/2 cup butter
- 2 cups chopped celery
- 1 cup chopped onions
- 1/2 cup chopped green pepper
- 3 cloves garlic, minced
- 12 cups dry unseasoned cubed bread stuffing
- 1/2 cup shredded Parmesan cheese
- 1 (2.25 oz.) can sliced black olives, drained
- 1 tsp. dried basil
- 1 tbsp. minced fresh basil
- 1 tsp. rubbed sage
- 1/2 tsp. salt
- 1/4 tsp. pepper
- 4 cups chicken broth
- 2 eggs, beaten

Direction

- Cook and crumble sausage in a big skillet on medium heat till lightly browned and not pink anymore. Drain; put aside. Melt butter in the same skillet; sauté garlic, green pepper, onion and celery till tender.

- Mix seasonings, olives, parmesan cheese, veggies, sausage and bread stuffing in a big bowl. Mix eggs and broth; add to the bread mixture, gently mixing to combine.
- Put in a 3-qt. buttered baking dish then cover; bake for 1 hour at 325°F. Uncover; bake till lightly browned for 10 minutes more. Serve.

Nutrition Information

- Calories: 898 calories;
- Total Carbohydrate: 134 g
- Cholesterol: 77 mg
- Total Fat: 26.3 g
- Protein: 28.2 g
- Sodium: 3671 mg

181.Kale And Butter Beans Soup With Pesto

"A great soup for cold days!"
Serving: 4 | Prep: 15m | Ready in: 35m

Ingredients

- 1/4 cup olive oil, divided
- 1 onion, diced small
- 1 carrot, diced small
- 3 cloves garlic, pressed
- 2 links Merguez sausage, casing removed and discarded
- 1 (16 oz.) can butter beans (large lima beans), drained and rinsed
- 1 cup water
- 1 tomato, diced small
- 4 leaves kale, stems removed and leaves coarsely chopped
- 2 tbsps. basil pesto
- 10 leaves fresh basil leaves

Direction

- Heat 2 tbsp. olive oil in heavy pot on medium heat; stir and cook garlic, carrot and onion in hot oil for 3 minutes till onion is translucent.
- Break sausage meat to small pieces. Mix into veggie mixture; mix and cook for 5 minutes till meat is slightly golden. Mix tomato, water and butter beans into sausage mixture; cook and simmer for 5 minutes till tomatoes soften.
- Mix pesto and kale into sausage mixture; mix and cook for 3-5 minutes till kale slightly wilts. Take pot off heat. Mix basil leaves into soup.

Nutrition Information

- Calories: 417 calories;
- Total Carbohydrate: 28.5 g
- Cholesterol: 34 mg
- Total Fat: 27.5 g
- Protein: 15.9 g
- Sodium: 489 mg

---

182. Killer Chicken With Mushroom, Asparagus, And Red Bell Pepper

"This Asian-style chicken is super tasty. I often spice it up, but you can let the fresh flavors speak for themselves. If you want a vegetarian option, you can leave out the chicken and use 2 eggs instead."
Serving: 4 | Prep: 20m | Ready in: 1h10m

Ingredients

- 2 cups basmati rice
- 4 cups water
- 1 tbsp. vegetable oil
- 1 red onion, cut into 1/2-inch slices
- 3 1/2 lbs. skinless, boneless chicken thighs, cut into 2-inch strips
- 1 tbsp. minced fresh ginger root
- 6 cloves garlic, minced
- 3 cups cremini mushrooms, cut in half
- 12 fresh asparagus, trimmed and cut into 2-inch pieces

- 2 small red bell peppers, cut into 1/2-inch strips
- 1 tbsp. fish sauce
- 1 egg
- 2 cups fresh basil leaves
- 1 cup fresh cilantro leaves, chopped
- 2 tbsps. sesame seeds, for garnish
- tamari soy sauce to taste

Direction

- In a saucepan, boil water and rice together. Lower the heat to medium-low, put a cover on and simmer for 35-40 minutes until the rice is soft and liquid is absorbed.
- Once the rice has almost done, in a big skillet, heat oil over high heat. In the hot oil, cook the onion for 2-3 minutes until tender. Add ginger, garlic and chicken to the skillet and keep stirring and cooking for 7-10 minutes until the chicken is entirely browned. Fold fish sauce, bell peppers, asparagus and mushrooms into the chicken mixture, keep cooking for 5 minutes until just hot. Crack the egg and scramble it into the mixture. Add basil leaves to the mixture, cook for 30 seconds until the leaves have slightly wilted. Take the pan away from heat immediately. Enjoy on top of the basmati rice, drizzle tamari soy sauce over and use sesame seeds and cilantro to garnish.

Nutrition Information

- Calories: 1095 calories;
- Total Carbohydrate: 86.7 g
- Cholesterol: 270 mg
- Total Fat: 47.7 g
- Protein: 77.8 g
- Sodium: 610 mg

183. Leftover Ham And Bacon Hash

"A great hash recipe."
Serving: 4 | Prep: 10m | Ready in: 1h

Ingredients

- 1 tbsp. Dijon mustard
- 2 tbsps. olive oil
- 3/4 tsp. kosher salt
- 1 tsp. freshly ground black pepper
- 2 lbs. yellow potatoes, diced
- 8 oz. button mushrooms, quartered
- 1 1/2 cups cubed ham (Smithfield® Anytime Favorites Cubed Ham or Smithfield® Hickory Smoked Spiral Sliced Ham, cubed)
- 4 slices Smithfield® Hometown Original Bacon
- 2/3 cup jarred roasted red peppers, drained and roughly chopped
- 3/4 cup fresh mozzarella cheese, cubed
- 4 eggs, fried, poached, or to preference (optional)
- 1/3 cup thinly sliced fresh basil leaves

Direction

- Preheat an oven to 425°F. Whisk pepper, salt, oil and mustard till combined in a big bowl; add mushrooms and potatoes. Toss till coated.
- Evenly spread potato mixture on 2 nonstick/lightly oiled rimmed baking pans. Roast for 35-40 minutes in oven till mushrooms and potatoes start to brown, mixing halfway through cooking. Add any leftover ham/bacon into mixture; mix.
- Add roasted peppers into oven-safe serving casserole (optional). Put cheese on top. Bake till cheese starts to melt and is soft for 10-15 more minutes. Top hash using sliced basil and eggs cooked to your preference.

Nutrition Information

- Calories: 555 calories;
- Total Carbohydrate: 49.7 g
- Cholesterol: 237 mg

- Total Fat: 24.4 g
- Protein: 35.2 g
- Sodium: 2023 mg

184. Lemon, Garlic, And Asparagus Warm Caprese Pasta Salad

"There is nothing like a summer tomatoes' sweetness mixed with the peppery sweetness fresh basil offers, the zing of lemon and richness of garlic that really makes an amazing treat for summertime."
Serving: 6 | Prep: 20m | Ready in: 40m

Ingredients

- 1 lb. mezze (short) penne pasta
- 1 bunch fresh asparagus, trimmed and cut into thirds
- 1/4 cup olive oil
- 3 tbsps. butter
- 2 tsps. lemon juice, or more to taste
- 1/2 large shallot, minced
- 2 large cloves garlic, minced
- 1 large grilled chicken breast, sliced thinly and halved (optional)
- 1 roma (plum) tomato, diced
- 8 leaves fresh basil, torn

Direction

- In a big pot, fill with lightly salted water and bring to a boil. Stir in penne and bring back to a boil. Cook pasta without a cover for about 11 minutes, while stirring sometimes, until cooked through but still firm to the bite. Drain.
- Put into a saucepan the asparagus, then add a small amount of water and place on moderate heat. Allow asparagus to steam, covered, for 3-4 minutes, until tender and bright green. Drain.
- In a big saucepan, heat olive oil, butter and lemon juice on moderately low heat until butter is melted. Cook and stir shallot in hot butter and oil mixture for 1-2 minutes, until it

just starts to soften. Stir garlic into shallot mixture and cook for 3 minutes longer, until garlic and shallot are opaque. Stir chicken and asparagus into the mixture and cook for about 5 minutes, until heated through.
- Toss chicken, vegetables and pasta together to combine, then mix in basil and tomato and serve warm.

Nutrition Information

- Calories: 446 calories;
- Total Carbohydrate: 60 g
- Cholesterol: 23 mg
- Total Fat: 17.6 g
- Protein: 15 g
- Sodium: 54 mg

185. Lemon-basil Quinoa Salad

""Since quinoa seems to be so common, I made this and shared with everyone. A recipe that is perfect for outdoor parties that won't spoil in the sun.""
Serving: 4 | Prep: 15m | Ready in: 30m

Ingredients

- 2 cups low-sodium chicken broth
- 1 cup quinoa
- 1 large lemon, zested and juiced
- 1/2 cup roasted red peppers, drained and diced
- 1/4 cup dried cranberries
- 2 tbsps. minced red onion
- 2 tbsps. chopped fresh basil

Direction

- Place quinoa and chicken broth in a saucepan then bring to a boil. Minimize heat to medium-low, then simmer for 15 to 20 minutes, covered, until broth has been absorbed and quinoa is softened.
- Mix together in a bowl the lemon juice, lemon zest and quinoa. Mix in basil, onion, cranberries and red peppers; combine well by tossing.

Nutrition Information

- Calories: 205 calories;
- Total Carbohydrate: 38.8 g
- Cholesterol: 2 mg
- Total Fat: 3 g
- Protein: 8.4 g
- Sodium: 157 mg

186. Lemon-herb Turkey

"This is the recipe of a roasted turkey that is so flavorful and mouth-watering."
Serving: 12 | Prep: 30m | Ready in: 2h40m

Ingredients

- 3 tbsps. chopped fresh marjoram
- 3 tbsps. chopped fresh rosemary
- 3 tbsps. chopped fresh thyme
- 3 tbsps. chopped fresh basil
- 3 tbsps. garlic, minced
- 1 pinch ground black pepper to taste
- 1 (12 lb.) whole turkey, neck and giblets removed
- 1/4 cup olive oil
- 2 large lemons, juiced, lemon halves reserved
- 1 tbsp. all-purpose flour
- 1 turkey-size oven roasting bag

Direction

- Set the oven to 350°F (175°c) for preheating. In a small dish, mix the basil, black pepper, rosemary, marjoram, garlic, and thyme; put the mixture aside.
- Lift the skin of the turkey away from the meat gently. Brush the meat with olive oil lightly. Sprinkle it with lemon juice, and then with 2/3 of the mixed herbs. Slowly pat the skin of the turkey into the meat. Sprinkle the turkey cavity with the remaining herbs. Add the squeezed lemon halves. Fill the turkey roasting bag with the flour. Shake the bag well to coat evenly. Place the turkey inside the bag. Use a nylon tie to seal the end of the bag. Place

the bag into the deep roasting pan and cut its top into six 1/2-inch slits.
- Bake the turkey inside the preheated oven for 2-2 1/2 hours until the juices run clear and the bone is no longer pink. The inserted instant-read thermometer into the thigh's thickest part, the one that is near on the bone, should read 180°F or 82°C. Remove the turkey from the oven. Use a doubled sheet of aluminum foil to cover the turkey. Let the turkey rest in a warm area for 10-15 minutes before slicing it.

Nutrition Information

- Calories: 722 calories;
- Total Carbohydrate: 3.6 g
- Cholesterol: 264 mg
- Total Fat: 36 g
- Protein: 91.2 g
- Sodium: 221 mg

187. Lenie's Herbal Fish

"Bake any fish fillet, fresh herbs and various veggies to have a tasty meal."
Serving: 6 | Prep: 15m | Ready in: 50m

Ingredients

- 3 tbsps. olive oil
- 3 onions, thinly sliced
- 1 red bell pepper, thinly sliced
- 1/2 green bell pepper, sliced
- 3 shallots, thinly sliced
- 1/2 zucchini, thinly sliced
- 1/2 yellow squash, thinly sliced
- 1 large tomato, cubed
- 1/2 (6 oz.) can black olives, halved
- 2 tbsps. balsamic vinegar
- salt and pepper to taste
- 2 lbs. cod fillets
- 1/3 cup chopped fresh chives
- 1/3 cup chopped fresh basil leaves
- 1/3 cup chopped fresh cilantro

Direction

- Preheat oven to 175 degrees C (350 degrees F).
- In a big frying pan, heat the oil. Mix shallots, green and red bell peppers and onion. Cook for 3 minutes. Mix in balsamic vinegar, olives, tomato, squash and zucchini. Sauté till vegetables are just softened. Use pepper and salt to season to taste.
- In an oiled 9x11 inch baking pan, spread half of vegetables. Cover the vegetables with half cup of the herbs.
- On top of herbs and vegetables, arrange the fillets. Spread the second half of the vegetables on top of the fish and drizzle the rest of the herbs onto the vegetables. Use foil to cover the plate and bake for 25 minutes.

Nutrition Information

- Calories: 261 calories;
- Total Carbohydrate: 15.2 g
- Cholesterol: 55 mg
- Total Fat: 9.5 g
- Protein: 29 g
- Sodium: 328 mg

188. Light Tuscan Garlic Chicken

"A low-calorie and low-fat option."
Serving: 4 | Prep: 20m | Ready in: 40m

Ingredients

- 6 oz. whole wheat linguine
- 20 asparagus spears, trimmed
- 1 tbsp. chopped fresh oregano
- 1 tbsp. chopped fresh basil
- 1 tbsp. chopped fresh thyme
- 1 tbsp. salt
- 2 tsps. freshly ground black pepper
- 4 (3 oz.) skinless, boneless chicken breast halves, pounded thin
- olive oil cooking spray
- 2 tsps. olive oil, divided
- 1 red bell pepper, cut into matchstick-sized pieces
- 3 cloves garlic, minced
- 2 cups low-fat buttermilk
- 1/2 cup white wine
- 1 tbsp. all-purpose flour
- 1/2 lb. fresh spinach
- 1/3 cup grated Parmesan cheese

Direction

- Boil big pot of lightly salted water; cook linguine at a boil for 10-12 minutes till tender yet firm to chew. Drain.
- Boil 2nd pot of water; cook asparagus for 3 minutes till bright green. Use tongs to remove asparagus; dunk in cold water immediately.
- Mix pepper, salt, thyme, basil and oregano in small bowl. Spray cooking spray on chicken breasts; rub the herb mixture on chicken.
- Heat 1 tsp. of olive oil in a skillet on medium high heat; in hot oil, cook chicken for 3 minutes per side till not pink in middle and lightly browned.
- Heat the leftover 1 tsp. of olive oil in a saucepan on medium high heat; mix and cook garlic and red bell pepper in hot oil for 1 minute till fragrant. Mix flour, wine and buttermilk into red bell pepper mixture; mix and cook for 2-4 minutes till sauce is thick. Add spinach; cook for 2-3 minutes till spinach wilts. Mix Parmesan cheese into the sauce till melted.
- To warm, run hot water on asparagus. Divide linguine to serving plates evenly; put chicken, asparagus and sauce on top.

Nutrition Information

- Calories: 414 calories;
- Total Carbohydrate: 44.8 g
- Cholesterol: 64 mg
- Total Fat: 8.2 g
- Protein: 36.8 g
- Sodium: 2080 mg

189. Lighter Spaghetti Alfredo With Cauliflower

"A light and delicious cauliflower spaghetti Alfredo."
Serving: 4 | Prep: 20m | Ready in: 1h

Ingredients

- 3 cloves garlic, lightly crushed
- 2 tbsps. olive oil
- 1 head cauliflower, cored and separated into florets
- 4 cups water
- 1/2 tsp. dried Italian herb seasoning
- 1/2 tsp. crushed red pepper flakes
- salt and freshly ground black pepper to taste
- 1 (14 oz.) package spaghetti
- 1/2 cup fine dried bread crumbs
- 1/3 cup grated Parmesan cheese
- 1 tbsp. olive oil
- salt to taste
- 2 tbsps. chopped fresh basil
- 1/4 cup heavy whipping cream
- 1/2 cup grated Parmesan cheese, plus extra for garnishing
- freshly ground black pepper to taste
- 1/2 lemon, juiced

Direction

- In a large pot, cook, while stirring, garlic cloves with 2 tbsps. of olive oil on medium for 2-3 minutes until browned a little and fragrance spreads. Season with black pepper, salt, red pepper flakes, Italian herbs, then pour in water and cauliflower. Boil, covered, this mixture for about 10 minutes until cauliflower is softened.
- Boil lightly salted water in a big pot. Put in spaghetti, cook and stir from time to time for 12 minutes until al-dente. Drain off water and pour into a big serving bowl.
- In the meantime, bring a skillet to medium heat and mix in 1 tbsp. of olive oil, a third cup of Parmesan cheese and bread crumbs; then cook, while stirring, for 2-3 minutes until the mixture is browned and cheese is melted.

- Remove from heat; season with salt and mix in basil, then put aside.
- Pour cream into the pot with the cauliflower mixture and use a stick blender to make creamy and lumps-free puree. Whisk in half a cup of Parmesan cheese until totally melted, and then add freshly ground black pepper to season.
- Mix lemon juice in pasta and stir with Alfredo sauce to coat. Sprinkle with Parmesan cheese and seasoned bread crumbs, and then serve.

Nutrition Information

- Calories: 660 calories;
- Total Carbohydrate: 91.4 g
- Cholesterol: 35 mg
- Total Fat: 23.1 g
- Protein: 23.6 g
- Sodium: 413 mg

190. Lime-curry Tofu Stir-fry

"This is a tasty sweet, sour dish with tofu which is marinated in the same sauce used on the dish. It helps the tofu really soak up the flavor from the sauce."
Serving: 4 | Prep: 20m | Ready in: 30m

Ingredients

- 2 tbsps. peanut oil
- 1 (16 oz.) package extra-firm tofu, cut into bite-sized cubes
- 1 tbsp. minced fresh ginger root
- 2 tbsps. red curry paste
- 1 lb. zucchini, diced
- 1 red bell pepper, diced
- 3 tbsps. lime juice
- 3 tbsps. soy sauce
- 2 tbsps. maple syrup
- 1 (14 oz.) can coconut milk
- 1/2 cup chopped fresh basil

Direction

- In a wok or large skillet, heat the peanut oil over high heat. Put in the tofu and stir-fry until it turns golden brown. Take out the tofu and put aside, reserve the remaining oil in the wok.

- Toss the ginger and curry paste into the hot oil for a few seconds until the curry paste gets fragrant and the ginger starts to turn golden. Put in bell pepper and the zucchini; cook while stirring for 1 minute. Pour in tofu, coconut milk, maple syrup, soy sauce, and lime juice. Simmer the coconut milk and cook for a few minutes until the vegetables become tender and the tofu is hot. Right before serving, mix in the chopped basil.

Nutrition Information

- Calories: 425 calories;
- Total Carbohydrate: 20.9 g
- Cholesterol: 0 mg
- Total Fat: 38.8 g
- Protein: 18.4 g
- Sodium: 856 mg

191. Linguine With Clam Sauce And Baby Portobello Mushrooms

"So satisfying."
Serving: 4 | Prep: 15m | Ready in: 1h

Ingredients

- 1 tbsp. olive oil
- 3 cloves garlic, chopped
- 1 (8 oz.) package baby portobello mushrooms, sliced and chopped
- 4 (6.5 oz.) cans chopped clams with juice
- 4 cubes chicken bouillon
- 1 tbsp. chopped fresh parsley
- 1 tsp. dried basil
- 1 tsp. dried oregano
- 1 tbsp. Worcestershire sauce
- 1 (16 oz.) package uncooked linguini pasta
- 1/2 cup butter

Direction

- Warm olive oil in a saucepan on medium heat. Mix in mushrooms and garlic; cook till mushrooms are tender. Mix in Worcestershire sauce, oregano, basil, parsley, chicken bouillon and clam juice. Put heat on high; put on a quick boil. Lower heat to medium then simmer for 30 minutes.
- Meanwhile, boil a big pot of lightly salted water. Add pasta; cook for 8-10 minutes till al dente. Drain; put aside.
- Mix butter and chopped clams into sauce; simmer for 15 more minutes. Put on cooked pasta; serve.

Nutrition Information

- Calories: 941 calories;
- Total Carbohydrate: 97 g
- Cholesterol: 185 mg
- Total Fat: 33 g
- Protein: 64.7 g
- Sodium: 1574 mg

192. Linguine With Mushrooms & Ham

"Honey ham and basil give this dish an unforgettable flavor."
Serving: 4 | Prep: 15m | Ready in: 45m

Ingredients

- 1 (8 oz.) package linguine pasta
- 1 tbsp. butter
- 1 onion, finely chopped
- 3 cloves garlic, minced
- 1 cup sliced fresh mushrooms
- 1 1/2 cups whipping cream
- 1/4 lb. cooked ham, julienned
- 1 tsp. fresh basil leaves, chopped
- freshly ground black pepper

Direction

- Heat a big pot of slightly salted water to a boil. Put in linguine pasta, and cook until al dente, about 8-10 minutes; drain.
- In a sauté pan on medium heat, melt butter. In butter, cook and stir mushrooms, garlic, and onion until tender. Lower the heat; gradually mix in cream. Keep cooking till sauce thickens; put in basil and ham; simmer 10 minutes more.
- Toss cream sauce and linguine together in a big bowl, Use freshly ground black pepper to season.

Nutrition Information

- Calories: 626 calories;
- Total Carbohydrate: 48.1 g
- Cholesterol: 146 mg
- Total Fat: 42.6 g
- Protein: 15.6 g
- Sodium: 423 mg

---

193. Liv And Zack's Romantic Heart Pizza

"This homemade pizza recipe is great to serve your guests. You need to make sure that you add copious amounts of any pizza toppings you like. In this recipe, we use zucchini, pepperoni, and mushrooms."
Serving: 8 | Prep: 25m | Ready in: 2h59m

Ingredients

- Pizza Dough:
- 3 cups spelt flour
- 6 1/2 tbsps. spelt flour
- 1 tbsp. instant yeast
- 1 tsp. salt
- olive oil, divided, or as needed
- 1 cup lukewarm water
- Pizza Sauce:
- 1/2 onion, finely diced
- 3 cups tomato puree
- 2 cloves garlic, crushed
- 1/4 cup chopped fresh basil, or to taste
- 1 2/3 (16 oz.) packages mozzarella cheese, shredded
- salt to taste
- olive oil, divided, or as needed

Direction

- In a bowl, sift together 1 tsp. salt, yeast and 3 cups plus 6 1/2 tbsps. flour. Add 1 tbsp. olive oil into the lukewarm water in a bowl; steadily stir into the dough, kneading by hands until elastic.
- Remove the dough to a lightly oil-coated bowl with 1 1/2 tsps. oil and use a towel to cover. Put in a warm place to rise for 1 1/2 hours until the volume doubles.
- Punch the dough down, cover again and let it rise for another 30-45 minutes.
- In a pot, heat 1 tbsp. olive oil over medium heat. Cook onion for 5 minutes until opaque, tossing sometimes. Add garlic and tomato puree, mix in basil. Cook for 4 minutes until simmering, tossing sometimes. Lower the heat to medium-low. Put a cover on and cook for another 15 minutes until the flavors combine. Lower the heat to low.
- Turn the oven to 350°F (175°C) to preheat. Use the leftover 1 1/2 tsps. olive oil to grease 2 baking sheets.
- Roll each dough half into a pizza crust, pinching up the dough edges if desired. On the pizzas, generously scoop the sauce, fully cover them. Distribute the mozzarella cheese among the pizzas.
- Put in the preheated oven and bake for 10-20 minutes until pizza is browned on the bottom and the mozzarella cheese melts golden brown. Let it cool before enjoying together, about several minutes.

Nutrition Information

- Calories: 495 calories;
- Total Carbohydrate: 47.4 g
- Cholesterol: 61 mg
- Total Fat: 21.2 g
- Protein: 31.9 g

- Sodium: 1273 mg

194. Lobster Tomato Sauce

"Delicious and rich tomato sauce with lobster."
Serving: 6 | Prep: 20m | Ready in: 1h35m

Ingredients

- 1/4 cup olive oil
- 1 onion, chopped
- 1 small garlic clove, crushed
- 1 tbsp. chopped fresh parsley
- 6 (6 oz.) lobster tails, thawed
- 1 (28 oz.) can crushed tomatoes
- 1 (8 oz.) can tomato sauce
- 3 tbsps. chopped fresh basil
- salt and ground black pepper to taste

Direction

- In a large saucepan over medium heat, heat olive oil.
- Stir in garlic and onion; cook in hot oil for about 8 minutes until they are browned lightly.
- Add lobster tails and parsley into garlic and onion, stir well; cook for 10-15 minutes until the shells is bright red.
- Add in black pepper, salt, basil, tomato sauce and crushed tomatoes, stir; let it simmer with occasional stirs for 1 hour over low heat.
- Take off the lobster tails from the sauce; shake to remove all excess sauce from the shells. Serve lobster pieces separately or take lobster meat off the shells and mix into sauce to serve to your liking.

Nutrition Information

- Calories: 295 calories;
- Total Carbohydrate: 15.1 g
- Cholesterol: 101 mg
- Total Fat: 13.7 g
- Protein: 29.3 g
- Sodium: 891 mg

195. Lori's Spicy Chipotle Lasagna

"" Convert a non-pasta lover to swoon with this lasagna recipe. Packed with flavors of cheese and herbs, even those on a diet will be bound to try it."
Serving: 12 | Prep: 35m | Ready in: 2h

Ingredients

- 1 lb. lean ground beef
- 1 lb. bulk hot Italian sausage
- 1 onion, chopped
- 1 pint sliced fresh mushrooms
- 3 cloves garlic, minced
- 1 chipotle chile in adobo sauce, chopped
- 1 (6 oz.) can tomato paste
- 2 (15 oz.) cans stewed tomatoes
- sea salt and ground black pepper to taste
- 1/2 cup chopped fresh basil
- 1/4 cup chopped fresh oregano
- 2 (8 oz.) packages cream cheese, at room temperature
- 1 lb. frozen chopped spinach, thawed
- 9 lasagna noodles
- 2 (8 oz.) balls of fresh mozzarella, sliced
- 2 zucchini, thinly sliced lengthwise
- 1 cup grated Asiago cheese
- 1 cup grated Parmesan cheese

Direction

- In a Dutch oven or big saucepan set on medium-high heat, cook Italian sausage and ground beef until light brown in color. Drain off excess oil. Cook garlic, onions, and mushroom for 5 minutes or until the onions become clear and tender. Add in tomato paste, chipotle chili, and stewed tomatoes. Let the mixture boil; lower the heat to medium-low and leave to simmer for 15 minutes. Add pepper and salt to taste. Mix in oregano and basil and simmer for 5 more minutes, then take off from heat.
- Meanwhile, combine chopped spinach and cream cheese. The water released by the soggy

spinach will thin out the mixture, making it more sour cream-like.

- Preheat the oven to 400°F or 200°C.
- Grease the bottom of a 9x13-inch baking tray or layer with aluminum foil. At the bottom of the pan, layer 3 pieces of lasagna noodles and top with a third of the made spinach mixture. Pour in a third of the chipotle meat sauce and spread evenly. Top the layer with a third of the mozzarella cheese and a third of the zucchini. Sprinkle a third of the Parmesan cheese and a third of the Asiago cheese at the top. Repeat these layers twice, topping everything off with the cheeses.
- Cover the pan with aluminum foil; bake in the preheated oven for 40 minutes. Remove the foil and return to oven to bake for 15 to 20 minutes or until the top becomes bubbly.

Nutrition Information

- Calories: 581 calories;
- Total Carbohydrate: 27.5 g
- Cholesterol: 128 mg
- Total Fat: 38.5 g
- Protein: 32.6 g
- Sodium: 969 mg

---

196. Lots O'veggies Sausage Spaghetti Sauce

"This recipe has ground beef, Italian sausage, and tons of veggies and herbs. The longer you cook it, the better it will taste! Be sure to use fresh basil and do not use the canned tomatoes that have corn syrup in them. You can add crush red pepper or use hot Italian sausage to make a spicier sauce."
Serving: 10 | Prep: 30m | Ready in: 3h30m

Ingredients

- 1 lb. sweet Italian sausage, casings removed
- 1 lb. lean ground beef
- 1/4 cup olive oil
- 1 large onion, diced
- 1 green bell pepper, diced
- 1 red bell pepper, diced
- 1 zucchini, quartered and sliced
- 12 oz. mushrooms, sliced
- 2 carrots, shredded
- 4 oz. fresh basil, julienned
- 1 (10 oz.) package frozen chopped spinach, thawed and drained
- 1 tbsp. chopped fresh thyme
- 1 tbsp. fresh oregano
- 4 cloves garlic, crushed
- 1 tbsp. white sugar
- salt and pepper to taste
- 3 (28 oz.) cans peeled and diced tomatoes

Direction

- In a medium pan, cook the ground beef and sausage over medium heat until brown. Drain the meat and reserve 2 tbsps. of drippings then set meat aside.
- In a Dutch oven or big stockpot, heat oil over medium heat and cook onions in oil until they become translucent. Stir in carrots, mushrooms, zucchini, and red and green bell peppers, cook just until tender. Add the browned ground beef and sausage. Stir in pepper, salt, sugar, garlic, oregano, thyme, spinach, and basil, then cook for 2-5 minutes. Pour in the tomatoes and mix well, then lower the heat. Simmer while covered for 3 hours, occasionally stirring.

Nutrition Information

- Calories: 339 calories;
- Total Carbohydrate: 18.3 g
- Cholesterol: 45 mg
- Total Fat: 20.7 g
- Protein: 18.7 g
- Sodium: 803 mg

197. Lucky's Quickie Chickie

"The crucial ingredient in this recipe is fresh basil to give it an explosion of flavor with a dash of sweet and sour. Make a fast weeknight meal and accompany with a salad and your favorite vegetable."
Serving: 2 | Prep: 10m | Ready in: 20m

Ingredients

- 2 tsps. olive oil
- 6 oz. chicken tenderloin strips
- 1/4 tsp. salt
- 1/8 tsp. freshly ground black pepper
- 2 tbsps. chopped fresh basil
- 1 1/2 tsps. honey
- 1 1/2 tsps. balsamic vinegar, or more to taste

Direction

- On medium-high heat, pour olive oil in a non-stick pan and heat. Sprinkle pepper and salt on the chicken. Cook while regularly stirring the chicken in the hot oil for 3-5 minutes until it's not pink in the middle. Mix honey, balsamic vinegar, and basil into the chicken and stir Cook for another minute.

Nutrition Information

- Calories: 157 calories;
- Total Carbohydrate: 5.3 g
- Cholesterol: 48 mg
- Total Fat: 6.8 g
- Protein: 17.8 g
- Sodium: 334 mg

198. Margherita® Sun-dried Tomato And Salami Bruschetta

"A light and yummy appetizer."
Serving: 12 | Prep: 10m | Ready in: 30m

Ingredients

- 1 (10 oz.) (12-inch) French baguette
- 1/4 cup olive oil
- 3 cloves garlic, minced
- 2 oz. finely diced, thickly sliced deli Margherita® Genoa or Hard Salami*
- 1/4 cup drained, finely chopped sun-dried tomatoes (packed in oil)
- 1/4 cup finely diced smoked provolone or smoked Gouda cheese
- 2 tbsps. finely chopped pitted calamata olives
- 2 tbsps. chopped fresh basil or Italian parsley

Direction

- Heat an oven to 375°F. Crosswise, cut bread to 1/2-inch thick slices; put on baking sheet. Mix garlic and oil; put on bread slices. Bake till bread toasts lightly for 15 minutes.
- Meanwhile, mix basil, olives, cheese, sun dried tomatoes and salami well; put aside. Add 1 tsp. oil from the bottled sun-dried tomatoes if it looks dry. Put salami mixture on toasts before servings. Yields 12 servings/24 pieces.

Nutrition Information

- Calories: 149 calories;
- Total Carbohydrate: 14.5 g
- Cholesterol: 7 mg
- Total Fat: 8.2 g
- Protein: 4.6 g
- Sodium: 302 mg

199. Maria's Tomato-basil Spaghetti Sauce

"This tomato sauce is homemade and contrary to popular belief, it does not take so long to prepare. Mix it up every time make it your own. This recipe will include title_directions for using fresh tomatoes, however you can feel free to used canned ones and that will work just as well."
Serving: 8 | Prep: 15m | Ready in: 40m

Ingredients

- 8 lbs. Roma (plum) tomatoes, peeled and chopped

- 1/2 cup extra-virgin olive oil
- 1 large onion, minced
- 1/4 cup grated Parmesan cheese
- 4 sprigs fresh basil, or more to taste, chopped
- 3 cloves garlic, minced
- 2 tbsps. red wine
- coarse salt and ground black pepper to taste

Direction

- Use a food processor to puree the tomatoes. Make sure you puree it until its smooth then strain with a fine-mesh sieve and pour it in a bowl.
- Prepare a large deep pot with some olive oil and place it over medium heat. In the same pot with the oil, mix red wine, garlic, basil, Parmesan cheese, onion, and strained tomatoes then season the mixture with salt and pepper. Let this boil and lower down the heat after to medium-low. Leave it to simmer for about 25 minutes until it thickens to the consistency you prefer.

Nutrition Information

- Calories: 231 calories;
- Total Carbohydrate: 20.2 g
- Cholesterol: 2 mg
- Total Fat: 15.7 g
- Protein: 5.3 g
- Sodium: 81 mg

200. Marinara Dipping Sauce

"This marinara sauce goes very well with warm bread. Garlic bread is tasty too."
Serving: 4 | Prep: 10m | Ready in: 55m

Ingredients

- 1 tbsp. olive oil
- 2 cloves garlic, chopped
- 5 tomatoes, peeled and finely chopped
- 1 tsp. white sugar
- 1/4 cup water

- 2 tsps. chopped fresh basil
- salt and pepper to taste

Direction

- Heat oil in a big skillet and sauté garlic until tender and lightly browned. Make sure to not burn the garlic. Mix in pepper, salt, basil, water, sugar and tomatoes.
- Boil the contents in the pan. Put a cover on and simmer over low heat for about 45 minutes, tossing sometimes. Enjoy warm.

Nutrition Information

- Calories: 64 calories;
- Total Carbohydrate: 7.6 g
- Cholesterol: 0 mg
- Total Fat: 3.7 g
- Protein: 1.5 g
- Sodium: 8 mg

201. Marinated Chicken And Pasta Salad

""Great for summer barbecues Australian recipe. You can serve the chicken warm, for a winter alternative!""
Serving: 6 | Prep: 1h | Ready in: 2h15m

Ingredients

- 3 tbsps. soy sauce
- 2 tbsps. honey
- 2 tbsps. tomato sauce
- 2 tbsps. plum sauce
- 1 tbsp. Worcestershire sauce
- 1 tsp. sesame seeds
- 1 tsp. chopped fresh basil
- 3 skinless, boneless chicken breast halves
- 2 cups elbow macaroni
- 2 tbsps. olive oil
- 1/2 cup low-fat mayonnaise
- 1/2 cup fat free sour cream
- 1 tsp. coarse grained prepared mustard
- 1 tbsp. honey
- 1 tbsp. tomato sauce

- 1 tsp. Worcestershire sauce
- 1/4 cup shredded sharp Cheddar cheese
- 1 avocados - peeled, pitted and sliced
- 1/2 cup cashews

Direction

- Mix in a large bowl the basil, sesame seeds, 1 tbsp. Worcestershire sauce, 2 tbsps. plum sauce, 2 tbsps. tomato sauce, 2 tbsps. honey and 3 tbsps. soy sauce. Put chicken in and flip to coat.
- Place in the refrigerator to marinate for at least 1 hour.
- Place a lightly salted water in a large pot and make it boil. Then put in the pasta and cook for 8 to 10 minutes or until al dente; drain and wash.
- Put olive oil in a skillet and heat on medium. Put the chicken and cook until not pink and juices run clear. Use paper towels to drain on. Let it cool, then slice into bite-size strips.
- Combine in a large bowl the 1 tsp. Worcestershire sauce, 1 tbsp. tomato sauce, 1 tbsp. honey, mustard, sour cream, and mayonnaise. Add in Cheddar cheese, chicken and cooked pasta. Gradually mix in sliced avocado and cashews just before serving.

Nutrition Information

- Calories: 446 calories;
- Total Carbohydrate: 48.9 g
- Cholesterol: 42 mg
- Total Fat: 17.9 g
- Protein: 23.9 g
- Sodium: 755 mg

202. Marinated Chicken Bruschetta

"The Italian tomato salsa gives this grilled chicken extra flavor. You can enjoy it with salad greens."
Serving: 6 | Prep: 10m | Ready in: 1h2m

Ingredients

- 3/4 cup Wish-Bone® Italian Dressing, divided
- 6 (5 oz.) skinless, boneless chicken breast halves
- 2 medium beefsteak tomatoes, chopped
- 1/4 cup diced red onion
- 1 tbsp. finely chopped fresh basil leaves* (optional)

Direction

- In a plastic bag or a big, shallow, nonaluminum baking dish, put the chicken and add 1/4 cup Wish-Bone® Italian Dressing on top. Close the bag or put a cover on the baking dish, and put in a fridge to marinate for 30 minutes to 3 hours, flipping sometimes.
- In the meantime, in a medium-sized bowl, mix together 1/4 cup dressing, basil, onion and tomatoes. Put a cover on and put in a fridge to marinate for a minimum of 30 minutes.
- Take the chicken out of the marinade, get rid of the marinade. Broil or grill the chicken for 12 minutes until the chicken has fully cooked, flipping 1 time and brushing with the leftover 1/4 cup dressing often. Enjoy the chicken with the tomato mixture on top.

Nutrition Information

- Calories: 247 calories;
- Total Carbohydrate: 5.3 g
- Cholesterol: 81 mg
- Total Fat: 11.5 g
- Protein: 29.9 g
- Sodium: 563 mg

203. Marinated Grilled Shrimp

"You won't need cocktail sauce for your shrimps if you use this marinade recipe. Do not be intimated by the cayenne pepper; my young kids eat these, and more than we do! You can make these with fresh shrimps, frozen shrimps, and cook them indoors or outdoors. Eat with some baked potatoes, garlic bread, and a salad."
Serving: 6 | Prep: 15m | Ready in: 55m

Ingredients

- 3 cloves garlic, minced
- 1/3 cup olive oil
- 1/4 cup tomato sauce
- 2 tbsps. red wine vinegar
- 2 tbsps. chopped fresh basil
- 1/2 tsp. salt
- 1/4 tsp. cayenne pepper
- 2 lbs. fresh shrimp, peeled and deveined
- skewers

Direction

- Mix together red wine vinegar, tomato sauce, olive oil, and garlic in a large bowl. Sprinkle with salt, cayenne pepper, and basil. Put in the shrimps and stir to coat. Cover and refrigerate for half up to a full hour, stirring occasionally.
- Preheat grill at medium. Skewer the shrimps, impaling near the tail and coming out near the head. Discard its marinade.
- Lightly grease the grate. Grill for 2 to 3 minutes each side or until flesh is opaque.

Nutrition Information

- Calories: 273 calories;
- Total Carbohydrate: 2.8 g
- Cholesterol: 230 mg
- Total Fat: 14.7 g
- Protein: 31 g
- Sodium: 472 mg

204. Marinated Pesto Rosso Salad

"It's a greatly delicious vegetarian salad perfect for everyone with shaved Parmigiano-Reggiano atop."
Serving: 8 | Prep: 40m | Ready in: 1h56m

Ingredients

- 1 (8 oz.) package sun-dried tomato pasta
- 1 cup asparagus tips
- 1 1/2 cups thinly sliced roasted red peppers
- 1 cup halved yellow pear tomatoes
- 1 cup thinly sliced red onion
- 1 cup thinly sliced zucchini
- 1 cup thinly sliced yellow summer squash
- 1 cup purple cauliflower florets
- 1 cup thinly sliced fennel
- 1/2 cup chopped Italian flat-leaf parsley
- Pesto Rosso Dressing:
- 2 cups sun-dried tomatoes packed in oil, drained and oil reserved
- 2 cups fresh basil leaves
- 1/2 cup grated Parmigiano-Reggiano cheese
- 1/4 cup mascarpone cheese
- 4 cloves roasted garlic
- 1 1/2 tsps. kosher salt
- 1 tsp. ground black pepper
- 1 1/4 cups extra-virgin olive oil

Direction

- Bring lightly salted water in a big pot to a boil. Cook pasta at a boil for 11 minutes, while stirring sometimes, until softened yet firm to the bite. Drain and allow pasta to chill.
- Bring lightly salted water in a pot to a boil. Put in asparagus tips, cook without a cover for 3 minutes, until bright green. Drain in a colander and plunge in ice water promptly for a few minutes to prevent from cooking further. Drain.
- In a big bowl, combine together parsley, fennel, cauliflower, yellow squash, zucchini, tomatoes, onion, roasted red peppers, asparagus tips and pasta.
- In a food processor, mix together pepper, salt, roasted garlic, mascarpone cheese, Parmigiano-Reggiano cheese, basil leaves and

sun-dried tomatoes. Blend together and gradually put in olive oil and reserved sun-dried tomato oil, then processing until dressing is smooth.

- Drizzle over pasta-vegetable mixture with the dressing, then season to taste with salt and pepper. Before serving, chill for an hour.

Nutrition Information

- Calories: 574 calories;
- Total Carbohydrate: 36.3 g
- Cholesterol: 13 mg
- Total Fat: 44.5 g
- Protein: 10 g
- Sodium: 678 mg

---

205. Meatballs Divine

"It might be a little complicated but the result is absolutely satisfied. Don't miss it or you will regret forever."
Serving: 12 | Prep: 1h | Ready in: 3h

Ingredients

- 1/2 cup chopped fresh flat-leaf parsley
- 2 large eggs
- 3 tbsps. Worcestershire sauce
- 6 leaves fresh basil, or to taste
- 3 cloves garlic, minced
- 1 1/2 tsps. kosher salt
- 1 tsp. ground black pepper
- 1 tsp. Italian seasoning
- 1 tsp. olive oil
- 1 large yellow onion, finely chopped
- 1 cup shredded mozzarella cheese
- 2/3 cup freshly grated Parmesan cheese
- 3 tbsps. ricotta cheese
- 2 lbs. ground beef chuck
- 1 lb. Italian pork sausage
- 2 cups fresh bread crumbs
- 1 cup olive oil for frying
- 6 cups bottled marinara sauce, or more to taste

Direction

- Process Italian seasoning, black pepper, kosher salt, garlic, basil leaves, Worcestershire sauce, eggs, and parsley in a food processor until herbs are finely chopped.
- In a skillet, heat 1 tsp. olive oil on medium-high heat. Cook and stir onion in hot oil until transparent and almost caramelized, for approximately 10 minutes. Take away from heat.
- Combine ricotta cheese, Parmesan cheese, mozzarella cheese, onion, and egg mixture in a large bowl. Put in fresh bread crumbs, Italian sausage, and ground beef to egg mixture; combine. Form into 1 1/2 -inch meatballs.
- Start preheating the oven at 400°F (200°C).
- Heat 1 cup olive oil over medium-high heat in a large nonstick pan. Cook meatballs in hot oil until seared finely all around evenly, for 4 to 5 minutes each meatball; place to a nonstick baking sheet.
- Bake meatballs in the prepared oven until cooked thoroughly, for 15 minutes.
- Heat marinara sauce over medium heat in a large pot. Remove meatballs to the marinara sauce with a slotted spoon. Heat mixture to a boil, lower the heat to low, and simmer for a minimum of 1 hour.

Nutrition Information

- Calories: 469 calories;
- Total Carbohydrate: 25.4 g
- Cholesterol: 106 mg
- Total Fat: 28.7 g
- Protein: 26 g
- Sodium: 1349 mg

206. Mediterranean Brown Rice Pilaf

"It's a fantastic and tasty combination of Mediterranean flavors that is quick to make as well as healthy."
Serving: 6 | Prep: 30m | Ready in: 1h22m

Ingredients

- 1 (14.5 oz.) can chicken broth
- 1 cup uncooked brown rice
- 1/2 tsp. dried rosemary (optional)
- 2 tbsps. olive oil
- 2 cloves garlic, minced
- 1 onion, chopped
- 2 shallots
- 1/4 cup chopped green bell pepper
- 1 (15 oz.) can chickpeas, drained
- 1/4 cup drained chopped sun-dried tomatoes
- 2 eggs, slightly beaten
- salt and ground black pepper to taste
- 1/4 cup pine nuts
- 1/4 cup fresh basil

Direction

- In a saucepan, bring chicken broth to a boil, then put in rosemary and rice. Lower the heat and simmer for approximately 45 minutes, until broth is absorbed and rice is softened.
- In a big saucepan, heat olive oil on medium heat. Put in garlic then stir in shallots and onion. Cook for around 5 minutes until tender while stirring often. Put in green bell pepper and cook for approximately 1 minute until tender. Mix into the vegetable mixture with tomatoes and chickpeas, then cook for around a minute until heated through.
- Scoop cooked rice into the vegetable mixture. Add eggs and stir until whole mixture is dry. Season to taste with pepper and salt, then take away from the heat. Stir in basil and pine nuts.

Nutrition Information

- Calories: 311 calories;
- Total Carbohydrate: 44 g
- Cholesterol: 64 mg
- Total Fat: 11.3 g
- Protein: 9.7 g
- Sodium: 496 mg

207. Mediterranean Chicken Sandwich

"This dish is chicken cooked with capers, kalamata olives, onion, bell pepper, and garlic, and then stacked into hoagie buns with feta cheeses and mozzarella."
Serving: 8 | Prep: 40m | Ready in: 1h

Ingredients

- 4 skinless, boneless chicken breast halves , cut into cubes
- 1 tbsp. olive oil
- 1 tbsp. minced garlic
- 1 tsp. red pepper flakes
- 1 pinch salt and freshly ground black pepper to taste
- 1 yellow bell pepper, diced
- 1 onion, diced
- 1/4 cup pitted kalamata olives, diced
- 1/4 cup capers, drained
- 1 cup halved cherry tomatoes
- 1 lb. shredded mozzarella cheese
- 1 cup crumbled feta cheese
- 4 Italian-style hoagie buns, split lengthwise and toasted
- 1/4 cup artichoke aioli (see footnote for recipe link)
- 1/4 cup chopped fresh basil

Direction

- In a big bowl, mix together black pepper, salt, red pepper flakes, garlic, olive oil and chicken; mix to coat.
- Place a Dutch oven or a big pot on medium-high heat. Add the chicken mixture and cook for 5 minutes until the middle of the chicken is not pink anymore, tossing often. Add onion and yellow bell pepper, cook for 5 minutes until the onion starts to get tender. Stir in capers and olives until blended. Mix in

mozzarella cheese until melted. Take away from the heat and mix in feta cheese.

- Spread 1 tbsp. artichoke aioli over each hoagie roll. Evenly divide the chicken mixture between the 4 sandwiches. Sprinkle 1 tbsp. basil over each sandwich.

Nutrition Information

- Calories: 494 calories;
- Total Carbohydrate: 40.6 g
- Cholesterol: 85 mg
- Total Fat: 20.8 g
- Protein: 34.7 g
- Sodium: 1185 mg

208. Mediterranean Farfalle

"Great as a meal or alongside sandwiches or grilled meats."
Serving: 7

Ingredients

- 1 (12 oz.) package farfalle pasta
- 1 lb. chorizo sausage, crumbled
- 1/4 cup fresh basil leaves, cut into thin strips
- 1/2 cup pine nuts
- 2 cloves garlic, minced
- 1/2 cup grated Parmesan cheese
- 1 cup diced tomato
- 1/2 cup olive oil
- 3/8 cup red wine

Direction

- In boiling salted water, allow pasta to cook till al dente.
- Meanwhile, over medium heat, brown the ham. Add and brown the nuts; keep form burning. Put garlic, and take off heat.
- Drain the pasta. Toss together tomatoes, cheese, basil, ham mixture and pasta in a big bowl. Mix together vinegar and olive oil; put atop pasta, then toss. Serve.

Nutrition Information

- Calories: 700 calories;
- Total Carbohydrate: 39.4 g
- Cholesterol: 62 mg
- Total Fat: 48 g
- Protein: 26.9 g
- Sodium: 894 mg

209. Mediterranean-twist Salmon

"Level up your usual salmon dish with this yummy recipe! It is great served over couscous! You may use 1 cup of tomatoes rather than 1/2 cup if you want to."
Serving: 2 | Prep: 10m | Ready in: 30m

Ingredients

- Salmon:
- 1 tsp. olive oil
- 2 (4 oz.) fillets salmon
- Sauce:
- 2 tbsps. olive oil
- 1 clove garlic, minced
- 1/2 cup chopped tomatoes, or more to taste
- 1 tbsp. balsamic vinegar
- 6 fresh basil leaves, chopped

Direction

- In a saucepan, put in 1 tsp. of olive oil and let it heat up over medium heat setting. Put in the salmon and let it cook in hot oil for 5-7 minutes on every side until the fish meat can be flaked apart easily using a fork and it has been cooked thoroughly.
- In another saucepan, put in 2 tbsps. of olive oil and let it heat up over medium heat setting then put in the garlic and sauté it for about 1 minute until you can smell the garlic aroma. Put in the tomatoes and let it cook for about 5 minutes until it is thoroughly heated. Add in the balsamic vinegar then followed by the basil. Let the tomato mixture cook for about 3 minutes while stirring it until the flavors have combined.

- Transfer the cooked salmon onto a plate and spoon over the prepared tomato sauce.

Nutrition Information

- Calories: 347 calories;
- Total Carbohydrate: 3.8 g
- Cholesterol: 76 mg
- Total Fat: 25.6 g
- Protein: 24.8 g
- Sodium: 63 mg

210. Mexi-italian Salsa

"This is a combination between bruschetta and salsa and a hit at picnics and parties all the time."
Serving: 10 | Prep: 25m | Ready in: 25m

Ingredients

- 3 roma (plum) tomatoes, chopped
- 1/2 onion, chopped
- 1 (2.25 oz.) can sliced black olives, drained
- 1 (6 oz.) can marinated artichoke hearts, drained and chopped
- 2 tbsps. lemon juice
- 2 cloves garlic, minced
- 3 tbsps. chopped fresh basil
- 1/4 tsp. crushed red pepper flakes
- 1/4 tsp. Italian seasoning
- 1/4 tsp. ground cumin
- 3 tbsps. chopped fresh cilantro
- 1/4 tsp. salt
- 1/8 tsp. ground black pepper

Direction

- In a bowl, cautiously mix the artichoke hearts, olives, onion, and tomatoes; reserve. In another bowl, mix pepper, salt, cilantro, cumin, Italian seasoning, red pepper flakes, basil, garlic, and lemon juice. Add the dressing into the tomato mixture and fold.

Nutrition Information

- Calories: 30 calories;

- Total Carbohydrate: 4.1 g
- Cholesterol: 0 mg
- Total Fat: 1.7 g
- Protein: 1 g
- Sodium: 178 mg

211.Mexican Bean And Squash Soup

"A spicy, flavorsome soup."
Serving: 8 | Prep: 40m | Ready in: 1h22m

Ingredients

- 2 tbsps. olive oil
- 2 cups butternut squash - peeled, seeded, and cut into 3/4-inch chunks
- 1 small yellow onion, finely chopped
- 1/4 cup finely chopped celery
- 1/2 cup finely chopped carrot
- 3 cloves garlic, minced
- 2 canned Chipotle peppers in adobo sauce, seeded and minced
- 1 tbsp. chopped fresh basil leaves
- 1 tbsp. chopped fresh parsley
- 1 tsp. cumin
- 1 (15 oz.) can diced tomatoes
- 2 quarts chicken broth
- 1 (15.5 oz.) can cannellini beans, drained
- 1 cup corn kernels, fresh, canned, or frozen
- 2 limes, cut into wedges
- 1 (10 oz.) bag tortilla chips, for topping
- 1 cup sour cream, for topping
- 1 (8 oz.) package shredded Mexican blend cheese, for topping

Direction

- In a deep pot, heat olive oil over medium-high heat. Mix in squash, and allow to cook for 5 to 7 minutes till it starts to become tender. Put the carrots, celery and onion. Let cook for 5 minutes till onion is transparent. Mix in the cumin, parsley, basil, chipotle peppers and garlic; let cook for 2 minutes longer. Add in chicken broth and tomatoes. Lower heat to medium, and let simmer for 30 minutes till vegetables are soft. Mix in corn and cannellini beans; allow to cook just till heated through.

- To serve, into the bowls, scoop the soup. Juice lime on top of every bowl, and put tortilla chips, a spoonful of sour cream, and a sprinkling of the Mexican cheese on top.

Nutrition Information

- Calories: 464 calories;
- Total Carbohydrate: 43.8 g
- Cholesterol: 40 mg
- Total Fat: 27.6 g
- Protein: 13.8 g
- Sodium: 602 mg

212. Mini Crab Cakes

"Crab cakes made with Greek nonfat yogurt are smaller than normal chomps of ecstasy."
Serving: 18 | Prep: 20m | Ready in: 40m

Ingredients

- 1 (16 oz.) can fancy lump crabmeat, well drained and picked through for cartilage
- 1 egg, lightly beaten
- 1 cup Dannon Oikos Plain Greek Nonfat Yogurt
- 1/4 cup finely chopped red bell pepper
- 1/4 cup thinly sliced green onion
- 1 tsp. finely grated zest of one lemon
- Fresh cracked pepper to taste
- 1 cup plain or panko breadcrumbs, divided
- Cooking spray
- 2 tbsps. chopped parsley
- 2 tbsps. chopped basil
- 2 tbsps. lemon juice

Direction

- Combine 1/2 cup breadcrumbs, lemon zest fresh cracked pepper, green onion, red pepper, 1/3 cup yogurt, egg and crabmeat.

- Use a small ice cream scoop or tbsp. to shape mini crab cakes then coat crab cakes in the reserved breadcrumbs, put them on a parchment lined baking sheet. Grease lightly with cooking spray.
- Bake in a preheated oven at 400°F until lightly golden, about 12 to 15 minutes.
- Blend together basil, chopped parsley, lemon juice and remaining yogurt. Add cracked black pepper for seasoning. Enjoy the crab cakes with sauce.

Nutrition Information

- Calories: 56 calories;
- Total Carbohydrate: 5.4 g
- Cholesterol: 30 mg
- Total Fat: 0.8 g
- Protein: 7.9 g
- Sodium: 134 mg

213. Mini Turkey Loaves With Feta, Basil, And Balsamic Sauce

""You can serve these mini and healthy loaves at a party. As the loaves cook, it will shrink. So you don't need to worry if you fill the cups up to the top.""
Serving: 6 | Prep: 10m | Ready in: 25m

Ingredients

- 1 lb. ground turkey
- 4 green onions, chopped
- 1/4 cup crumbled feta cheese
- 1 tbsp. chopped fresh basil
- 1 tsp. Worcestershire sauce
- 1/2 cup balsamic vinegar

Direction

- Set the oven to 350°F (175°C) for preheating.
- In a bowl, mix the Worcestershire sauce, green onions, ground turkey, feta cheese, and basil. Divide the turkey mixture among the 6 muffin cups.

- Let them bake inside the preheated oven for 15-20 minutes until the center is no longer pink and an instant-read thermometer pricked in the middle of the meatloaves registers at least 165°F (74°C).
- Meanwhile, pour balsamic vinegar in a small saucepan and heat it over medium-low heat. Cook and stir regularly for 10-15 minutes until it is reduced into a consistency of syrup. Drizzle the reduced balsamic all over the loaves.

Nutrition Information

- Calories: 145 calories;
- Total Carbohydrate: 4.3 g
- Cholesterol: 61 mg
- Total Fat: 7.1 g
- Protein: 16.1 g
- Sodium: 128 mg

214. Mock Caprese Salad

"Make this low-calorie dish with fat-free cottage cheese."
Serving: 2 | Prep: 10m | Ready in: 10m

Ingredients

- 1 cup fat-free cottage cheese
- 2 tomatoes, chopped
- 1 tbsp. chopped fresh basil leaves, or to taste
- 1/2 tsp. salt
- freshly ground black pepper to taste
- 2 tbsps. balsamic vinegar (optional)

Direction

- In a bowl, combine black pepper, salt, basil, tomatoes and cottage cheese. Add balsamic vinegar and stir.

Nutrition Information

- Calories: 120 calories;
- Total Carbohydrate: 13.2 g
- Cholesterol: 5 mg
- Total Fat: 0.3 g

- Protein: 15.6 g
- Sodium: 1032 mg

215. Morning Bruschetta

"A modern egg recipe for breakfast."
Serving: 6 | Prep: 15m | Ready in: 49m

Ingredients

- 1 loaf Italian bread, cut into 1-inch-thick slices on the diagonal
- 3 tbsps. olive oil, divided
- salt and ground black pepper to taste
- 3 cloves garlic, minced
- 2 (14 oz.) cans diced tomatoes
- 6 eggs
- 1/4 cup grated Parmesan cheese
- 1 tbsp. slivered fresh basil leaves

Direction

- Set oven to 200° C (400° F) and start preheating.
- On a baking sheet, place bread slices. Drizzle with 2 tbsps. olive oil and season with pepper and salt.
- Place in the preheated oven and bake 15 minutes until crisp. Take out of the oven. Leave the oven on.
- In an oven-safe skillet on medium heat, heat the rest 1 tbsp. of olive oil. Stir and cook garlic 3-4 minutes till garlic is fragrant. Mix in tomatoes and season with pepper and salt. Simmer 10 minutes, stirring often, until breaking down into a sauce.
- With a wooden spoon, make six wells in the tomatoes. Crack an egg into each of the wells. Sprinkle with Parmesan cheese and top with basil leaves.
- Put skillet into the preheated oven and bake 6 minutes until yolks are still runny and whites are set.
- With a big spoon, scoop each egg and place it on each bread slice. Spoon the rest of tomatoes atop.

Nutrition Information

- Calories: 470 calories;
- Total Carbohydrate: 61.4 g
- Cholesterol: 167 mg
- Total Fat: 16 g
- Protein: 17.9 g
- Sodium: 1001 mg

---

216. Mushrooms In White Wine Sauce

"A good side dish for those that love mushroom. I love preparing this for dinners on holidays in place the usual vegetable fare."
Serving: 6 | Prep: 15m | Ready in: 35m

Ingredients

- 1/4 cup peanut or vegetable oil
- 1/3 cup chopped onion
- 1 clove garlic, minced
- 1 lb. mushrooms, sliced
- 3/4 cup water, divided
- 1/4 cup dry white wine
- 1 cube chicken bouillon
- 1/4 tsp. dried basil
- salt and pepper to taste
- 1 tbsp. cornstarch

Direction

- Over medium heat, heat oil in a large skillet and mix in garlic and onions. Cook for 5 minutes until tender. Mix in wine, mushrooms, chicken bouillon, and 1/2 cup water. Season with pepper, salt, and basil. Heat to boil, decrease the heat and allow to simmer while uncovered for 10 minutes while stirring often. Combine together cornstarch with 1/4 cup of water. Mix into the mushrooms and then cook for about 5 minutes until thickened.

Nutrition Information

- Calories: 115 calories;

- Total Carbohydrate: 4.9 g
- Cholesterol: < 1 mg
- Total Fat: 9.3 g
- Protein: 2.6 g
- Sodium: 198 mg

---

217. Mussels In White Wine Sauce

"Yummy way to prepare mussels."
Serving: 4 | Prep: 15m | Ready in: 40m

Ingredients

- 4 cups mussels
- 2 tbsps. olive oil
- 2 tbsps. butter
- 2 tbsps. chopped garlic
- 2 tbsps. chopped shallots
- 2 cups beef broth, divided
- 2 tbsps. anise-flavored liqueur
- 1/2 jalapeno pepper, seeded and minced
- 1/2 red chile pepper, seeded and minced
- 1 cup white wine
- 10 leaves fresh basil, chopped
- 1/4 cup light cream
- 2 tsps. cornstarch
- 1 lemon, juiced

Direction

- In a bowl of cold water, submerge mussels for a minimum of 10 minutes; take off from water and using a stiff brush, scour to get rid of dirt if necessary. With a sharp knife, take off beard if necessary.
- In a big stockpot over medium heat, melt butter with olive oil; cook and mix shallots and garlic for 2 to 3 minutes till browned slightly. To garlic-shallot mixture, put red chili pepper, jalapeno pepper, anise-flavored liqueur and a cup beef broth; boil. Turn heat to medium-low and allow to simmer for 5 minutes till peppers have become tender.
- Into broth mixture, mix basil, leftover 1 cup beef broth and wine; allow to simmer.

- In a bowl, beat cornstarch and light cream till cornstarch is dissolved; put to the broth mixture and boil. To the boiling broth mixture, put lemon juice and mussels and with a lid, cover the stockpot; allow to cook for 5 minutes till shells open. Throw any shells that remain closed.

Nutrition Information

- Calories: 362 calories;
- Total Carbohydrate: 15.9 g
- Cholesterol: 67 mg
- Total Fat: 19.2 g
- Protein: 20.6 g
- Sodium: 876 mg

---

218. Naan Bread Margherita Pizza With Prosciutto

"I used naan bread as the pizza base in this recipe, and it works.""
Serving: 2 | Prep: 15m | Ready in: 25m

Ingredients

- 2 naan breads
- 2 tsps. olive oil, or as needed
- 1 green onion, sliced
- 1 clove garlic, finely chopped
- 8 slices mozzarella cheese
- 1 large roma tomato, thinly sliced
- salt and ground black pepper to taste
- 1 slice prosciutto, sliced
- 6 leaves fresh basil, roughly chopped
- 2 tbsps. grated Parmesan cheese

Direction

- Set oven to 350°F (175°C) to preheat. Line aluminum foil over a baking sheet.
- Arrange naan breads on the prepared baking sheet; brush olive oil over each naan. Spread with garlic and green onion. Place 4 slices of mozzarella cheese on each naan. Layer top with tomato slices. Sprinkle pepper and salt

over tomatoes to season. Top tomatoes with prosciutto, basil, and Parmesan cheese.
- Bake for about 8 minutes in the preheated oven until cheese is melted and edges of pizza are crispy. Turn the broiler of the oven on; allow to broil for 2 minutes until cheese is bubbling and lightly browned.

Nutrition Information

- Calories: 626 calories;
- Total Carbohydrate: 49.8 g
- Cholesterol: 92 mg
- Total Fat: 29.4 g
- Protein: 41.1 g
- Sodium: 1222 mg

---

219. Nat's Shrimp And Veggie Stuffed Zucchini

"You can enjoy this dish on its own or as a side dish."
Serving: 4 | Prep: 20m | Ready in: 55m

Ingredients

- 1 extra large zucchini
- 1/4 cup olive oil, divided
- 6 cloves garlic, finely chopped
- 1 shallot, finely chopped
- 1/2 lb. large shrimp - shelled, deveined, and cut in half
- 1 large tomato - peeled, seeded and diced
- 8 cremini mushrooms, quartered
- 1/4 cup grated Parmesan cheese
- 8 leaves fresh basil, torn
- ground black pepper to taste
- kosher salt to taste
- garlic powder to taste
- 1/4 cup grated Parmesan cheese, divided

Direction

- Turn on the oven's broiler to preheat and put the oven rack approximately 6-in. from the heat source. Oil a baking sheet lightly.

- Halve the zucchini lengthwise and spoon out the pulp and seeds, keeping a thick flesh shell. Brush approximately 1 tbsp. of olive oil over both zucchini halves, and put them on the prepared baking sheet with the cut sides facing down. Bake the zucchini for 5-10 minutes until the zucchini are hot and start to release moisture beads. Take the zucchini out of the oven.
- Lower the oven heat to 450°F (230°C).
- In a skillet, heat 2 tbsps. of olive oil over medium-low heat, and stir and cook shallot and garlic for 5 minutes until translucent. Take away from heat and cool.
- In a bowl, put the cooked shallot and garlic, basil, 1/4 cup of Parmesan cheese, mushrooms, diced tomato, shrimp and 1 tbsp. of olive oil, and mix to combine. Use garlic powder, salt and black pepper to season to taste. Stuff into the zucchini halves with the mixture, and sprinkle approximately 2 tbsps. of Parmesan cheese over each zucchini.
- Put the stuffed zucchini in the preheated oven and bake for 20 minutes until the filling has fully cooked and hot as well as the cheese is browned.

Nutrition Information

- Calories: 267 calories;
- Total Carbohydrate: 13 g
- Cholesterol: 95 mg
- Total Fat: 17.4 g
- Protein: 17.4 g
- Sodium: 376 mg

220. No Name Orange Roughy

"A random recipe I came up with. It is cooked in a skillet with none frying. Make another distinct flavor by mixing a half lb. of chopped mushrooms with tomatoes and white wine."

Serving: 4 | Prep: 10m | Ready in: 30m

Ingredients

- 1 tsp. olive oil
- 3 green onions, chopped
- 1 cup dry white wine
- 1 (14.5 oz.) can whole peeled tomatoes with liquid, chopped
- 4 (4 oz.) fillets orange roughy
- 1 tbsp. chopped fresh basil
- 1/4 tsp. ground black pepper
- 1 pinch dried thyme, crushed
- 1 pinch dried rosemary, crushed
- 1/4 cup sliced black olives, drained
- 1/2 lb. crumbled feta cheese

Direction

- In a medium frying pan, heat olive oil over medium heat. Mix in green onions, then cook for 5 - 10 minutes until tender.
- Mix tomatoes and white wine along with the green onions, then boil. Put the orange roughy fillets into the white wine mixture. Flavor with rosemary, thyme, pepper, and basil. Decrease heat, then simmer for 15 - 20 minutes, until fish can be easily flaked using a fork. Take fish fillets away from the skillet.
- Sprinkle feta cheese and black olives over fish fillets.

Nutrition Information

- Calories: 329 calories;
- Total Carbohydrate: 9.9 g
- Cholesterol: 117 mg
- Total Fat: 15.1 g
- Protein: 27.6 g
- Sodium: 936 mg

221. Nomato Sauce (tomato-free Marinara Sauce)

"A restricted version of the paleo diet."
Serving: 2 | Prep: 25m | Ready in: 57m

Ingredients

- 1/4 kabocha squash, peeled and cut into small cubes
- 3 carrots, cut into small cubes
- 1/2 red beet, cut into small cubes
- 1 1/2 tsps. olive oil
- 1/3 yellow onion, finely chopped
- 1 clove garlic, minced
- 5 leaves fresh sage, finely chopped
- 1 tbsp. capers (optional)
- 1 tbsp. dried Italian herbs
- 1 pinch Himalayan salt to taste
- 1/2 cup water, or more if needed
- 1/2 lemon, juiced
- 5 leaves fresh basil, chopped

Direction

- In food processor, mix beet, carrots and kabocha squash; pulse till roughly grated.
- In a saucepan, heat olive oil till sizzling over medium heat. Put in sage, garlic and onion; cook and mix for a minute, or till onion is aromatic. Mix in salt, Italian herbs, capers and grated kabocha squash mixture.
- In the saucepan, put the water. Place cover on and let sauce simmer for half an hour, putting additional water if necessary, or till kabocha squash mixture is tender. Using a fork, crush mixture to create a smoother sauce.
- Mix basil and lemon juice into sauce and allow the flavors to blend for a minute.

Nutrition Information

- Calories: 160 calories;
- Total Carbohydrate: 32.1 g
- Cholesterol: 0 mg
- Total Fat: 4.5 g
- Protein: 3.8 g
- Sodium: 252 mg

222. Nonna's Tuscan Salad Dressing

"This dressing is tasty yet very easy to make. You can drizzle it over basil leaves, summer tomatoes or use it with mixed greens, romaine or spinach."
Serving: 8 | Prep: 5m | Ready in: 1h5m

Ingredients

- 3 tbsps. mayonnaise
- 1/3 cup red wine vinegar
- 1/2 cup water
- 2 tsps. lemon juice
- 2 tbsps. grated Parmesan cheese
- 3 tbsps. olive oil
- 1 small clove garlic, minced (optional)
- 1/4 tsp. dried oregano
- 1/4 tsp. dried basil
- 1/8 tsp. ground black pepper, or to taste

Direction

- In a blender, put black pepper, basil, oregano, garlic, olive oil, Parmesan cheese, lemon juice, water, vinegar and mayonnaise. Process for 2 minutes, and then add to a salad dressing container, and chill for a minimum of 60 minutes. Before using, shake well.

Nutrition Information

- Calories: 91 calories;
- Total Carbohydrate: 1.2 g
- Cholesterol: 3 mg
- Total Fat: 9.5 g
- Protein: 0.6 g
- Sodium: 49 mg

223. Orange Chicken Kabobs

"You will need to marinate your cubed chicken for a minimum of 2 hours. I also chop my vegetables and add them to the bag with a small amount of the marinade. You can prepare this in the morning and all left to do for the dinner is to assemble the kabobs and grill them. It goes very well with wild rice or brown rice."
Serving: 4 | Prep: 15m | Ready in: 2h30m

Ingredients

- 1/4 cup orange marmalade
- 2 tbsps. balsamic vinegar
- 2 tbsps. red wine
- 1 tbsp. olive oil
- 1 tbsp. chopped fresh chives
- 1 tbsp. chopped fresh basil
- 1 large garlic clove, minced
- 1/4 tsp. dried sage
- 1/8 tsp. garlic salt
- 1/8 tsp. kosher salt
- 1 (6 oz.) package fresh mushrooms, or to taste
- 1 bell pepper, chopped, or to taste
- 1/2 red onion, chopped, or to taste
- 2 skinless, boneless chicken breast halves, cubed
- 1 cup chopped fresh pineapple, or to taste
- skewers

Direction

- In a bowl, combine kosher salt, garlic salt, sage, garlic, basil, chives, olive oil, red wine, balsamic vinegar and orange marmalade until the marinade is smooth. Add approximately 1/4 of the marinade to a resealable plastic bag, add red onion, bell pepper and mushrooms. Squeeze the air out of the bag and seal.
- Add the leftover marinade to another resealable bag; add chicken. Squeeze the air out of the bag and seal. Put the chicken and vegetables in the fridge to marinate for 2-8 hours.
- Take the chicken and vegetables out of the bag and get rid of the marinade. On skewers, thread pineapple, chicken and vegetables.

- Set an outdoor grill to medium-high heat to preheat and lightly grease the grate.
- On the preheated grill, cook kabobs for 5-10 minutes on each side until the middle of the chicken is not pink anymore.

Nutrition Information

- Calories: 197 calories;
- Total Carbohydrate: 24.6 g
- Cholesterol: 32 mg
- Total Fat: 5 g
- Protein: 14 g
- Sodium: 162 mg

224. Oven Roasted Grape Tomatoes

"A great, hearty side dish for summertime."
Serving: 2 | Prep: 15m | Ready in: 45m

Ingredients

- 1 lb. grape tomatoes, halved
- 1 tbsp. olive oil
- 2 cloves garlic, minced
- 5 fresh basil leaves, chopped
- 1 tsp. chopped fresh thyme
- salt to taste

Direction

- Preheat the oven to 175°C or 350°F.
- In a big square of aluminum foil, put the tomatoes. Sprinkle olive oil on tomatoes and put salt, thyme, basil and garlic on top. Wrap tomato mixture with foil securing tightly to retain juices inside.
- In the preheated oven, bake for about half an hour till tomatoes are soft. Slightly cool.

Nutrition Information

- Calories: 113 calories;
- Total Carbohydrate: 11.7 g
- Cholesterol: 0 mg
- Total Fat: 7.5 g

- Protein: 2.2 g
- Sodium: 99 mg

225. Oven-ready Lasagna With Meat Sauce And Bechamel

"This dish is meat sauce and béchamel layered with cheese and lasagna noodles."
Serving: 6 | Prep: 20m | Ready in: 45m

Ingredients

- 1 (9 oz.) box Barilla® Oven Ready Lasagne
- 1 quart milk
- 6 tbsps. butter
- 5 tbsps. all-purpose flour
- Salt and black pepper to taste
- 1/4 tsp. ground nutmeg
- 1 cup grated Parmesan cheese
- 1 (24 oz.) jar Barilla® Meat Sauce
- 1/2 cup fresh basil leaves, julienned

Direction

- Turn the oven to 375°F to preheat.
- To prepare the béchamel: In a saucepan, simmer milk. In the meantime, melt butter in another pan, mix in flour and cook for 2-3 minutes. Mix the hot milk into the flour-butter mixture. Stir vigorously and simmer for 5 minutes. Take the pan away from the heat. Use 3/4 of cheese, nutmeg, pepper and salt to season.
- Add 1/5 of the béchamel and 1/5 of the Barilla sauce to the bottom of a 13x9-in. baking dish, put basil on top. Put on 3 noodles to cover and continue layering until having 3 more layers. Add basil and the leftover Parmigiano cheese for the top layer. Use foil to cover.
- Bake for 20 minutes until the corners are light brown and bubbly. Allow the lasagna to sit before enjoying, about 5 minutes.

Nutrition Information

- Calories: 496 calories;

- Total Carbohydrate: 55 g
- Cholesterol: 68 mg
- Total Fat: 20.8 g
- Protein: 19.1 g
- Sodium: 882 mg

226. Pad Kee Mao

"Many vendors in Bangkok made this "drunken" stir-fry."
Serving: 4 | Prep: 20m | Ready in: 1h40m

Ingredients

- 3 1/2 oz. dried Thai-style rice noodles, wide (such as Chantaboon Rice Noodles)
- 1 1/2 tsps. olive oil
- 2 cloves garlic, minced
- 1/2 tsp. thick soy sauce
- 2 tsps. white sugar
- 1 1/2 tsps. olive oil
- 2 cloves garlic, minced
- 1/2 lb. pork (any cut), thinly sliced
- 1 serrano pepper, minced, or more to taste
- 30 fresh basil leaves, chopped
- 1/2 tsp. thick soy sauce
- 1 tsp. white sugar
- 1 tsp. salt
- 1/2 cup bean sprouts

Direction

- Put dry rice noodles inside a bowl. Cover using hot water and soak for about an hour until soft and white. Drain noodles then put aside.
- In a big skillet or wok, heat 1 1/2 tsp. of olive oil on low heat. Sauté 2 minced garlic cloves for 2-3 minutes until it starts to crisp and brown in color. Mix in 2 tsps. of sugar, 1/2 tsp. of thick soy sauce, and soaked noodles until noodles absorb soy sauce and become brown in color for about 3 minutes. Take noodles out of skillet.
- Heat leftover 1 1/2 tsps. of olive oil in a wok on low heat. Mix in leftover 2 minced garlic cloves then cook for 2-3 minutes until it starts

to brown and crisp. Bring heat up to medium-high and mix in salt, 1 tsp. of sugar, 1/2 tsp. of thick soy sauce, basil, serrano pepper, and pork. Sauté for about 5 minutes until pork isn't pink and the meat edges are starting to brown. Put noodles back in wok and mix in bean sprouts. Sauté for about 5 more minutes until heated through.

Nutrition Information

- Calories: 218 calories;
- Total Carbohydrate: 26.2 g
- Cholesterol: 22 mg
- Total Fat: 9.1 g
- Protein: 7.2 g
- Sodium: 707 mg

227. Paleo Artichoke Bruschetta

"Bruschetta serve with grilled vegetables or sliced cucumbers."
Serving: 4 | Prep: 10m | Ready in: 10m

Ingredients

- 1 (14 oz.) can artichoke hearts, drained and chopped
- 2 cloves garlic, minced
- 1 tsp. sea salt
- 1/2 tsp. freshly ground black pepper
- 1/2 red bell pepper, finely chopped
- 1/4 cup extra-virgin olive oil
- 3 tbsps. minced fresh basil
- 2 tbsps. finely chopped red onion
- 1 tbsp. drained capers

Direction

- In a big bowl, combine black pepper, sea salt, garlic and artichoke hearts together; put onion, basil, olive oil and red bell pepper and mix well. Atop artichoke mixture with capers.

Nutrition Information

- Calories: 169 calories;

- Total Carbohydrate: 8.6 g
- Cholesterol: 0 mg
- Total Fat: 14.1 g
- Protein: 2.6 g
- Sodium: 869 mg

228. Panzanella Panini

"This sandwich is the combination of sandwiches and salad."
Serving: 1 | Prep: 10m | Ready in: 15m

Ingredients

- 1 French deli roll, split
- 1 tsp. balsamic vinegar
- 2 slices mozzarella cheese
- 1 small tomato, sliced
- 4 fresh basil leaves
- olive oil

Direction

- Preheat a skillet on the medium low heat.
- Drizzle cut sides of roll along with balsamic vinegar. Layer 1 mozzarella cheese slice, tomato slices, basil leaves, and the leftover mozzarella cheese slice over the roll. Close the sandwich; using olive oil to rub the outside of sandwich.
- Put sandwich into the preheated skillet; press by add another heavy skillet on top of it. Cook for roughly 3 minutes till bread becomes toasted and golden. Turn the sandwich over; place the skillet on top. Cook second side for roughly extra 2 minutes till becomes toasted.

Nutrition Information

- Calories: 402 calories;
- Total Carbohydrate: 29.9 g
- Cholesterol: 36 mg
- Total Fat: 24.1 g
- Protein: 18.5 g
- Sodium: 613 mg

229. Parmesan And Basil Chicken Salad

"Unusual but tasty chicken salad recipe."
Serving: 4 | Prep: 15m | Ready in: 1h50m

Ingredients

- 2 whole skinless, boneless chicken breasts
- salt and pepper to taste
- 1 cup mayonnaise
- 1 cup chopped fresh basil
- 2 cloves crushed garlic
- 3 stalks celery, chopped
- 2/3 cup grated Parmesan cheese

Direction

- Season chicken with pepper and salt. Roast 190° C (375° F) until juices run clear, about 35 minutes. Allow to cool then cut into chunks.
- Puree celery, garlic, basil and mayonnaise in a food processor.
- Mix together Parmesan cheese, pureed mixture and the chunked chicken then toss. Chill in the fridge. Serve.

Nutrition Information

- Calories: 592 calories;
- Total Carbohydrate: 3.9 g
- Cholesterol: 101 mg
- Total Fat: 49.1 g
- Protein: 33.5 g
- Sodium: 618 mg

230. Parmesan Zucchini Patties

"This dish is very delicious."
Serving: 7 | Prep: 25m | Ready in: 35m

Ingredients

- 2 tbsps. vegetable oil
- 4 cups shredded zucchini
- 2 large onions, chopped
- 2 cloves garlic, minced
- 1 tbsp. chopped fresh basil
- 2 tbsps. chopped parsley
- 1/8 tsp. ground black pepper
- 1/8 tsp. ground thyme
- 3 eggs, lightly beaten
- 1 cup crushed saltine crackers
- 1 cup grated Parmesan cheese
- 1/4 cup vegetable oil, or as needed
- 2 tbsps. grated Parmesan cheese, or to taste (optional)

Direction

- In a big skillet, heat 2 tbsps. vegetable oil over medium heat. In the hot oil, stir and cook garlic, onion and zucchini for 5 minutes until the moisture evaporates and the vegetables are limp. Mix thyme, black pepper, parsley and basil into the vegetables; take away from the heat. Remove the zucchini mixture into a big mixing bowl.
- Mix 1 cup Parmesan cheese, crushed crackers and eggs into the zucchini mixture until it holds together; form into 14 patties, about 3-inch each.
- In a skillet, pour vegetable oil enough until reaching 1/2-in. deep, heat over medium-high heat.
- In the hot oil, cook the patties in batches of 3-4, for 2 minutes on each side until turning fully brown. Sprinkle more Parmesan cheese over and enjoy.

Nutrition Information

- Calories: 261 calories;
- Total Carbohydrate: 14.3 g
- Cholesterol: 91 mg
- Total Fat: 18.8 g
- Protein: 9.9 g
- Sodium: 343 mg

231. Pasta Alla Norma (eggplant Pasta)

""Like many traditional Italian dishes, you only need a few ingredients with excellent quality.""
Serving: 4 | Prep: 20m | Ready in: 3h5m

Ingredients

- 3 eggplant
- coarse salt
- 5 tbsps. extra virgin olive oil, divided
- 1 clove garlic
- 1 (18 oz.) can whole peeled tomatoes
- salt and freshly ground black pepper to taste
- 1 small bunch fresh basil, chopped, divided
- 1 (16 oz.) package spaghetti
- 1 (8 oz.) container ricotta cheese, or to taste

Direction

- Rinse the eggplants and cut the ends off. Slice the eggplant into 1/3-inch pieces. Arrange the slices in a large-sized bowl in a layer. Sprinkle each layer with coarse salt. Allow them to sit for at least 2 hours until all the bitterness is drawn out.
- Meanwhile, prepare for the tomato sauce. Put 2 tbsp. of olive oil in a saucepan and heat it over medium heat. Cook the garlic for 2 minutes until browned. Remove the garlic and add the peeled tomatoes. Bring the mixture to a boil. Cook for 5 minutes until the tomatoes begin to break down. Lower the heat. Simmer the mixture for 20 minutes until the sauce is thick. Season the mixture with salt and pepper. Toss in 2/3 of the basil. Simmer the mixture for 3 more minutes.
- Wash the slices of eggplant under the cold running water. Use paper towels to pat the slices until dry. Pour the remaining 3 tbsp. of olive oil in a large skillet; heat it over medium-high. Working in batches, fry the eggplant slices for 3-5 minutes per side until golden brown. Let them drain on paper towels. Slice them into small cubes.
- Boil a large pot of lightly salted water. Cook the spaghetti in boiling water for 12 minutes while occasionally stirring it until tender but still firm to the bite; drain.
- Stir the eggplant slices into the tomato sauce. Simmer the mixture over low heat for 10 minutes. Mix in ricotta thoroughly. Season the mixture with the remaining basil, salt, and pepper. Stir in drained spaghetti. Cook for 3 minutes until warm.

Nutrition Information

- Calories: 770 calories;
- Total Carbohydrate: 115.7 g
- Cholesterol: 18 mg
- Total Fat: 24.1 g
- Protein: 26.7 g
- Sodium: 1746 mg

232. Pasta Pomodoro

"This tomato and garlic pasta dish is light and simple to make. It can also be served as a main course by adding in cooked chunks of shrimp or chicken breast."
Serving: 4 | Prep: 15m | Ready in: 30m

Ingredients

- 1 (16 oz.) package angel hair pasta
- 1/4 cup olive oil
- 1/2 onion, chopped
- 4 cloves garlic, minced
- 2 cups roma (plum) tomatoes, diced
- 2 tbsps. balsamic vinegar
- 1 (10.75 oz.) can low-sodium chicken broth
- crushed red pepper to taste
- freshly ground black pepper to taste
- 2 tbsps. chopped fresh basil
- 1/4 cup grated Parmesan cheese

Direction

- Boil a large saucepan filled with lightly salted water, then add the pasta. Cook until the pasta has gone al dente which is for about 8 minutes. Drain.
- In a large deep skillet, pour in the olive oil and place over a high heat. Sauté garlic and onions

until slightly brown. Decrease heat to a medium-high then add chicken broth, vinegar, and tomatoes, letting it simmer for 8 minutes.

- Sir in the cooked pasta, basil, black pepper, and red pepper, then combine by tossing with the sauce completely. Simmer for 5 minutes more and serve with a topping of grated cheese.

Nutrition Information

- Calories: 500 calories;
- Total Carbohydrate: 69.7 g
- Cholesterol: 6 mg
- Total Fat: 18.3 g
- Protein: 16.2 g
- Sodium: 350 mg

233. Pasta With Asparagus Pesto

"You can use shell pasta for orecchiette."
Serving: 4 | Prep: 10m | Ready in: 30m

Ingredients

- 2 tbsps. pine nuts
- 1 cup water, or as needed
- 1 1/2 lbs. fresh asparagus, trimmed and cut into 1 1/2-inch pieces
- 3/4 cup packed fresh basil, divided
- 1/4 cup olive oil
- 1 clove garlic, crushed
- 1 tsp. salt
- 1/4 tsp. ground black pepper
- 1/3 cup grated Pecorino-Romano cheese, plus more for garnish
- 1 (16 oz.) package orecchiette pasta

Direction

- Heat skillet on medium high heat then add pine nuts; mix and cook pine nuts for 5 minutes till toasted and fragrant.
- Put 1-in. depth enough water in a skillet; boil. Add asparagus; cook for 5 minutes till tender. Take the asparagus from the skillet; keep 1/2

cup of cooking water. Put 1/2 cup asparagus tips aside.

- Blend black pepper, salt, garlic, olive oil, 1/2 cup basil, reserved 1/2 cup of cooking water, pine nuts and leftover asparagus till smooth in a blender; keep the middle lid piece off to release the steam. Add the Pecorino-Romano cheese and blend till smooth.
- Boil a big pot of lightly salted water; cook orecchiette pasta in the boiling water for 10 minutes till cooked through yet firm to chew, occasionally mixing. Drain; put pasta back in the pot.
- Slice leftover 1/4 cup basil. Add reserved asparagus tips, asparagus sauce and sliced basil to pasta; toss to mix evenly. Garnish using more Pecorino-Romano cheese.

Nutrition Information

- Calories: 598 calories;
- Total Carbohydrate: 89.8 g
- Cholesterol: 3 mg
- Total Fat: 18.9 g
- Protein: 20.4 g
- Sodium: 647 mg

234. Pasta With Vietnamese Pesto

"You can use an equal amount of lemon zest that's grated instead of fresh lemon grass."
Serving: 4 | Prep: 30m | Ready in: 35m

Ingredients

- 1 lb. dried rice noodles
- 1 1/2 cups chopped fresh cilantro
- 1/2 cup sweet Thai basil
- 2 cloves garlic, halved
- 1/2 tsp. minced lemon grass bulb
- 1 jalapeno pepper, seeded and minced
- 1 tbsp. vegetarian fish sauce
- 4 tbsps. chopped, unsalted dry-roasted peanuts
- 7 tbsps. canola oil
- 1/2 lime, cut into wedges

- salt and pepper to taste

Direction

- In a big bowl, soak rice noodles for half an hour in cold water. Drain noodles then put aside.
- Pesto: Combine 2 tbsps. peanuts, salt or imitation fish sauce, jalapeno peppers, lemon grass, garlic cloves, basil, and chopped cilantro in a food processor or blender. Whirl until peanuts and herbs are chopped coarsely. As machine runs, run a thin stream of oil into it. Add leftover peanuts then run machine in short spurts to coarsely chop peanuts.
- In a big skillet, put soaked rice noodles and half a cup of water on medium-high heat. Mix until majority of water absorbs and noodles become tender.
- Add nearly all the pesto and mix it well. Add several tbsps. of water if pesto begins clumping.
- Taste pasta and add more pepper, salt, imitation fish sauce, lime juice, or pesto if you want. Top pasta with leftover 2 tbsps. of peanuts then immediately serve.

Nutrition Information

- Calories: 694 calories;
- Total Carbohydrate: 98.8 g
- Cholesterol: 0 mg
- Total Fat: 29.8 g
- Protein: 6.8 g
- Sodium: 217 mg

235. Pea Pesto Open-faced Sandwiches

""Toasted bread slices cover with basil pesto and pea and add a fried egg on top - perfect for breakfast, lunch, or even dinner."
Serving: 4 | Prep: 5m | Ready in: 10m

Ingredients

- 1/2 cup fresh basil
- 1 cup peas, fresh or frozen (thawed)
- 1 clove garlic, smashed
- 1 tsp. salt
- 1/2 tsp. ground black pepper
- 1/2 cup extra virgin olive oil
- 4 Eggland's Best Eggs, large
- 4 slices toasted bread

Direction

- Combine extra virgin olive oil, pepper, salt, garlic, peas, and basil in a food processor. Process until blended and smooth.
- Toast bread for 3-4 minutes in oven (350°F) or toaster.
- Carefully break Eggland's Best egg onto surface of a small non-stick sauté pan over medium heat.
- Fry until egg yolk is cooked and transparent membrane looks white.
- Remove the cooked egg and do again for each egg.
- Top each toast with a tbsp. of pesto and spread evenly.
- Gently put each egg on top the pesto.
- Sprinkle virgin olive oil (optional), pepper, and extra salt on top.

Nutrition Information

- Calories: 384 calories;
- Total Carbohydrate: 13.5 g
- Cholesterol: 186 mg
- Total Fat: 33.2 g
- Protein: 7.7 g
- Sodium: 814 mg

236. Peach And Tomato Caprese Salad

"This dish is mozzarella, peaches, and heirloom tomatoes topped with balsamic vinaigrette."
Serving: 4 | Prep: 15m | Ready in: 15m

Ingredients

- 2 tbsps. extra-virgin olive oil
- 1 tbsp. balsamic vinegar
- 1 tsp. flaked salt, divided
- 2 large heirloom tomatoes, thinly sliced
- 2 ripe peaches - halved, pitted, and sliced into half moons
- 6 leaves fresh basil
- 1 (8 oz.) ball fresh mozzarella, thinly sliced

Direction

- In a bowl, combine 1 pinch flaked salt, balsamic vinegar and olive oil until the dressing is smooth.
- On a platter, alternately place tomato slices, the peach slices, the basil leaves, and mozzarella slices in layers. Drizzle over the salad with the dressing and sprinkle over the top with the leftover flaked salt.

Nutrition Information

- Calories: 254 calories;
- Total Carbohydrate: 8.4 g
- Cholesterol: 45 mg
- Total Fat: 19.1 g
- Protein: 11 g
- Sodium: 568 mg

237. Peach-basil Sangria

"You will love this easy to make sangria with basil"
Serving: 4 | Prep: 5m | Ready in: 10m

Ingredients

- 3/4 cup white sugar
- 1 cup loosely packed fresh basil leaves
- 3 1/2 cups peach nectar
- 1/4 cup fresh lemon juice
- 1 (750 milliliter) bottle white wine such as Pinot Grigio

Direction

- Mix lemon juice, half of the peach nectar, basil leaves and sugar in a saucepan. Simmer, using the back of the spoon to mash the basil leaves to infuse the flavor. Simmer till sugar melts, take off heat, and let rest to cool down.
- Into a pitcher packed with ice cubes strain the basil mixture. Add in wine and rest of the peach nectar. Mix quickly, serve.

238. Penne A La Vodka II

"You can prepare the sauce while the pasta is cooking. Sprinkle Parmesan cheese over."
Serving: 6 | Prep: 10m | Ready in: 45m

Ingredients

- 2 tbsps. olive oil
- 2 cloves garlic, minced
- 1 (28 oz.) can whole peeled tomatoes
- 1/2 cup chopped fresh basil
- salt and pepper to taste
- 1/4 cup vodka
- 1 lb. penne pasta
- 1 pint heavy cream

Direction

- In a big skillet, cook garlic with olive oil over medium heat for 1-2 minutes until soft. Mix in tomatoes, use a fork to crumble a bit. Mix in pepper, salt and basil, and simmer for 15 minutes. Mix in vodka and cook for another 15 minutes.

- Boil lightly salted water in a big pot. Put in pasta and cook until al dente, or about 8-10 minutes; strain.
- Mix the cream into the sauce and cook for another 10 minutes. Mix with the hot pasta.

Nutrition Information

- Calories: 632 calories;
- Total Carbohydrate: 62.9 g
- Cholesterol: 109 mg
- Total Fat: 35.8 g
- Protein: 12.9 g
- Sodium: 221 mg

239. Penne With Vegan Arrabbiata Sauce

"This recipe is meatless and best served with bread slices and a salad as a side."
Serving: 14 | Prep: 15m | Ready in: 3h20m

Ingredients

- 1 lb. penne pasta
- 1 cup extra virgin olive oil
- 7 cloves garlic, minced
- 7 (28 oz.) cans crushed tomatoes
- 2 1/2 tsps. crushed red pepper flakes
- 2 bay leaves
- 10 leaves fresh basil

Direction

- To cook the pasta, boil a large pot of water that's slightly salted. Add the chosen pasta to boiling water and cook for 8 to 10 minutes or until al dente. After it's cooked, drain water from pasta.
- In a separate pan, cook garlic in heated olive oil just until softened. Stir the remaining ingredients in the pan. Let this simmer while the heat is low for at least 3 hours.

- When the oil sauce has simmered, add the cooked penne pasta and let it sit for at least 5 minutes. Mix well, then serve warm.

Nutrition Information

- Calories: 389 calories;
- Total Carbohydrate: 52.9 g
- Cholesterol: 0 mg
- Total Fat: 17.9 g
- Protein: 10.9 g
- Sodium: 519 mg

240. Penne With Vodka Sauce And Bacon

"Several shots of vodka spike tomato sauce in this recipe. It goes with crispy bacon."
Serving: 4 | Prep: 10m | Ready in: 35m

Ingredients

- 1 (12 oz.) package penne pasta
- 2 slices bacon, chopped
- 1/2 cup chopped onion
- 3 cloves garlic, chopped
- 4 fluid oz. vodka
- 1 (28 oz.) can crushed tomatoes
- 1/4 cup heavy whipping cream
- 2 tsps. Worcestershire sauce
- 1/2 tsp. red pepper flakes, or to taste
- 4 tsps. dried basil
- ground black pepper to taste

Direction

- Boil lightly salted water in a big pot. Put in penne and cook for 11 minutes until soft yet firm to the bite, tossing sometimes.
- In a big saucepan, cook bacon over medium heat for 5 minutes until crispy, flipping sometimes. Put the bacon on paper towels to strain.
- Place the saucepan back on medium-low heat. Add garlic and onion, cook while mixing for 3 minutes until the onion is opaque. Raise the

heat to high, add vodka and boil it. Cook for 2 minutes until decreased by 1/2. Mix in red pepper flakes, Worcestershire sauce, heavy cream and tomatoes. Lower the heat to a simmer and cook for 10 minutes until the sauce is thick.

- Strain the pasta; put the sauce on top, and sprinkle black pepper, basil and bacon over.

Nutrition Information

- Calories: 527 calories;
- Total Carbohydrate: 81.2 g
- Cholesterol: 25 mg
- Total Fat: 10.1 g
- Protein: 17.2 g
- Sodium: 403 mg

241. Perfect Caprese Salad

"This salad will never fail to impress your guests, especially when served along with a toasted and buttered English muffin."
Serving: 6 | Prep: 20m | Ready in: 20m

Ingredients

- 4 plum tomatoes, sliced
- 12 small fresh mozzarella balls, sliced
- 1 avocado - peeled, pitted, and cubed
- 6 leaves fresh basil, cut into strips
- 1 (8 oz.) can sweet corn, drained
- 3 tbsps. extra-virgin olive oil
- 1 tbsp. white truffle oil
- 2 tbsps. balsamic vinegar
- salt and cracked black pepper to taste

Direction

- In a bowl, mix together corn, basil, avocado, mozzarella and tomatoes, then put in black pepper, salt, balsamic vinegar, truffle oil and olive oil. Gently toss to blend all ingredients together.

Nutrition Information

- Calories: 298 calories;
- Total Carbohydrate: 14.9 g
- Cholesterol: 31 mg
- Total Fat: 23.1 g
- Protein: 9.6 g
- Sodium: 178 mg

242. Pesto And Prawn Lasagna

"Prawns and pesto lasagna."
Serving: 6 | Prep: 20m | Ready in: 2h26m

Ingredients

- 2 cups fresh basil leaves
- 1 cup reduced fat cream of mushroom soup
- 1 tbsp. grated Parmesan cheese
- 1 tsp. olive oil
- 1/4 tsp. garlic powder
- 1 pinch salt and ground black pepper to taste
- 2 cups fresh spinach
- 6 sun-dried tomatoes, chopped
- 2 tbsps. butter
- 1 cup reduced fat cottage cheese
- olive oil cooking spray
- 1 cup chopped oyster mushrooms
- 1/2 cup chopped white mushrooms
- 9 dry lasagna noodles, uncooked
- 3 cups frozen king prawns
- 1/2 cup fresh mozzarella cheese, torn into pieces

Direction

- Mix together pepper, salt, garlic powder, olive oil, Parmesan cheese, cream of mushroom soup and basil. Using an immersion blender, puree till smooth.
- In a big microwave-safe bowl, mix together butter, sun-dried tomatoes and spinach. Microwave for 1 to 2 minutes till spinach wilts. Stir in pepper, salt and cottage cheese.
- Preheat an oven to 175 °C or 350 °F.

- On high heat, heat a big skillet. Coat in cooking spray. Put in white mushrooms and oyster mushrooms; cook and mix for 5 to 8 minutes till tender.
- Spread approximately 3 tbsps. of basil puree on the bottom of a square 8-inch baking pan. Spread 3 lasagna noodles over. Spread half of the spinach mixture evenly on top of noodles. Set half of the prawns over. Put 3 lasagna noodles to cover. Top with half of basil puree and put mushroom mixture on top to cover. Put the leftover 3 lasagna noodles to cover the top.
- Top the leftover prawns and spinach mixture evenly over lasagna noodles. On top, put the rest of basil puree. Scatter mozzarella cheese over. Cover using aluminum foil.
- In prepped oven, bake for approximately 90 minutes till sauce bubbles and noodles are tender. Take off aluminum foil and keep baking for about 30 minutes till mozzarella browns.

Nutrition Information

- Calories: 395 calories;
- Total Carbohydrate: 48.8 g
- Cholesterol: 121 mg
- Total Fat: 10.8 g
- Protein: 28.6 g
- Sodium: 1110 mg

243. Pesto Sauce

"Easy and quick pesto for pasta."
Serving: 16 | Prep: 10m | Ready in: 20m

Ingredients

- 3 cups fresh basil leaves
- 1 1/2 cups chopped walnuts
- 4 cloves garlic, peeled
- 1/4 cup grated Parmesan cheese
- 1 cup olive oil
- salt and pepper to taste

Direction

- Blend cheese, garlic, nuts and basil leaves in a food processor. Slowly pour oil in while mixing. Mix in pepper and salt.

Nutrition Information

- Calories: 199 calories;
- Total Carbohydrate: 2 g
- Cholesterol: 1 mg
- Total Fat: 21.1 g
- Protein: 2.4 g
- Sodium: 20 mg

244. Pizza Margherita From Fleischmann's®

"This is a traditional thin crust pizza."
Serving: 2

Ingredients

- Thin Crust:
- 1 1/4 cups all-purpose flour, divided, or more as needed
- 1 (.25 oz.) envelope Fleischmann's® Pizza Crust Yeast or RapidRise Yeast
- 1 1/2 tsps. sugar
- 3/4 tsp. salt
- 1/2 cup very warm water (120 degrees to 130 degrees F)*
- 2 tbsps. Mazola® Extra Virgin Olive Oil
- Toppings:
- 2 tbsps. Mazola® Extra Virgin Olive Oil
- 1 tsp. minced fresh garlic
- Freshly ground Spice Islands® Sea Salt Adjustable Grinder
- 2 medium tomatoes, thinly sliced
- 1/4 cup chopped fresh basil***
- 1 cup shredded Italian cheese blend
- 1 tsp. Spice Islands® Italian Herb Seasoning

Direction

- Preheat the oven to 425 degrees F.

- In a large bowl, mix 1 cup flour, salt, sugar, and undissolved yeast. Pour in very hot water and oil and then stir thoroughly for about 1 minute until blended.
- Slowly add plenty of the remaining flour to form a soft dough. The dough should form a ball and should be slightly gooey. Knead on a floured surface while adding more flour if need be for about 4 minutes until smooth and elastic. (If you're using RapidRise Yeast, allow the dough stand at this point for ten minutes.)
- Use floured hands to pat the dough to fill the greased baking sheet or pizza pan or roll the dough onto a floured counter to form a 12-inch circle. Transfer into the greased baking sheet or pizza pan. Pinch the edge of dough to form a rim.
- For the toppings: Mix garlic and oil. Rub atop the crust. Add freshly ground sea salt on top. Place in basil and tomato slices and drizzle with cheese. Complete with a drizzle of Italian herb seasoning.
- Bake for 12 to 15 minutes on lowest oven rack, until cheese forms bubble and crust is browned.

Nutrition Information

- Calories: 764 calories;
- Total Carbohydrate: 70.9 g
- Cholesterol: 44 mg
- Total Fat: 44.7 g
- Protein: 22.8 g
- Sodium: 1694 mg

245. Pollo Alla Cacciatore

"Chicken cacciatore recipe with herbs, tomatoes, olives, capers and caramelized onions."
Serving: 8 | Prep: 30m | Ready in: 2h24m

Ingredients

- 12 green olives, pitted
- 1 stalk celery, chopped
- 2 onions, sliced
- 1/2 cup water
- 2 tsps. white sugar
- 1 tbsp. extra-virgin olive oil
- 1 (2 lb.) whole chicken, cut into pieces
- 4 ripe tomatoes, diced
- 1 bunch fresh basil, chopped
- 1 lemon, juiced
- 2 tbsps. capers
- salt and ground black pepper to taste
- 1/4 cup extra-virgin olive oil, or to taste
- 5 potatoes, peeled and cubed

Direction

- Boil a small pot of water, then add celery and olives. Let it simmer for about 30 seconds until the celery turns bright green. Let it drain well.
- In a saucepan, mix together the sugar, water and onions on medium heat. Put cover and let it cook for about 30 minutes, stirring from time to time, until the onions become caramelized and soft.
- In a big frying pan, heat 1 tbsp of olive oil on medium heat. Cook the chicken pieces for around 4 minutes on each side, until it turns brown.
- Move the pieces of chicken to a big saucepan, then add pepper, salt, capers, lemon juice, basil, tomatoes, caramelized onions, celery and olives. Put cover and let it cook for about 1 hour on medium heat, until the chicken has no visible pink color in the middle.
- In a deep frypan, heat 1/4 cup of olive oil, then add potatoes and let it cook and stir for around 10 minutes, until it turns golden brown and becomes crisp. Mix the potatoes into the saucepan briefly prior to taking out of the heat.

Nutrition Information

- Calories: 342 calories;
- Total Carbohydrate: 34.6 g
- Cholesterol: 31 mg
- Total Fat: 17 g
- Protein: 15.1 g
- Sodium: 271 mg

246. Porcini Mushroom Pasta

"This dish is Tagliatelle pasta topped with a porcini mushroom sauce. The sauce is made with herbs, red wine, red bell pepper, and carrot."
Serving: 6

Ingredients

- 1 tbsp. olive oil
- 2 cloves garlic, minced
- 1/2 red onion, minced
- 1/2 cup red bell pepper, julienned
- 1/2 cup julienned carrots
- 1/2 cup dry red wine
- 1 cup rehydrated porcini mushrooms
- 1 1/2 cups crushed tomatoes
- 2 tsps. chopped fresh basil
- 1 tsp. dried rosemary, crushed
- salt and pepper to taste
- 6 cups tagliatelle (wide noodles)

Direction

- In a big skillet, heat oil over medium heat. Add onions and garlic, sauté for 4 minutes, and then add carrots as well as red bell pepper and sauté for another 4 minutes. Pour in red wine, increase the heat and boil for 1 minute; and then lower the heat to medium-low, add mushrooms and cook for 3 minutes.
- Add basil, rosemary and tomatoes and put in pepper and salt to taste. Simmer for 10 minutes and enjoy the sauce on top of the cooked noodles.

Nutrition Information

- Calories: 335 calories;
- Total Carbohydrate: 56.1 g
- Cholesterol: 0 mg
- Total Fat: 4.3 g
- Protein: 13.8 g
- Sodium: 19 mg

247. Pork Chops With Basil And Marsala

"This dish is pork chops dredged in garlic salt and flour, browned, and baked with Marsala wine and basil."
Serving: 6 | Prep: 15m | Ready in: 1h20m

Ingredients

- 1 cup all-purpose flour
- 1 tbsp. garlic salt
- 6 pork loin chops, 1 inch thick
- 1 tbsp. olive oil
- 2 tsps. dried basil
- 1/2 cup Marsala wine
- salt and pepper to taste

Direction

- Turn the oven to 350°F (175°C) to preheat.
- In a big resealable plastic bag, combine garlic salt and flour. In the bag, put the pork chops and shake to coat.
- In a skillet, heat oil over medium heat, and brown both sides of the chops. Remove to a baking dish and sprinkle basil over. Use aluminum foil to cover the pan.
- Bake in the preheated oven for 45 minutes. Take away the foil and add Marsala wine. Keep baking for 15 minutes, basting with the wine from time to time. Skim off and get rid of any fat and use pepper and salt to season the chops and enjoy.

Nutrition Information

- Calories: 211 calories;
- Total Carbohydrate: 19.3 g
- Cholesterol: 30 mg
- Total Fat: 6.2 g
- Protein: 13.2 g
- Sodium: 926 mg

248. Progresso® Baked Ziti Casserole

"Tasty Italian casserole for the whole family."
Serving: 6 | Prep: 20m | Ready in: 55m

Ingredients

- 1 1/2 cups uncooked ziti pasta
- 1 lb. bulk Italian pork sausage
- 1 (9 oz.) pouch Progresso™ Recipe Starters™ fire roasted tomato cooking sauce
- 1 cup ricotta cheese*
- 1/4 cup Parmesan cheese
- 1 egg
- 1 cup shredded mozzarella cheese
- Chopped fresh basil leaves (optional)

Direction

- Set oven to 375° F and start heating. Follow package instructions to cook and drain pasta.
- At the same time, cook sausage in a 12-in. skillet on medium-high heat until no longer pink, mixing occasionally; drain. Put in the cooked pasta, 1/4 tsp. pepper, and cooking sauce; combine well.
- Mix together egg, Parmesan cheese and ricotta cheese in a small bowl.
- Scoop pasta mixture to an ungreased 11x7-in. (2-qt.) glass baking dish. Scoop ricotta cheese mixture atop and sprinkle mozzarella cheese over. Spray cooking spray on sheet of foil; use foil to cover the baking dish with sprayed side down.
- Bake 25-30 minutes till the mixture is bubbly and hot and cheese is melted, taking foil out when there is 10 minutes left for baking. Sprinkle basil over top.

Nutrition Information

- Calories: 438 calories;
- Total Carbohydrate: 29.8 g
- Cholesterol: 88 mg
- Total Fat: 23.4 g
- Protein: 26 g
- Sodium: 977 mg

249. Queenie's Killer Tomato Bagel Sandwich

"This breakfast treat is very easy to prepare."
Serving: 1 | Prep: 10m | Ready in: 10m

Ingredients

- 1 bagel, split and toasted
- 2 tbsps. cream cheese
- 1 roma (plum) tomatoes, thinly sliced
- salt and pepper to taste
- 4 leaves fresh basil

Direction

- Spread on bagel halves with cream cheese, then put tomato slices on top of cream cheese layer. Use pepper and salt to sprinkle over top, then put fresh basil leaves on top.

Nutrition Information

- Calories: 358 calories;
- Total Carbohydrate: 50.8 g
- Cholesterol: 32 mg
- Total Fat: 11.7 g
- Protein: 12.1 g
- Sodium: 564 mg

250. Quick And Easy Greek Spaghetti

"This recipe only requires one pot to make. You can use fresh or canned ingredients. You can enjoy this dish with cheesy bread or crusty garlic bread."
Serving: 4 | Prep: 15m | Ready in: 55m

Ingredients

- 1 (8 oz.) package spaghetti
- extra-virgin olive oil, or as needed
- 1 (10 oz.) bag fresh spinach
- 1 (8 oz.) package sliced fresh mushrooms
- 1/4 cup red wine vinegar

- 1/4 cup balsamic vinegar
- 2 (14.5 oz.) cans diced tomatoes
- 1/4 cup chopped fresh basil
- 1 tbsp. chopped fresh parsley
- 1 (6 oz.) can sliced black olives, drained (optional)
- 2 oz. crumbled feta cheese, or to taste

Direction

- Allow lightly salted water in a big pot to come to a rolling boil. At a boil, cook spaghetti for 12 minutes until soft yet firm to the bite, tossing sometimes. Strain and put aside.
- In a big saucepan, heat olive oil over medium heat. In the hot oil, stir and cook mushrooms and spinach for 10 minutes until they release their liquid. Add balsamic vinegar and red wine vinegar, boil it. Mix black olives, parsley, basil and tomatoes into the boiling mixture, keep stirring and cooking for another 10 minutes until the flavors combine.
- Stir into the tomato mixture with the cooked spaghetti and lower the heat to medium-low. Simmer the sauce and pasta for 8-10 minutes until the flavors combine, mix feta cheese into the pasta. Sprinkle additional feta cheese over and enjoy.

Nutrition Information

- Calories: 413 calories;
- Total Carbohydrate: 60.7 g
- Cholesterol: 13 mg
- Total Fat: 11.7 g
- Protein: 16.1 g
- Sodium: 1095 mg

251. Quick And Easy Grilled Cheese

"It's a truly twist."
Serving: 1 | Prep: 10m | Ready in: 16m

Ingredients

- 1 tbsp. butter, softened
- 2 slices bread
- 2 slices sharp Cheddar cheese
- 1 tbsp. chopped parsley
- 1 tsp. chopped basil
- 1 tsp. oregano
- 1 tsp. chopped fresh rosemary
- 1 tsp. chopped fresh dill

Direction

- Spread on one side of each bread piece with 1/2 tsp. of butter, then lie on the side without butter on one of the bread slices with a Cheddar slice. Sprinkle on the unbuttered side of another bread slice with dill, rosemary, oregano, basil and parsley. Sandwich 2 bread slices together, buttered-sides facing outwards.
- Heat a skillet on medium heat. Once skillet is hot, lie the sandwich in the skillet gently, then cook until cheese is melted, about 3 minutes per side.

Nutrition Information

- Calories: 470 calories;
- Total Carbohydrate: 27.4 g
- Cholesterol: 90 mg
- Total Fat: 32.2 g
- Protein: 18.4 g
- Sodium: 777 mg

252. Quick Sun-dried Tomato And Basil Hummus

"This easy to whip hummus is great with sandwiches and burgers, and best served with crackers, pita wedges and chips."
Serving: 20 | Prep: 15m | Ready in: 15m

Ingredients

- 1 (15.5 oz.) can garbanzo beans, drained (reserve liquid) and rinsed
- 1/2 cup chopped sun-dried tomatoes (not oil-packed)
- 3 cloves garlic
- 2 tbsps. chopped fresh basil leaves
- 1/4 cup grated Parmesan cheese
- 1/4 cup olive oil
- salt and pepper to taste

Direction

- In a food processor, grind together the Parmesan cheese, basil, garlic, sun-dried tomatoes and garbanzo beans for 15 seconds.
- Stir in about 1/4 of the reserved liquid, then grind for 15 seconds more. Put in enough additional reserved liquid a small amount at a time then grind. Redo until you reach a chunky peanut butter consistency.
- Put in olive oil and grind for 15 seconds more. Put pepper and salt to season.

Nutrition Information

- Calories: 59 calories;
- Total Carbohydrate: 5.9 g
- Cholesterol: < 1 mg
- Total Fat: 3.3 g
- Protein: 1.7 g
- Sodium: 110 mg

253. Quinoa Salad With Grilled Vegetables And Cottage Cheese

"A great summer dish that makes a nice side dish, potluck, packed lunch or small snack. Make it ahead of time, because you can make a big batch and refrigerate it for later. It can go up to three days if properly stored.""
Serving: 6 | Prep: 20m | Ready in: 30m

Ingredients

- 1 medium zucchini
- 1 red bell pepper
- 1 yellow bell pepper
- 1 tbsp. Gay Lea Spreadables, melted
- 2 tbsps. balsamic vinegar
- 3 cups cooked quinoa
- 2 green onions, chopped
- 1/4 cup chopped fresh basil leaves
- 1/4 cup chopped fresh parsley leaves
- 1 cup Nordica 2% Cottage Cheese
- 2 tsps. finely grated lemon zest
- 2 tbsps. fresh lemon juice
- 1 clove garlic, minced
- 3/4 tsp. salt
- 3/4 tsp. pepper
- 1/4 cup toasted pine nuts

Direction

- Set grill to preheat at medium-high. Cut the zucchini into lengthwise strips. Remove the core and cut the peppers into quarters. Toss these veggies with half of the balsamic vinegar and the melted Spreadable. Grill them for 7-10 minutes, until soft and well-marked. Turn to cook all sides. Let cool to room temperature, then slice into bite-sized portions.
- Mix the sliced veggies with onion, cooked quinoa, parsley and basil. Mix cottage cheese with lemon juice and zest, salt, pepper, garlic, and the rest of the balsamic vinegar. Mix cottage cheese dressing with quinoa mixture. Combine well. Top with pine nuts if you wish.

Nutrition Information

- Calories: 226 calories;

- Total Carbohydrate: 28.7 g
- Cholesterol: 9 mg
- Total Fat: 7.7 g
- Protein: 11.7 g
- Sodium: 421 mg

254. Ravioli With Cherry Tomatoes And Cheese

"Sausage ravioli are particularly good."
Serving: 10 | Prep: 15m | Ready in: 1h20m

Ingredients

- 1 pint red and yellow cherry tomatoes, halved
- 1 (16 oz.) package shredded mozzarella cheese
- 1/3 cup fresh basil, chopped
- 1/2 cup olive oil
- 5 cloves garlic, minced
- 1 tbsp. chopped fresh parsley
- salt and pepper to taste
- 1 (25 oz.) package frozen ravioli

Direction

- Toss together the pepper, salt, parsley, garlic, olive oil, basil, mozzarella cheese, and cherry tomatoes in a big bowl. Let rest for about an hour.
- Boil a pot of lightly salted water, and cook ravioli for about 5 minutes till heated through and tender. Let drain, and toss together with the cherry tomato mixture, serve.

Nutrition Information

- Calories: 452 calories;
- Total Carbohydrate: 32.4 g
- Cholesterol: 59 mg
- Total Fat: 26.8 g
- Protein: 21.4 g
- Sodium: 689 mg

255. Red And Yellow Cherry Tomato Salad

"This recipe is a great way to use summer tomatoes."
Serving: 4 | Prep: 15m | Ready in: 15m

Ingredients

- 6 cups red and yellow cherry tomatoes, some halved
- salt and ground black pepper to taste
- 2/3 cup buttermilk
- 1/4 cup sour cream
- 3 tbsps. chopped fresh basil
- 1 shallot, minced
- 2 cloves garlic, minced

Direction

- In a big serving bowl, put tomatoes, use pepper and salt to season and mix.
- In another bowl, whisk together garlic, shallot, basil, sour cream and buttermilk using a whisk; use pepper and salt to season. Drizzle over the tomatoes with the dressing and mix to coat.

Nutrition Information

- Calories: 106 calories;
- Total Carbohydrate: 15.6 g
- Cholesterol: 8 mg
- Total Fat: 4.1 g
- Protein: 4.2 g
- Sodium: 111 mg

256. Red Cabbage Slaw With A Twist

""I attempted to create a salad filled with colors and interesting flavors. I especially wanted to use ginger as it has an abundance of great properties!""
Serving: 6 | Prep: 20m | Ready in: 20m

Ingredients

- 3 cups thinly sliced red cabbage

- 3/4 cup diced red bell pepper
- 2 shallots, diced
- 1 (1 inch) piece fresh ginger, peeled and minced
- 10 leaves fresh basil, snipped
- 1/4 cup mayonnaise
- 1 lemon, juiced
- 2 tbsps. olive oil
- 1 1/2 tsps. wasabi paste
- freshly ground multi-colored peppercorns to taste
- 1/4 cup toasted pine nuts
- 2 tbsps. salted sunflower kernels

Direction

- In a big bowl, mix basil, ginger, shallots, red bell pepper and cabbage together. In a separate bowl, combine ground pepper, wasabi paste, olive oil, lemon juice and mayonnaise before stirring it into the cabbage mixture. Finish off with sunflower kernels and pine nuts over the top.

Nutrition Information

- Calories: 193 calories;
- Total Carbohydrate: 11.2 g
- Cholesterol: 3 mg
- Total Fat: 16.4 g
- Protein: 3.4 g
- Sodium: 92 mg

257. Red Curry Butternut Squash

"This dish will certain be one of your favorites!"
Serving: 6 | Prep: 15m | Ready in: 40m

Ingredients

- 1 bunch green onions
- 1 tbsp. vegetable oil
- 2 tbsps. tomato paste
- 1 tbsp. red curry powder
- 1 tsp. ground cumin
- 1 tsp. red curry paste

- 3 cloves garlic, crushed
- 1 (14 oz.) can coconut milk
- 3 tbsps. fish sauce
- 1 1/2 tbsps. brown sugar
- 1 (3 lb.) butternut squash - peeled, seeded, and cut into 1-inch cubes
- 1/4 cup torn fresh basil leaves

Direction

- Chop the green onions; for garnish, reserve one tbsp. of the chopped green onion tops. In a heavy saucepan or Dutch oven, heat the vegetable oil over medium heat; sauté red curry paste, cumin, red curry powder, tomato paste and larger portion of green onions in hot oil for 5 mins or until the seasonings and green onions give off toasted smell and sizzle. Mix the garlic into the green onion mixture; sauté for one more minute or until the garlic is fragrant.
- Put the coconut milk into the Dutch oven. Stir until the mixture is thoroughly combined. Mix the brown sugar and fish sauce into the coconut milk sauce, stirring to dissolve the brown sugar. Bring the sauce to a simmer.
- Mix the butternut squash cubes into the sauce. Adjust the heat to medium-low, cover with a lid. Stir gently every 5 mins for about 20 mins in total or until the squash are tender. The squash is easily overcooked so watch it carefully. Mix the basil leaves into the butternut squash. Taste for spiciness and salt; if needed, adjust the seasoning. Place into the serving dish and scatter with the reserved green onions.

Nutrition Information

- Calories: 291 calories;
- Total Carbohydrate: 37.2 g
- Cholesterol: 0 mg
- Total Fat: 17.2 g
- Protein: 5.5 g
- Sodium: 632 mg

258. Red Curry Flank Steak

"This Thai red curry beef recipe is so wonderful."
Serving: 4 | Prep: 5m | Ready in: 1h20m

Ingredients

- 1/4 cup seasoned rice vinegar
- 3 tbsps. fish sauce
- 1 tbsp. freshly grated ginger
- 3 cloves garlic, crushed
- 1 tsp. hot sauce
- 1 tsp. red curry powder
- 1/2 tsp. red curry paste
- 1 (1 1/2-lb.) flank steak
- 1 bunch fresh basil

Direction

- Mix red curry paste, red curry powder, hot sauce, garlic, grated ginger, fish sauce and rice vinegar in the shallow dish. Put them aside.
- Puncture the flank steak a few times using the fork and put into vinegar mixture. Keep it covered and let marinate at the room temperature for 60 minutes.
- Preheat the outdoor grill to high heat, and grease grate lightly with oil.
- Add the steak onto grill and top steak with basil. Grill the steak for 6 minutes. Take out the basil, flip the meat, and add the basil back over the steak. Cook steak roughly 6 minutes longer or till steak starts to firm and hot and pink a bit in middle. The instant-read thermometer inserted to middle should register 54 degrees C (130 degrees F).

Nutrition Information

- Calories: 176 calories;
- Total Carbohydrate: 5.5 g
- Cholesterol: 37 mg
- Total Fat: 7.1 g
- Protein: 21.6 g
- Sodium: 1220 mg

259. Red Pepper Pesto Pasta

"This pesto is very delicious."
Serving: 6 | Prep: 5m | Ready in: 20m

Ingredients

- 1 lb. penne pasta
- 2 bunches fresh basil leaves
- 1 cup roasted red pepper
- 3/4 cup grated Parmesan cheese
- 1 cup olive oil
- salt and pepper to taste

Direction

- Boil lightly salted water in a big pot. Mix penne into the water and boil again. Cook for 11 minutes until pasta is mostly soft but remains firm to the bite, strain. Remove the drained pasta to a big bowl.
- In the bowl of a food processor, put Parmesan cheese, red pepper and basil; add olive oil to the mixture in a stream as it processes until smooth. Use pepper and salt to season. Drizzle over the cooked pasta with the sauce and mix to coat.

Nutrition Information

- Calories: 678 calories;
- Total Carbohydrate: 61.4 g
- Cholesterol: 9 mg
- Total Fat: 41 g
- Protein: 16.2 g
- Sodium: 286 mg

260. Red Pepper Scallops On Potato Pancakes

"Fun and fast."
Serving: 4 | Prep: 15m | Ready in: 55m

Ingredients

- 1/2 red bell pepper
- 3/4 cup cold mashed potatoes

- 1 egg, beaten
- 2 tbsps. dry bread crumbs
- 1 pinch salt and freshly ground black pepper to taste
- 1 lb. scallops
- 1 tsp. olive oil
- cayenne pepper to taste
- 1/4 cup fresh whole basil leaves, or to taste
- 1 tbsp. butter
- 1 tbsp. capers
- 1/4 cup water

Direction

- Put oven rack 6 inches from heat source; preheat oven broiler. Line aluminum foil on a baking sheet; put pepper on prepped baking sheet, cut side down.
- Cook pepper under preheated broiler for 5-8 minutes till pepper skin blisters and blackens. Put blackened pepper into a bowl; seal with plastic wrap tightly. Let pepper steam for 20 minutes while it cools. Remove then discard skin; slice pepper thinly.
- Mix black pepper, salt, breadcrumbs, egg and mashed potatoes till smooth in a bowl.
- Heat olive oil in big nonstick skillet on medium heat; drop batter by spoonfuls in batches into hot oil. Flatten out to make small pancake; cook for 7 minutes till crispy and golden on 1 side. Flip; cook for 5-7 minutes longer till crispy and golden on other side. Use paper towel to wipe skillet clean.
- Put scallops in a bowl; season with salt, cayenne pepper and olive oil.
- Heat the same nonstick skillet on high heat. Put scallops in middle of skillet; put red peppers in a pile in skillet's side. Cook scallops for 3-4 minutes till golden curst develops. Put scallops onto a plate; keep peppers in skillet.
- Mix and cook capers, butter, basil and peppers in hot skillet. Add water to skillet; mix sauce. Take off heat.
- In 1 layer, put pancakes on a platter/plates; on each pancake, put 2-3 scallops. Put pepper sauce on top.

Nutrition Information

- Calories: 296 calories;
- Total Carbohydrate: 19.5 g
- Cholesterol: 109 mg
- Total Fat: 15.5 g
- Protein: 19.1 g
- Sodium: 657 mg

261. Red, White, And Blue Bruschetta

"Toasted baguette topped with a bean mixture."
Serving: 6 | Prep: 25m | Ready in: 30m

Ingredients

- 1 (15 oz.) can great northern beans, drained (reserve liquid)
- 1/4 cup chopped fresh thyme
- 2 oz. crumbled Gorgonzola cheese
- 4 sun-dried tomatoes, drained and minced
- 1/2 tsp. ground black pepper
- 1 clove garlic, minced
- 1 multigrain baguette, cut into 3/4-inch thick slices on the bias
- 1 clove garlic, halved
- 1 (4 oz.) log goat cheese, softened
- 12 leaves fresh basil, or as needed

Direction

- Place the oven rack 6 inches away from the heat source and preheat the broiler.
- In a saucepan, add 1/4 cup of liquid and heat the great northern beans over low heat. Add 1 clove of minced garlic, black pepper, sun-dried tomatoes, Gorgonzola cheese, and thyme and stir together. Melt the Gorgonzola cheese on a gentle heat. Keep warm.
- On a baking sheet, toast the baguette slices for 1 minute under the broiler. Keep an eye on them. Take the baguette out and rub a garlic clove over each slice. Spread a layer of goat cheese over each slice of bread and add a basil

leaf on top. Add the bean mixture on top, then serve.

Nutrition Information

- Calories: 354 calories;
- Total Carbohydrate: 49 g
- Cholesterol: 25 mg
- Total Fat: 9.7 g
- Protein: 18.4 g
- Sodium: 590 mg

262. Refreshing Blueberry Soda

"You can use fresh mint leaves as the substitution for basil leaves."
Serving: 8 | Prep: 10m | Ready in: 30m

Ingredients

- 1 cup water
- 1 cup white sugar
- 2 cups fresh basil
- 2 cups blueberries
- 1/2 cup water
- 2 tbsps. lemon juice
- 4 cups carbonated sparkling water

Direction

- In a saucepan, heat 1 cup of water to a boil. Mix basil and sugar into the water, bring back to a boil. Cook in boiling water for 10 minutes then take away from heat right away. Chill 10 minutes in the fridge until lightly cooled.
- In a blender, blend lemon juice, 1/2 cup water and blueberries until smooth; transfer to a pitcher. Take basil leaves out of the simple-syrup mixture and discard. Mix syrup into the blueberry mixture. Pour carbonated water into the mixture; mix gradually.

Nutrition Information

- Calories: 121 calories;
- Total Carbohydrate: 30.9 g
- Cholesterol: 0 mg

- Total Fat: 0.2 g
- Protein: 0.6 g
- Sodium: 6 mg

263. Ricotta And Margherita® Salami Manicotti

"Margherita® Genoa Salami with mozzarella cheeses, Romano and ricotta."
Serving: 6 | Prep: 10m | Ready in: 1h30m

Ingredients

- 1 (15 oz.) container ricotta cheese
- 8 oz. Margherita® Genoa Salami, sliced 1/8 inch thick, chopped*
- 1/4 cup shredded Romano or Parmesan cheese
- 1/2 cup chopped fresh basil or Italian parsley, divided
- 12 manicotti pasta shells, uncooked
- 1 (24 oz.) jar pasta sauce with mushrooms
- 1 cup water
- 2 cups shredded mozzarella cheese

Direction

- Heat the oven to 350 °F. Mix a quarter cup basil, Romano cheese, salami and ricotta cheese; combine thoroughly. In the uncooked manicotti shells, place the mixture.
- Mix water and pasta sauce; in the bottom of 13x9-inch baking dish, place a cup of mixture. Set the manicotti shells on top of the sauce; scoop the rest of the sauce on top of shells covering entirely.
- Cover the dish using foil; bake for an hour to an hour and 5 minutes or till pasta is soft once pricked with a knife. Remove the cover; place mozzarella cheese on top. Put back into oven; bake for 10 minutes or till bubbly and cheese is melted. Put leftover a quarter cup basil on top.

Nutrition Information

- Calories: 579 calories;

- Total Carbohydrate: 45.3 g
- Cholesterol: 91 mg
- Total Fat: 29.6 g
- Protein: 32.8 g
- Sodium: 1485 mg

264. Ricotta Spaghetti

"This recipe is sure to become your favorite!"
Serving: 6 | Prep: 10m | Ready in: 25m

Ingredients

- 3/4 lb. spaghetti
- 1 clove garlic, minced
- 1 cup part-skim ricotta cheese
- 2 tsps. chopped fresh basil
- salt and ground black pepper to taste
- 2 tbsps. grated Parmesan cheese

Direction

- Fill lightly salted water in a large pot and bring to a rolling boil over high heat. Stir in the spaghetti when water is boiling, then bring back to a boil. Cook pasta, uncovered, for about 12 mins, stirring occasionally, until pasta has cooked through yet still firm to bite. Let it drain well in a colander placed in the sink, saving two tbsps. cooking water.
- In a saucepan, stir basil, ricotta, and garlic over medium-low for about 4 mins until hot. Season with pepper and salt to taste; stir in reserved water from cooking the pasta and spaghetti. Sprinkle with the Parmesan cheese. Enjoy.

Nutrition Information

- Calories: 275 calories;
- Total Carbohydrate: 44.7 g
- Cholesterol: 14 mg
- Total Fat: 4.6 g
- Protein: 12.8 g
- Sodium: 80 mg

265. Rigatoni Al Segreto (rigatoni With Secret Sauce)

""My version of the famous Rigatoni al Segreto recipe of NYC popular Italian restaurants. This has a generous amount of butter.""
Serving: 4 | Prep: 15m | Ready in: 1h10m

Ingredients

- 4 tbsps. olive oil
- 1 cup diced onion
- 1 tsp. salt, plus more to taste
- 2 cloves garlic, crushed (or more to taste)
- 1 pinch red pepper flakes
- 1 (28 oz.) can San Marzano (Italian) tomatoes, blended smooth
- 1/2 cup water (to rinse out can of tomatoes)
- 1 (8 oz.) package uncooked rigatoni pasta
- 1/2 cup fresh basil leaves, thinly sliced
- 4 tbsps. cold butter, cubed
- 1 cup grated Parmigiano-Reggiano cheese, plus more for serving

Direction

- In a saucepan, warm oil in medium-high fire. Once warm, mix in onions and salt. Let it cook for about 5 minutes until it begins to become transparent. Mix in garlic and stir for about 60 seconds. Mix in blended tomato sauce and chili flakes. Let it simmer and regulate heat from medium to medium-low heat. Continue to simmer gently for 45 to 60 minutes with occasional stirring. Lower down heat to low.
- Allow to boil a big pot of lightly salted water. Once boiling, cook rigatoni for 8 minutes or 5 minutes from doneness with occasional stirring until al dente.
- Add 2/3 of the basil to the sauce. Mix in butter. Dissolve butter and mix in cheese in 3 additions.
- Strain pasta and decant to sauce. Evenly coat rigatoni pasta with sauce by stirring. Garnish with grated cheese and then serve.

Nutrition Information

- Calories: 596 calories;
- Total Carbohydrate: 57.9 g
- Cholesterol: 48 mg
- Total Fat: 33 g
- Protein: 17.7 g
- Sodium: 1431 mg

---

266. Rigatoni With Eggplant, Peppers, And Tomatoes

"I got this recipe from one of my Italian. You can enjoy it with Parmesan cheese if you want."
Serving: 6 | Prep: 30m | Ready in: 1h

Ingredients

- 2 tbsps. olive oil
- 2 eggplants, diced with skin
- 1 red bell pepper, sliced
- 2 cloves garlic, minced
- salt and black pepper to taste
- 1 tbsp. olive oil
- 6 tomatoes - peeled, seeded, and chopped
- 1 sprig fresh thyme, chopped
- 1 lb. rigatoni pasta
- 12 basil leaves, chopped
- 12 black olives, sliced

Direction

- In a big skillet, heat 2 tbsps. of olive oil over medium-high heat. In the hot oil, cook diced eggplant for 10 minutes until turning light brown, tossing often. Mix in garlic and red pepper, use pepper and salt to season. Lower the heat to medium-low, put a cover on and cook for 20 minutes until the vegetables are soft.
- In the meantime, in a saucepan, heat 1 tbsp. of olive oil over medium-high heat. Mix in chopped tomatoes and simmer it, use pepper, salt and fresh thyme to season. Lower the heat to medium-low and simmer for 15 minutes until the tomatoes have slightly decreased.

- Boil lightly salted water in a big pot, mix in rigatoni and cook without a cover for 13 minutes until soft but remain firm to the bite, tossing sometimes. Strain and put back into the pot.
- Mix the eggplant mixture into the pasta together with olives and basil. Top with the tomato sauce using a spoon and enjoy.

Nutrition Information

- Calories: 400 calories;
- Total Carbohydrate: 65.4 g
- Cholesterol: 0 mg
- Total Fat: 9.9 g
- Protein: 12.4 g
- Sodium: 96 mg

---

267. Rigatoni With Pizza Accents

"This recipe was passed from generation to generation."
Serving: 8

Ingredients

- 1 (16 oz.) package rigatoni pasta
- 2 lbs. Italian sausage
- 2 onions, chopped
- 2 cloves garlic, minced
- 1 green bell pepper, chopped
- 1 lb. fresh mushrooms, sliced
- 2 (14.5 oz.) cans stewed tomatoes, undrained
- 2 (6 oz.) cans tomato paste
- 3 1/2 oz. sliced pepperoni sausage
- 1 tbsp. chopped fresh basil
- 1/2 lb. diced pepperoni
- salt and ground black pepper to taste

Direction

- In a big pot filled with boiling salted water, cook rigatoni pasta until al dente; drain thoroughly and put aside.
- Fry sausage in a big skillet until cooked through yet not brown. Put in minced garlic and chopped onion. Mix and cook until soft.

Put in sliced mushrooms; cook 5 minutes. Put in chopped green pepper; slowly cook until soft. Drain to remove excess fat.

- Mix in pepperoni, fresh basil, tomato paste, and tomatoes with their juice; heat to a boil. Lower heat; put in cooked rigatoni noodles. Season to taste with pepper and salt.
- Allow to simmer, mixing occasionally, about 20 minutes until most liquid is cooked off.

Nutrition Information

- Calories: 780 calories;
- Total Carbohydrate: 66.2 g
- Cholesterol: 87 mg
- Total Fat: 41.2 g
- Protein: 37.3 g
- Sodium: 2183 mg

268. Ro's Spaghetti And Meatballs

""These comfort meatballs bring back childhood memories.""
Serving: 6 | Prep: 25m | Ready in: 1h15m

Ingredients

- Tomato Sauce:
- 1/4 cup olive oil
- 3 cloves garlic, minced
- 1 large onion, sliced
- 2 (14 oz.) cans diced tomatoes
- 2 tbsps. chopped fresh basil
- Meatballs:
- 8 oz. ground beef
- 1 cup graham cracker crumbs
- 2 eggs
- 2 tbsps. grated Parmesan cheese
- 1/4 cup chopped fresh parsley
- 3 tbsps. olive oil
- 1 (12 oz.) package spaghetti
- salt and pepper to taste
- chopped fresh basil
- grated Parmesan cheese

Direction

- In a large saucepan, combine 2 tbsps. of chopped basil, tomatoes, onion, garlic and 1/4 cup of olive oil; allow to boil. Season with pepper and salt. Lower the heat; gently simmer for at least 40 minutes.
- Meanwhile, in a large bowl, combine 3 tbsps. of olive oil, parsley, 2 tbsps. of Parmesan cheese, eggs, graham cracker crumbs and ground beef together. Stir properly with clean hands; roll into 20 walnut-sized meatballs. Place a large skillet on medium-high heat; fry in the meatballs for around 10 minutes, till cooked through and well browned. Place the cooked meatballs into the tomato sauce; gently simmer while boiling the pasta.
- Pour salted water into a large pot; allow to boil; mix in spaghetti. Cook the pasta for around 12 minutes, till cooked through but still firm to bite. Strain properly. Toss the spaghetti with the meatballs and sauce carefully. Sprinkle each plate with Parmesan cheese and fresh basil. Serve.

Nutrition Information

- Calories: 551 calories;
- Total Carbohydrate: 61.7 g
- Cholesterol: 88 mg
- Total Fat: 25.4 g
- Protein: 19.6 g
- Sodium: 400 mg

269. Roasted Cauliflower Pasta Toss

"A simple creamy meatless dish carrying only 500 calories/serving to enjoy for a weeknight meal."
Serving: 6 | Prep: 10m | Ready in: 1h

Ingredients

- 1 (2 lb.) cauliflower
- 2 tbsps. Gay Lea Spreadables, Original or Gay Lea Salted Butter, melted

- 3 large cloves garlic, minced
- 1/2 tsp. salt, divided
- 1/2 tsp. pepper, divided
- 1 cup Gay Lea Gold 18% Sour Cream
- 1/2 cup grated Parmesan cheese, or as needed
- 1 lb. short pasta, such as rotini
- 1/2 cup finely chopped sun-dried tomatoes
- 1/2 cup finely chopped fresh basil leaves

Direction

- Set an oven to 190°C (375°F) and start preheating.
- Cut cauliflower and break into small florets. Toss 1/2 each of pepper and salt, the garlic, and melted butter together with cauliflower. Scatter over a rimmed baking sheet lined with parchment paper. Roast and stir once until brown and golden, for 30-40 minutes.
- Put a cup of cauliflower (250 ml) into a food processor. Put in the remaining pepper and salt, Parmesan cheese, and sour cream; then process until smooth.
- In the meantime, in a large pot with boiling salted water, cook the pasta. Save 1 1/2 cups of the cooking water (375 ml), then drain the pasta.
- Toss the hot cooked pasta together with basil, sun-dried tomatoes, leftover roasted cauliflower and the sour cream mixture; put in enough amount of the saved pasta water to keep the pasta saucy and moist. Serve right away along with more Parmesan cheese on the table.

Nutrition Information

- Calories: 479 calories;
- Total Carbohydrate: 71 g
- Cholesterol: 40 mg
- Total Fat: 14 g
- Protein: 19 g
- Sodium: 511 mg

270. Roasted Eggplant Sandwiches

""The eggplant is roasted on a grain roll with basil, Boursin® cheese, and fresh tomato.""
Serving: 2 | Prep: 15m | Ready in: 30m

Ingredients

- 1 tbsp. olive oil, or as needed
- 1 small eggplant, halved lengthwise and sliced
- 2 (6 inch) whole-grain sandwich rolls, split
- 1/4 cup Greek yogurt
- 1 tbsp. garlic-and-herb spreadable cheese (such as Boursin®)
- 2 cloves garlic, minced
- 1 Roma (plum) tomato, sliced
- 1/4 cup chopped fresh basil leaves

Direction

- Position the oven rack 6-inches away from the heat source. Set the oven's broiler to preheating.
- Coat both sides of eggplant slices with olive oil. Place the eggplant slices on a baking sheet.
- Place it under the broiler and cook each side for 5 minutes until browned lightly and tender.
- Place the split rolls under the broiler, cut-sides up, and then toast for 2-3 minutes until browned lightly.
- In a small bowl, mix the garlic, cheese, and yogurt until smooth. Spread the mixture all over the rolls. Distribute the slices of eggplant among the rolls. To finish the sandwiches up, add the basil and slices of tomato.

Nutrition Information

- Calories: 389 calories;
- Total Carbohydrate: 51 g
- Cholesterol: 14 mg
- Total Fat: 16.8 g
- Protein: 10.7 g
- Sodium: 487 mg

271. Roasted Peppers In Oil (peperoni Arrostiti Sotto Olio)

""My Italian mother-in-law taught me how to make these. She doesn't write down any of her recipes but rather, she just makes them the way she always has for years. They can also be used in different dishes like for example bruschetta or pureed with cream over pasta, etc. Usually, I would just make them as a side dish for any meal on our dinner table.""

Serving: 6 | Prep: 10m | Ready in: 30m

Ingredients

- 1 red bell pepper
- 1 yellow bell pepper
- 1 orange bell pepper
- 3/4 cup extra-virgin olive oil
- 1 clove garlic, minced
- 5 leaves fresh basil leaves, finely sliced
- 1/2 tsp. dried oregano
- 1/2 tsp. salt
- 1/4 tsp. ground black pepper

Direction

- The outdoor grill should be preheated for high heat and the grate should be lightly oiled. Lower down the grill heat to medium.
- Get whole peppers and grill them, turning them about every 5 minutes until all their sides are charred. Put them in a plastic food storage bag, tie it shut and leave them peppers to cool.
- In a 1-pint glass jar (or a bigger one if the size of the peppers are big), mix together the olive oil, basil, garlic, oregano, salt, and pepper.
- Take the cooled peppers out of the bag and remove the charred skins. Slice the peppers in half and take out the seeds and stems. Cut the peppers into long strips and put the strips in the oil mixture. Mix it properly to make sure that the peppers are well covered in oil then serve. Leftover peppers can be stored in the refrigerator for up to 5 days.

Nutrition Information

- Calories: 270 calories;
- Total Carbohydrate: 4 g
- Cholesterol: 0 mg
- Total Fat: 28.2 g
- Protein: 0.7 g
- Sodium: 196 mg

272. Roasted Red Pepper Aioli

"A scrumptious dressing for fish, poultry and burgers that is lively and velvety."

Serving: 20 | Prep: 10m | Ready in: 10m

Ingredients

- 2 whole roasted red peppers
- 2/3 cup fresh basil leaves
- 2 tbsps. lemon juice
- 3 cloves garlic, peeled and halved, or more to taste
- 1 1/2 cups light mayonnaise (such as Hellmann's® Light)
- 2 tsps. white sugar
- 1 tsp. salt, or to taste
- 1 tsp. ground black pepper, or to taste

Direction

- In a food processor, put basil and roasted red peppers; pulse until coarsely chopped and mixed. Put in the lemon juice; pulse 3 times. Scatter the garlic halves on the mixture; pulse to chop for 4 to 5 times. Put in sugar and mayonnaise; pulse for 5 to 7 times, until smooth. Add salt and pepper to season.

Nutrition Information

- Calories: 64 calories;
- Total Carbohydrate: 2.8 g
- Cholesterol: 6 mg
- Total Fat: 6 g
- Protein: 0.4 g
- Sodium: 270 mg

273. Roasted Tomato Caprese Salad

"A new version of the typical Caprese salad!"
Serving: 6 | Prep: 15m | Ready in: 2h45m

Ingredients

- 8 roma (plum) tomatoes, halved lengthwise and seeded
- 1/4 cup extra-virgin olive oil
- 1 1/2 tbsps. balsamic vinegar
- 1 1/2 tsps. minced garlic
- 2 tsps. white sugar
- sea salt to taste
- ground black pepper to taste
- 1 (16 oz.) package fresh salted mozzarella cheese, sliced 1/4-inch thick
- 8 leaves fresh basil, cut in very thin strips
- 1 tbsp. extra-virgin olive oil, or to taste
- 1 1/2 tsps. balsamic vinegar, or to taste

Direction

- Set oven to 275°F (135°C) and start preheating
- Cut tomatoes and lay them, cut sides up, on a baking sheet. Drizzle with 1 1/2 tbsp. balsamic vinegar and 1/4 cup olive oil, sprinkle with black pepper, sea salt, sugar and garlic.
- Roast tomatoes in preheated oven for about 2 hours until juices becomes sticky and thick and they start to turn brown. Allow tomatoes to cool to room temperature.
- On a serving platter, place in slices of mozzarella cheese and tomato halves, arrange cheese and tomatoes alternatively to make a pretty pattern; add basil on top of salad. Drizzle with 1 1/2 tsp. balsamic vinegar and 1 tbsp. extra-virgin olive oil

Nutrition Information

- Calories: 346 calories;
- Total Carbohydrate: 7.4 g
- Cholesterol: 60 mg
- Total Fat: 28 g
- Protein: 14.4 g
- Sodium: 167 mg

274. Roasted Tomato Sauce

""Roasting the tomatoes draws out the sweet flavor mixing very well with the roasted garlic.""
Serving: 2 | Prep: 10m | Ready in: 50m

Ingredients

- 1 lb. roma (plum) tomatoes, halved and seeded
- 2 cloves garlic, peeled
- 1 tbsp. olive oil
- 1 pinch salt and freshly ground black pepper to taste
- 10 leaves basil, torn

Direction

- Set the oven at 375°F (190°C) and start preheating. Use aluminum foil or parchment paper to line a baking sheet.
- Arrange tomato halves skin-side down on the prepared baking sheet. Include in garlic cloves. Equally drizzle garlic and tomatoes with olive oil; flavor with pepper and salt.
- Roast in the preheated oven for around 25 minutes till tomatoes are bubbling. Turn the heat up to 425°F (220°C). Roast for 10 more minutes till the tomatoes just start to brown. Turn off the heat. Let the tomatoes stand in the hot oven, door closed for around 5 minutes till further caramelized.
- Move garlic and roasted tomatoes to a bowl. Include in basil; use a wooden spoon to crush the mixture and break apart the tomatoes; leave them a tad chunky. Remove peels, if you want. Serve over your favorite cooked pasta.

Nutrition Information

- Calories: 106 calories;
- Total Carbohydrate: 10 g
- Cholesterol: 0 mg
- Total Fat: 7.2 g
- Protein: 2.3 g

- Sodium: 90 mg

275. Ron's Grilled Shrimp

"This mouth-watering grilled shrimp is marinated in a flavorful mix of basil, citrus juices, parsley, cilantro, and garlic. Use metal or soaked wooden skewers if you don't own a grill basket and remember to flip skewers once when cooking."
Serving: 4 | Prep: 15m | Ready in: 2h21m

Ingredients

- 1/4 cup lime juice
- 1/4 cup lemon juice
- 1/3 cup olive oil
- 2 tbsps. red wine vinegar
- 2 tbsps. finely chopped fresh cilantro
- 2 tbsps. finely chopped fresh parsley
- 2 tbsps. finely chopped fresh basil
- 1/4 tsp. salt
- 1/4 tsp. pepper
- 1 tbsp. minced garlic
- 1/2 tsp. crushed red pepper
- 2 lbs. jumbo shrimp, peeled and deveined

Direction

- In a big bowl, mix together vinegar, lime juice, olive oil, and lemon juice. Stir in crushed red pepper, cilantro, garlic, parsley, pepper, salt, and basil until well combined.
- Toss shrimp in the mixture until coated then cover and let it chill in the refrigerator for 1-2 hours, stirring intermittently.
- Preheat the grill on medium-high heat.
- Arrange the marinated shrimp in a grill basket. Grill for 5-6 minutes until the shrimp is non-transparent in the middle and pink on the outside. Keep on stirring as it cooks.

Nutrition Information

- Calories: 350 calories;
- Total Carbohydrate: 4.3 g
- Cholesterol: 346 mg
- Total Fat: 20 g

- Protein: 37.5 g
- Sodium: 546 mg

276. Rosemary Roasted Turkey

"Moist and full of flavor turkey"
Serving: 16 | Prep: 25m | Ready in: 4h45m

Ingredients

- 3/4 cup olive oil
- 3 tbsps. minced garlic
- 2 tbsps. chopped fresh rosemary
- 1 tbsp. chopped fresh basil
- 1 tbsp. Italian seasoning
- 1 tsp. ground black pepper
- salt to taste
- 1 (12 lb.) whole turkey

Direction

- Preheat the oven to 165°C or 325°F.
- Combine the salt, black pepper, Italian seasoning, basil, rosemary, garlic and olive oil in a small bowl. Reserve.
- Rinse turkey inside and out; pat it dry. Get rid any big fat deposits. Loosen the breast skin by gently working fingers between breast and skin. Loosen it to the end of drumstick, ensuring not to tear the skin.
- Apply a liberal amount of rosemary mixture beneath the breast skin and down the thigh and leg with your hand. Massage the rest of the rosemary mixture on the outer part of breast. Secure the skin over any exposed breast meat with toothpicks.
- In roasting pan, put turkey on rack. Into the base of pan, put approximately a quarter inch of water. In the prepped oven, roast for 3 to 4 hours, or till the inner temperature of turkey reads 80°C or 180°F.

Nutrition Information

- Calories: 596 calories;
- Total Carbohydrate: 0.8 g
- Cholesterol: 198 mg

- Total Fat: 33.7 g
- Protein: 68.1 g
- Sodium: 165 mg

277. Rustic Tomato Basil Tart

"This delicious piecrust is made with Mozzarella cheese."
Serving: 6 | Prep: 15m | Ready in: 40m

Ingredients

- 1 refrigerated rolled ready-to-use pie crust
- 3 medium plum tomatoes, thinly sliced crosswise
- 1 tbsp. balsamic glaze
- 1/4 cup chopped fresh basil
- 1 3/4 cups Sargento ® Shredded Reduced Sodium Mozzarella Cheese, divided

Direction

- On a baking sheet, unroll the pie crust. Put 1 cup cheese on top, except 1 1/2-in. the border around the edges. Arrange 1 layer of the tomatoes over the cheese. Evenly drizzle over the tomatoes with balsamic glaze, put the leftover cheese and basil on top.
- Fold over the filling with the pie crust edges, tucking and pressing the edges down onto the tart.
- Put on the lowest oven rack of a preheated 375 degrees F oven and bake until turning golden brown, or about 25 minutes. Let it sit for 15 minutes. Slice into wedges. Enjoy at room temperature or warm.

Nutrition Information

- Calories: 254 calories;
- Total Carbohydrate: 15.6 g
- Cholesterol: 12 mg
- Total Fat: 15.3 g
- Protein: 11.5 g
- Sodium: 391 mg

278. Saigon Noodle Salad

"A great way to use leftover grilled shrimp or meat."
Serving: 4 | Prep: 25m | Ready in: 30m

Ingredients

- Dressing:
- 1/4 cup water, or more to taste
- 3 tbsps. lime juice
- 3 tbsps. fish sauce
- 3 tbsps. brown sugar, or more to taste
- 1 clove garlic, minced
- 1 tsp. minced fresh ginger root
- 1/2 tsp. Sriracha chile sauce
- Salad:
- 1 (8 oz.) package (linguine-width) rice noodles
- 2 cups thinly sliced Napa (Chinese) cabbage
- 1 1/2 cups matchstick-cut carrots
- 8 oz. grilled shrimp
- 1 cup bean sprouts
- 1/2 English cucumber, halved lengthwise and cut into thin slices
- 2 green onions, thinly sliced
- 2 2/3 tbsps. chopped fresh mint
- 2 2/3 tbsps. chopped fresh cilantro
- 2 2/3 tbsps. chopped fresh basil
- 1/2 cup coarsely chopped peanuts

Direction

- Mix Sriracha, ginger, garlic, brown sugar, fish sauce, lime juice, and water in a bowl until sugar melts.
- Put a big pot of water on a full boil. Take off from heat then soak the rice noodles for a minute in hot water. Mix to separate noodles then keep soaking for about another 3 minutes until noodles become tender. Drain then rinse using cold water until it's cool. Shake the noodles in a colander to drain as much water as you can.
- Mix basil, cilantro, mint, green onions, cucumber slices, bean sprouts, shrimp, carrots, cabbage, and noodles in a big bowl. Drizzle dressing on salad then coat by tossing. Put chopped peanuts on top.

Nutrition Information

- Calories: 450 calories;
- Total Carbohydrate: 71 g
- Cholesterol: 109 mg
- Total Fat: 10.1 g
- Protein: 20.4 g
- Sodium: 1265 mg

279. Salmon Fillets With Creamy Dill

"This is family recipe for how Alaskans prepare a tasty salmon dish. You can use silver, king or red salmon. You can serve together with wild rice!"
Serving: 4 | Prep: 5m | Ready in: 45m

Ingredients

- 1 1/2 cups mayonnaise
- 1/2 cup prepared mustard
- 1 tsp. chopped fresh thyme
- 1 tsp. dried oregano
- 1 tsp. chopped fresh basil leaves
- 1 1/2 lbs. salmon fillets
- 2 tsps. dried dill, or to taste

Direction

- Preheat an oven to 190 degrees C (375 degrees F).
- Mix together mustard and mayonnaise in a bowl. Mix in basil, thyme, and oregano. Put the salmon fillets onto a baking sheet and then brush with mayonnaise mixture. Drizzle dill weed on top.
- Bake for about 30 to 40 minutes until salmon flakes easily with a fork.

Nutrition Information

- Calories: 861 calories;
- Total Carbohydrate: 4.8 g
- Cholesterol: 107 mg
- Total Fat: 76.8 g
- Protein: 38.6 g
- Sodium: 895 mg

280. Sauceless Garden Lasagna

""Don't let your garden produce of tomatoes and zucchini go to waste by trying this flavorful lasagna recipe. Need not worry if you don't have pasta sauce on stock because adding herbs to the vegetable mixture will do the trick. Even picky eaters will be pleased by this recipe!""
Serving: 6 | Prep: 20m | Ready in: 1h5m

Ingredients

- 1 medium zucchini, halved lengthwise and sliced
- 1/3 cup chopped red onion
- 1 cup shredded mozzarella cheese, divided
- 1/2 cup crumbled feta cheese
- 2 portobello mushrooms, sliced
- 4 cups fresh baby spinach
- 1/4 cup chopped fresh basil
- 1 tbsp. chopped fresh oregano
- 3 cloves garlic, minced
- 3 tbsps. olive oil
- 1/4 cup balsamic vinegar
- 1 tsp. sugar
- 1/2 tsp. salt
- 1/4 tsp. freshly ground black pepper
- 1 (8 oz.) package no-boil lasagna noodles
- 9 roma (plum) tomatoes, thinly sliced

Direction

- Preheat the oven at 350°F (175°C). Use a cooking spray to slightly grease a 9x9 inch baking dish.
- Mix spinach, zucchini, garlic, red onion, feta cheese, 1/2 cup of mozzarella cheese and mushrooms together in a big bowl. Put in balsamic vinegar and olive oil then mix in with salt, pepper, sugar, basil and oregano. Mix the mixture thoroughly.
- In the greased baking dish, put lasagna noodles at the bottom. Put a layer of tomato slices on top of the lasagna noodles. Put a good amount of spinach mixture evenly on top. It's normal for this dish to shrink in size while cooking. Put slices of tomatoes on top of

the spinach mixture then put a layer of lasagna noodles again. Put another layer of tomatoes on top and do whole layering process again until the baking dish is filled to the top, finish off the layers with the spinach mixture. Top with the remaining cheese.

- Put in the preheated oven and bake for 35-45 minutes or until the vegetables and noodles are soft. Let the lasagna set and cool down a bit before slicing then serve warm.

Nutrition Information

- Calories: 286 calories;
- Total Carbohydrate: 25.3 g
- Cholesterol: 32 mg
- Total Fat: 15.5 g
- Protein: 12.9 g
- Sodium: 576 mg

281. Sausage Mushroom Pizza

""Pizzas can be made on the grill completely.""
Serving: 8 | Prep: 30m | Ready in: 52m

Ingredients

- Reynolds Wrap® Heavy Duty Aluminum Foil
- 2 tbsps. cornmeal
- 2 lbs. frozen pizza dough, thawed or Whole Wheat Sesame Dough (below)
- 1/2 cup pizza sauce
- 1/8 tsp. crushed red pepper
- 8 oz. bulk Italian sausage, cooked and drained
- 1 cup thinly sliced fresh mushrooms
- 8 oz. shredded Italian cheese blend
- Grated Parmesan cheese (optional)
- Snipped fresh basil (optional)

Direction

- Set the oven to 450°F for preheating. Use the Reynolds Wrap® Heavy Duty Aluminum Foil to cover the two large baking sheets. Sprinkle the sheets with cornmeal.
- Split the thawed pizza dough or whole wheat sesame seed dough into 8 equal portions.

Cover the dough and allow it to rest for 10 minutes.

- On a lightly floured surface, unroll each of the dough into a 6-inch circle. Place the rolled dough onto the prepared baking sheets. Use a fork to prick the crusts. Make sure you won't let them rise.
- Let them bake for 7 minutes until browned slightly. Mix the crushed red pepper and pizza sauce in a small bowl. Spread the pizza sauce on top of each crust. Then place the sausage and mushrooms on top. Drizzle with Italian blend cheese. Let them bake for 5 more minutes until the cheese has melted. Sprinkle with fresh basil and/or Parmesan cheese if desired.
- For the grilling, use Reynolds Wrap® Heavy Duty Aluminum Foil to line the grill rack. Preheat the grill and then lower the heat to medium-hot. Coat each top of the dough with 1 tbsp. of olive oil using a brush. Arrange the dough circles onto the foil-lined grill rack, oiled-sides down. Cover the grill and cook the dough for 1 minute until the bottom is firm and browned. Place the dough circles onto the clean surface, positioning them grilled-side up. Place the pizza toppings on top following the directions above. Place the assembled pizzas back into the foil-lined grill rack. Cover the grill and cook for 2-3 minutes until the cheese has melted and the bottom is browned. To ensure even browning, rearrange the pizzas as needed.

Nutrition Information

- Calories: 477 calories;
- Total Carbohydrate: 59.3 g
- Cholesterol: 32 mg
- Total Fat: 16.7 g
- Protein: 20.6 g
- Sodium: 1304 mg

282. Savino's Herb And Olive Chicken Salad

"A simple chicken salad recipe."
Serving: 4 | Prep: 15m | Ready in: 15m

Ingredients

- 1/2 cup mayonnaise
- 1 tsp. minced fresh oregano
- 1 tsp. minced fresh basil
- 1 tsp. minced fresh rosemary
- 1/2 tsp. minced onion
- 1 pinch salt and cracked black pepper to taste
- 4 cooked boneless chicken breast halves, diced
- 1 (10 oz.) can large pitted black olives, drained and sliced thin

Direction

- In a bowl, whisk pepper, salt, onion, rosemary, basil, oregano and mayonnaise. Add chicken; mix to coat then fold olives into mixture.

Nutrition Information

- Calories: 683 calories;
- Total Carbohydrate: 5.4 g
- Cholesterol: 175 mg
- Total Fat: 45.7 g
- Protein: 61.1 g
- Sodium: 903 mg

283. Savory Tomato Bread Pudding

"A delicious bread pudding, great to serve at parties or any occasion."
Serving: 10 | Prep: 15m | Ready in: 45m

Ingredients

- 1/4 cup raisins
- 1/4 cup white Zinfandel wine
- 3 tbsps. brown sugar
- 2 (14.5 oz.) cans diced tomatoes, drained

- 1 tsp. Worcestershire sauce
- 3 tbsps. chopped fresh basil leaves
- 1 pinch cayenne pepper
- 1/4 cup butter
- 1 (1 lb.) loaf day-old bread, cubed
- 1 cup shredded Monterey Jack cheese

Direction

- Preheat an oven to 200°C or 400°F. Oil a baking dish, 9x13-inch in size or other of similar size.
- Mix the cayenne pepper, basil, Worcestershire sauce, tomatoes, brown sugar, wine and raisins in a small saucepan. Let to simmer for 10 minutes over medium-low heat.
- Melt butter in a big skillet. Coat bread cubes in butter by tossing, then toss with Monterey Jack cheese; put to prepped baking dish. Put tomato mixture on top of the bread.
- In the preheated oven, bake for 25 minutes to half an hour, or till top is toasted nicely.

Nutrition Information

- Calories: 253 calories;
- Total Carbohydrate: 33.2 g
- Cholesterol: 22 mg
- Total Fat: 9.5 g
- Protein: 7.1 g
- Sodium: 537 mg

284. Seared Steak And Charred Nectarine Salad With Feta, Pecans, And Basil

""This tangy nectarine salad has the all the tasty flavors of basil, steak, and feta. It is sure to come up on your weekly menu more than once!""
Serving: 2 | Prep: 15m | Ready in: 30m

Ingredients

- 2 tbsps. olive oil, divided
- 10 oz. beef sirloin steak
- salt and black pepper to taste

- 1 nectarine, pitted and thinly sliced
- 1 shallot, minced
- 2 tbsps. red wine vinegar
- 1 (4 oz.) package mixed spring greens
- 1/2 oz. basil, thinly sliced
- 1 oz. crumbled feta
- 1 oz. pecans

Direction

- Preheat an oven to 200 degrees C or 400 degrees F.
- In a large skillet, heat 1/2 tbsp. of olive oil over medium heat. Season a steak with salt and pepper on all sides and sear in the hot skillet for 3-4 minutes on each side, until evenly browned.
- Transfer the steak into a baking sheet and finish cooking in the oven until cooked to preferred doneness, for 5 - 7 minutes. Remove from oven and set aside for 5 minutes to rest.
- Using the same skillet, place the nectarines over high heat and sear on all sides for 1-2 minutes until charred and caramelized.
- In a large salad bowl, whisk together the remaining 1 1/2 tbsps. olive oil, red wine vinegar, and shallots to make the vinaigrette, and season with salt and pepper. Add basil and spring mix, tossing to combine.
- On a cutting board, slice steak thinly going against the grain. Arrange pecans, feta, nectarines, and steak over salad.

Nutrition Information

- Calories: 501 calories;
- Total Carbohydrate: 16.9 g
- Cholesterol: 99 mg
- Total Fat: 33.3 g
- Protein: 35.9 g
- Sodium: 1427 mg

285. Shrimp Goat Cheese Watermelon Salad Stack

"A twist on the traditional caprese salad. The ring mold can be replaced with triangles or squares but 1/4-inch thick watermelon pieces that are flat is very important."
Serving: 4 | Prep: 25m | Ready in: 35m

Ingredients

- 8 large shrimp, peeled and deveined
- 1 tsp. onion powder
- 1 tsp. garlic powder
- 1/2 tsp. salt
- 1/2 tsp. smoked paprika
- 1/4 tsp. chipotle pepper powder (optional)
- 1 seedless watermelon, cut crosswise into 2-inch thick slices
- 1 (8 oz.) goat cheese log, cut into 8 slices
- 2 tsps. balsamic vinegar
- 4 sprigs fresh basil

Direction

- Turn on the oven to 220°C (430°F) to preheat.
- Season the shrimp with chipotle pepper powder, smoked paprika, salt, garlic powder and onion powder all over. Place the shrimp onto a baking dish.
- Place the shrimp into the preheated oven for 8 minutes to get a bright pink color on the shrimp without the center being transparent.
- Cut the watermelon into circle shapes with the ring mold (make sure that the mold's diameter is a bit larger than the diameter of the goat cheese slices). Divide the circle shapes to twelve 1/4-inch thick slices.
- Put a watermelon slice onto a plate. Form a salad stack by placing 1 cheese slice, 1 watermelon slice, 1 cheese slice, 1 watermelon slice and 2 shrimps. Continue following this order until the shrimp, cheese and watermelon slices run out. Top each stack with balsamic vinegar drizzles and basil to garnish.

Nutrition Information

- Calories: 584 calories;

- Total Carbohydrate: 88 g
- Cholesterol: 109 mg
- Total Fat: 19.1 g
- Protein: 26.3 g
- Sodium: 669 mg

286. Shrimp Scampi With Linguini

"The classic garlic pasta has stepped up its game with an addition of lemon juice and wine."
Serving: 4 | Prep: 25m | Ready in: 45m

Ingredients

- 1 (16 oz.) package linguine
- 1/4 cup olive oil
- 1/4 cup butter
- 6 cloves garlic, minced
- 1 lb. peeled and deveined medium shrimp
- 3/4 cup white wine
- 1/2 cup lemon juice
- 1/4 tsp. crushed red pepper
- 1 tbsp. chopped fresh basil
- 1/2 tsp. salt
- 1/2 pint grape tomatoes, halved
- 2 tbsps. grated Pecorino Romano cheese
- 1 tbsp. chopped fresh parsley

Direction

- Bring lightly salted water to a rolling boil on high heat in a large pot. Mix in linguine once the water is boiling, bring back to a boil. Cook the pasta without a cover while stirring sometimes, for about 11 minutes until the pasta is cooked through. Drain pasta well in a colander set in a sink. Bring the linguine to a big mixing bowl.
- In a big skillet, heat butter and olive oil on medium heat until butter melts. Cook, while stirring garlic in oil and butter for 2-3 minutes. Put in shrimp and cook, stirring often, for another 4-5 minutes. Mix in salt, basil, red pepper, lemon juice and wine; cook for additional 60 seconds. Stir in tomatoes and cook for another 60 seconds, remove from the

heat and transfer them to the linguine bowl. Add parsley and Pecorino Romano cheese over the sauce and pasta; toss to combine well.

Nutrition Information

- Calories: 707 calories;
- Total Carbohydrate: 68.6 g
- Cholesterol: 289 mg
- Total Fat: 29.7 g
- Protein: 33.3 g
- Sodium: 652 mg

287. Shrimp With Penne And Squash

"Delicious shrimp pasta!"
Serving: 5 | Prep: 20m | Ready in: 35m

Ingredients

- 1/2 lb. dried penne pasta
- 2 tbsps. olive oil
- 4 cups thinly sliced yellow squash
- 3 cups thinly sliced zucchini
- 1 lb. medium shrimp - peeled and deveined
- 1/4 cup fresh lemon juice
- 1 tsp. dried basil
- 1 tsp. dried oregano
- 1/2 tsp. salt
- 1/4 tsp. black pepper
- 3 cloves garlic, minced
- 1/2 cup minced fresh chives or green onions
- 1/4 cup freshly grated Parmesan cheese

Direction

- In a large pot, add lightly salted water then bring to a boil. Then add pasta and cook till al dente for about 8-10 minutes; strain then transfer into a large bowl.
- In the meantime, in a large skillet, warm oil over medium heat. Then add in zucchini and squash and cook for 10 minutes. Stir shrimp in, cook for 3 minutes. Stir garlic, pepper, salt,

oregano, basil, and lemon juice in. Then cook for 2 more minutes.

- In a large bowl, pour sauce and shrimp with pasta. Use Parmesan and chives to dredge on, and stir to blend.

Nutrition Information

- Calories: 365 calories;
- Total Carbohydrate: 43 g
- Cholesterol: 142 mg
- Total Fat: 9.6 g
- Protein: 28.3 g
- Sodium: 441 mg

288. Sicilian Garlic Sauce

"This sauce can be serve over barbequed meats or hot spaghetti."
Serving: 8 | Prep: 15m | Ready in: 15m

Ingredients

- 1/2 cup raw almonds
- 7 cloves garlic
- 5 leaves fresh basil
- 2 tsps. minced fresh parsley
- 1 tsp. salt
- 1/2 tsp. black pepper
- 1/4 cup extra-virgin olive oil
- 1 (14.5 oz.) can diced tomatoes

Direction

- Place almonds in a food processor and grind finely. Put in pepper, salt, parsley, basil, and garlic cloves; process until basil and garlic are minced. Add diced tomatoes and olive oil; continue to process until tomatoes are in small pieces and the sauce is blended.

Nutrition Information

- Calories: 129 calories;
- Total Carbohydrate: 4.4 g
- Cholesterol: 0 mg
- Total Fat: 11.5 g

- Protein: 2.5 g
- Sodium: 371 mg

289. Simmering Marinara With Brie

"Yummy!"
Serving: 4 | Prep: 5m | Ready in: 55m

Ingredients

- 1 tbsp. olive oil
- 6 cloves garlic, minced
- 2 lbs. roma (plum) tomatoes, chopped
- 1/2 cup chopped fresh basil
- 8 oz. Brie cheese

Direction

- In a large skillet, heat olive oil over medium heat. Sauté the garlic but don't let brown. Stir in 1/2 basil and tomatoes. Lower the heat; simmer for 45 mins.
- Mix in the remaining basil. Discard rind from Brie. Put into pan. Let cheese melt without stirring; combine by stirring. Take away from the heat. Enjoy sauce immediately.

Nutrition Information

- Calories: 268 calories;
- Total Carbohydrate: 10.8 g
- Cholesterol: 57 mg
- Total Fat: 19.6 g
- Protein: 14.2 g
- Sodium: 369 mg

290. Slow Cooker Thai Curried Beef

"This slow cooker Thai dish is great for a busy family. You can prepare it ahead and enjoy it later."
Serving: 8 | Prep: 15m | Ready in: 7h8m

Ingredients

- 2 lbs. lean stew beef
- 1/8 tsp. salt
- 2 cups diced onion
- 4 cloves garlic, minced
- 1 (13.5 oz.) can coconut milk
- 3/4 cup beef broth
- 3 tbsps. red curry paste
- 2 tbsps. lime juice
- 2 tbsps. peanut oil
- 2 jalapeno chile peppers, seeded and minced
- 1 tbsp. brown sugar
- 2 cups baby spinach
- water
- 4 cups jasmine rice
- 1/2 cup fresh basil leaves (optional)

Direction

- Place a big skillet on medium-high heat to preheat. Stir and cook beef for 2 minutes on each side until turning brown. Strain the excess grease. Remove the beef to a 4-qt. slow cooker and sprinkle salt over.
- In the same skillet, mix together garlic and onion over medium-high heat; sauté for 5 minutes until soft. Add to the slow cooker with the beef.
- Mix brown sugar, jalapeno chile peppers, peanut oil, red curry paste, beef broth, lime juice and coconut milk into the slow cooker.
- Put the lid on and cook for 6-10 hours until on Low until the flavors blend.
- In a saucepan, boil rice and water. Lower the heat to medium-low, put a cover on and simmer for 20-25 minutes until the rice is soft and liquid is absorbed.

- Mix spinach into the slow cooker and cook for 15 minutes until wilted. Enjoy the beef mixture on top of rice and use basil leaves to garnish.

Nutrition Information

- Calories: 829 calories;
- Total Carbohydrate: 85.6 g
- Cholesterol: 99 mg
- Total Fat: 39.3 g
- Protein: 40.3 g
- Sodium: 299 mg

291. Smoked Sausage Frittata

"Save yourself from some boring breakfast or brunch meal by serving this flavorful dish with vegetables, Butterball smoked sausage and eggs in it."
Serving: 6 | Prep: 15m | Ready in: 45m

Ingredients

- 1 (14 oz.) package Butterball® Smoked Turkey Dinner Sausage, halved lengthwise, and cut into 1/4-inch-thick slices
- 1 cup diced green onions, white and green parts
- 1 1/2 tbsps. olive oil
- 10 large eggs, slightly beaten
- 3/4 cup shredded mozzarella cheese
- 1/3 cup freshly grated Parmesan cheese
- 16 torn fresh basil leaves
- 1/4 cup chopped sun-dried tomatoes
- 1/4 tsp. ground black pepper
- Freshly grated Parmesan cheese (optional)
- Fresh basil leaves (optional)

Direction

- Preheat the oven to 350°F.
- In a heavy and oven-safe 10-inch skillet, put in the oil, onions and sausage and let it cook in hot oil over medium heat setting for 5 minutes while stirring it until it turns light golden brown in color.
- In a medium-sized bowl, mix all the rest of the ingredients together. Add the egg mixture into

the sausage mixture and mix everything together. Let it cook over medium heat setting and use a rubber spatula to lift up the eggs 1 or 2 times so that the uncooked parts run under the cooked part. Allow the egg mixture to cook for about 6 minutes just until it has started to set.

- Put the skillet inside the preheated oven and let it bake for 5-7 minutes until the top surface of the mixture turns golden brown in color and the egg mixture has firmed up when touched.
- Take the skillet out from the oven. Use a spatula to gently loosen up the edges of the baked frittata. Flip the skillet over to release the frittata onto the serving platter. Slice the baked frittata into 4 equal portions. You may top each sliced frittata with basil and Parmesan cheese if you want.

Nutrition Information

- Calories: 325 calories;
- Total Carbohydrate: 3.8 g
- Cholesterol: 366 mg
- Total Fat: 19.6 g
- Protein: 32.9 g
- Sodium: 361 mg

---

292. Sorghum, Quail Egg, Avocado, Kumato®and Buffalo Mozzarella Bowl

""One bowl packed with delicious stuffs. Just combine Sorghum grains, avocado oil, vinegar, cumin and Sriracha salt together and top it off with buffalo mozzarella cheese, Kumato®, quail eggs and avocado and you're good to go.""
Serving: 2 | Prep: 20m | Ready in: 1h29m

Ingredients

- 3 cups water
- 1 cup sorghum grain
- 5 quail eggs
- 1/2 tsp. Sriracha salt, or to taste
- 1/4 tsp. ground cumin
- 2 tbsps. avocado oil, divided
- 1/2 tsp. vinegar
- 4 oz. fresh buffalo mozzarella
- 4 fresh basil leaves
- 1 avocado, sliced
- 1 Kumato® tomato, diced
- 4 radishes, sliced

Direction

- In a saucepan, let the sorghum and water boil. Lower the heat to medium-low setting then cover the pan. Let it simmer for about 1 hour until the liquid has been absorbed and the sorghum has softened.
- Put the eggs in a saucepan and let it cook in boiling water for 4 minutes. Remove the pan from heat then cover and let it stand for 5 minutes.
- In a bowl, combine the Sriracha salt, cumin and sorghum. Pour vinegar and 1 tbsp. of avocado oil over the sorghum mixture and mix until well combined; divide the mixture in 2 bowls.
- Run cold water over the quail eggs. Peel off the shells and cut each egg in 1/2. Place the halved eggs over the sorghum mixture.
- Use your hands to shred the mozzarella cheese and divide it between the 2 sorghum bowls. Sprinkle torn basil leaves on top of the mozzarella cheese. Distribute the radishes, avocado and tomatoes evenly in the 2 bowls.

Nutrition Information

- Calories: 870 calories;
- Total Carbohydrate: 91.1 g
- Cholesterol: 234 mg
- Total Fat: 46.1 g
- Protein: 24.1 g
- Sodium: 742 mg

293. Spaghetti Carbonara (paleo Style)

"Gluten-free, lactose-free and paleo pasta."
Serving: 4 | Prep: 10m | Ready in: 1h

Ingredients

- 1 large spaghetti squash, halved and seeded
- 1/4 cup extra-virgin olive oil
- 8 slices bacon, diced
- 1 large tomato, diced
- 1 tsp. salt
- 1 tsp. ground black pepper
- 4 large egg yolks
- 3 sprigs fresh basil

Direction

- Preheat an oven to 200°C/400°F. Put squash on baking sheet, cut side up.
- In preheated oven, bake squash for 45 minutes – 1 hour till tender. Use fork to scoop flesh out then shred squash to strands.
- In big skillet, heat olive oil on medium high heat; mix and cook bacon in hot oil for 5-10 minutes till cooked through and browned. Add shredded squash; mix and cook for 3-5 minutes till squash is soft. Mix pepper, salt and tomato into squash mixture; take skillet off heat.
- Mix egg yolks into squash mixture; don't let egg yolks touch skillet, till mixture is creamy. Put squash carbonara in serving bowl; put basil sprigs over as a garnish.

Nutrition Information

- Calories: 428 calories;
- Total Carbohydrate: 34.4 g
- Cholesterol: 225 mg
- Total Fat: 28.7 g
- Protein: 12.9 g
- Sodium: 1091 mg

294. Spaghetti Pasta Sauce

"Serve this amazing sauce on hot cooked spaghetti."
Serving: 6 | Prep: 15m | Ready in: 35m

Ingredients

- 1 tsp. olive oil
- 1 onion, chopped
- 1/2 cup prepared mincemeat, crumbled, or to taste
- 1 (28 oz.) jar prepared pasta sauce
- 1/2 cup tomato puree, or to taste (optional)
- 5 leaves fresh basil, chopped

Direction

- Heat olive oil in a pot on medium heat; stir and cook onion 10 minutes until lightly browned. Mix in mincemeat; cook and mix till mincemeat is hot and well combined with onion. Put in tomato puree and pasta sauce; blend in basil leaves. Heat the sauce to a simmer; cook 10 minutes until flavors have combined. Mix frequently.

Nutrition Information

- Calories: 185 calories;
- Total Carbohydrate: 33.2 g
- Cholesterol: 3 mg
- Total Fat: 4.5 g
- Protein: 3.1 g
- Sodium: 683 mg

295. Spaghetti With Salami And Bacon

"Have this pasta dish along with a nice glass of wine for a light and sophisticated dinner.""
Serving: 8 | Prep: 20m | Ready in: 30m

Ingredients

- 1 (16 oz.) package uncooked spaghetti
- 2 tbsps. olive oil
- 1 tbsp. butter

- 1/4 lb. hard salami, diced
- 2 slices bacon, chopped
- 1 clove garlic, chopped
- 1 leek, thinly sliced
- salt and pepper, to taste
- 2 tbsps. chopped fresh basil
- 2 tomatoes, diced
- 4 tbsps. grated Parmesan cheese

Direction

- Boil a big pot of lightly salted water. Cook pasta in boiling water for 8-10 minutes until cooked through, but still firm enough to the bite. Drain off water.
- In the meantime, heat butter and olive oil in a large skillet on medium heat. Cook bacon and salami on the skillet until crispy. Toss in leek and garlic, then add pepper and salt to season and cook for another 2 minutes. Stir in 1 tbsp. of basil and tomatoes and cook for an additional 1 minute.
- Combine the prepared pasta into the content of the skillet and add 3 tbsps. of Parmesan. Sprinkle on basil and the leftover Parmesan on top, then serve.

Nutrition Information

- Calories: 354 calories;
- Total Carbohydrate: 45.4 g
- Cholesterol: 24 mg
- Total Fat: 13.2 g
- Protein: 12.7 g
- Sodium: 387 mg

296. Speedy Chicken, Feta, And Orzo Salad

"Busy day? Whip up this quick and tasty cold pasta salad with feta, tomatoes, herbs, and grilled chicken. Best paired with hot rustic bread. You can also use buffalo mozzarella or goat cheese if you want."
Serving: 6 | Prep: 15m | Ready in: 30m

Ingredients

- 1 1/4 cups uncooked orzo pasta
- 3 cups chopped grilled chicken breasts
- 1 cup cherry tomatoes, halved
- 1/4 cup chopped red onion
- 2 tbsps. chopped fresh basil
- 1 tsp. chopped fresh oregano
- 1/4 cup red wine vinegar, or more to taste
- 2 tbsps. extra-virgin olive oil, or more to taste
- 1/8 tsp. kosher salt
- 1/8 tsp. cracked black pepper
- 1 (2 oz.) can sliced black olives, or to taste (optional)
- 2 oz. crumbled feta cheese

Direction

- Boil a big pot of water; add orzo. Cook for about 11mins while mixing from time to time, until the orzo is tender but firm to chew. Drain, then rinse under cold water.
- In a big bowl, mix oregano, basil, red onion, tomatoes, chicken and orzo together.
- In another bowl, whisk the pepper, salt, oil and vinegar. Drizzle on top of the pasta mixture, then toss to coat. Sprinkle feta cheese and olives on top.

Nutrition Information

- Calories: 369 calories;
- Total Carbohydrate: 34.8 g
- Cholesterol: 61 mg
- Total Fat: 13.4 g
- Protein: 26.6 g
- Sodium: 275 mg

297. Spicy Chicken Rigatoni (chicken Riggies)

"Rigatoni pasta topped with tomato-based sauce."
Serving: 6 | Prep: 15m | Ready in: 1h

Ingredients

- 1 (16 oz.) box rigatoni pasta
- 3 tbsps. butter
- 2 tbsps. olive oil
- 5 cloves garlic, minced, or more to taste
- 1 large shallot, chopped
- 3 boneless chicken thighs, cut into small pieces, or more to taste
- 5 fresh cherry peppers, thinly sliced, or more to taste
- 1 (16 oz.) can tomato sauce
- 1/4 cup dry sherry
- 1/2 cup whole milk
- 1 small bunch fresh basil leaves, torn

Direction

- Heat a big pot of slightly salted water to a boil. In the boiling water, cook rigatoni 13 minutes, stirring sometimes, until tender but firm to the bite. Drain.
- In a big skillet on medium-high heat, heat oil and butter. Put in shallot and garlic; stir and cook 2-3 minutes till shallots become translucent and the mixture is fragrant. Put in chicken; stir and cook 5 minutes till the internal temperature reaches 74° C (165° F) and chicken is no longer pink.
- Add cherry peppers to chicken mixture and combine; cook 5-7 minutes until soft. Mix in tomato sauce; combine well. Decrease to medium heat and simmer 7-10 minutes.
- Add sherry to the tomato sauce mixture; simmer 10 minutes, mixing occasionally. Add milk and simmer 5 minutes.
- Take away from heat; blend in torn basil leaves. Scoop tomato sauce over pasta; serve.

Nutrition Information

- Calories: 505 calories;
- Total Carbohydrate: 67.9 g
- Cholesterol: 52 mg
- Total Fat: 16.7 g
- Protein: 22.8 g
- Sodium: 542 mg

298. Spicy Creamy Tomato Sauce

"This creamy tomato sauce has a spicy kick to it with all the chili and basil in it."
Serving: 4 | Prep: 25m | Ready in: 50m

Ingredients

- 2 tbsps. olive oil
- 1 large red onion, chopped
- 1 clove garlic, crushed
- 2 (14 oz.) cans diced tomatoes
- 1 tsp. balsamic vinegar
- 1 tsp. white sugar
- 1 tbsp. chopped fresh basil
- 1 red chile pepper, seeded and minced
- 1/4 tsp. salt
- 1/4 tsp. ground black pepper
- 2/3 cup mascarpone cheese

Direction

- Start by heating olive oil in a skillet over medium heat. Stir and cook the onion for about 5 minutes until it is soft and translucent. Put in the garlic and cook it with the onion while stirring for another a minute. Next, add the sugar, balsamic vinegar, and tomatoes and stir. Let them cook while stirring sometimes over medium heat for 10 minutes. Mix in black pepper, salt, red chile pepper and basil, then cook for another 10 minutes. Lastly, remove from the heat, and mix in the mascarpone cheese.

Nutrition Information

- Calories: 287 calories;
- Total Carbohydrate: 12.6 g
- Cholesterol: 47 mg

- Total Fat: 24.2 g
- Protein: 5 g
- Sodium: 480 mg

299. Spicy Italian Sausage And Black Bean Soup

"A lovely Italian soup for both winter and simmer days."
Serving: 6 | Prep: 25m | Ready in: 2h20m

Ingredients

- 1 tsp. vegetable oil
- 1 lb. hot Italian sausage
- 5 cloves garlic, minced
- 1 large onion, diced
- 2 carrots, diced
- 1 russet potato, cubed
- 5 stalks celery, diced
- 1 (6 oz.) can tomato paste
- 1 cup red wine
- 1 (32 fluid oz.) container beef broth
- 1 (15 oz.) can black beans, rinsed and drained
- 1 (28 oz.) can diced tomatoes
- 1 cup uncooked rotini pasta
- 1 cup baby spinach leaves
- 1 1/2 tsps. dried oregano
- 1 bunch fresh basil, chopped
- salt and black pepper to taste

Direction

- In a large pot, cook the vegetable oil on medium heat. In the heated oil, cook the Italian sausages and frequently turn, for 10-15 minutes until the outside gets browned and no pink remained in the center. Chill by putting aside; reserve a tbsp. of grease and remove the remaining from the pot.
- Stir the celery, potato, carrot, onion, and garlic into the heated fat. Cook for 7 minutes until the onion gets translucent and the vegetables become tender. Stir the tomato paste until all lumps disappear; add in red wine. Boil on high heat and cook till liquid has reduced by half, occasionally stirring to deglaze the pan. Add in the diced tomatoes, black beans, and beef broth. Turn down the heat to medium-low; cover and simmer for an hour.
- Slice the chilled sausage into slices, about 1/2 inch thickness. Stir the sausage with the dried oregano, spinach, and rotini pasta into the soup. Bring to a simmer for 7-10 minutes until the pasta becomes tender. Stir the chopped basil in and use pepper and salt to season, then serve.

Nutrition Information

- Calories: 383 calories;
- Total Carbohydrate: 35.6 g
- Cholesterol: 41 mg
- Total Fat: 15.2 g
- Protein: 18.4 g
- Sodium: 1531 mg

300. Spicy Kale And Shrimp Soup

"A healthy and flavorful soup with the spice of curry paste, which you can adjust as you like and remember that a little can go a long way."
Serving: 8 | Prep: 15m | Ready in: 50m

Ingredients

- 1 tbsp. olive oil
- 2 cups sliced fresh mushrooms
- 1 cup chopped onion
- 1 cup chopped carrots
- 2 cloves garlic, minced
- 8 cups reduced-sodium chicken broth
- 1 tsp. chopped fresh basil
- 4 cups chopped kale (ribs removed)
- 1 tsp. red curry paste
- salt and ground black pepper to taste
- 1 lb. peeled and deveined shrimp
- 2 (8 oz.) cans chopped tomatoes
- 1 (8 oz.) can kidney beans, rinsed and drained
- 1 lemon, juiced

Direction

- Add oil to a big saucepan, heat over moderate-low heat. Stir and cook garlic, carrots, onion and mushrooms in hot oil for 5 to 7 minutes until tender.
- Add the chicken broth to the saucepan and put in basil. Boil, lower to low heat; let simmer while covered for about 10 minutes until the broth is seasoned with basil.
- Mix in pepper, salt, curry paste and kale and restart boiling; lower to low heat and let simmer for about 10 minutes until the kale gets soft.
- Mix the lemon juice, kidney beans, tomatoes and shrimp into the broth, let simmer for about 10 minutes until the meat turns opaque in the middle and the shrimp gets bright pink on the outside.

Nutrition Information

- Calories: 149 calories;
- Total Carbohydrate: 15 g
- Cholesterol: 90 mg
- Total Fat: 3.1 g
- Protein: 16.5 g
- Sodium: 392 mg

301. Spicy Tomato And Lentil Soup

"You can puree this in a blender, but it's best with a food mixer/hand blender."
Serving: 4 | Prep: 5m | Ready in: 30m

Ingredients

- 1 onion, finely chopped
- 1 tbsp. olive oil
- 1 chile pepper, chopped
- 1 cup red lentils
- 1 (14.5 oz.) can peeled and diced tomatoes
- 1 cup water
- salt and pepper to taste
- 1/2 tsp. ground cumin
- 1 tsp. dried basil

- 1/4 cup sour cream, for topping (optional)
- 2 sprigs fresh basil leaves for garnish (optional)

Direction

- Heat olive oil in a Dutch oven or a big saucepan. Brown onions in oil lightly. Add basil, cumin, lentils, chili pepper, tomatoes along with water to the pan; boil. Lower the heat to medium low; simmer till lentils are tender or for 20 minutes.
- Once the lentils are softened, puree the soup with a stick blender; season with pepper and salt to taste. Put sour cream in a squirt bottle for a special touch; squeeze a spiral over each soup bowl. Garnish with a fresh basil sprig.

Nutrition Information

- Calories: 239 calories;
- Total Carbohydrate: 32 g
- Cholesterol: 6 mg
- Total Fat: 7 g
- Protein: 12.8 g
- Sodium: 269 mg

302. Spinach Basil Pasta Salad

"This is a delicious salad, an alternative to the traditional pasta."
Serving: 10 | Prep: 15m | Ready in: 30m

Ingredients

- 1 (16 oz.) package bow tie pasta
- 1 (6 oz.) package spinach leaves
- 2 cups fresh basil leaves
- 1/2 cup extra virgin olive oil
- 3 cloves garlic, minced
- 4 oz. prosciutto, diced
- salt and ground black pepper to taste
- 3/4 cup freshly grated Parmesan cheese
- 1/2 cup toasted pine nuts

Direction

- With lightly salted water, fill a big pot and over high heat, bring to a rolling boil. When the water is boiling, mix in the bow tie pasta and bring back to a boil. Without cover, cook the pasta for about 12 minutes, mixing from time to time, till cooked through yet still firm to the bite. Wash with cold water to cool. Drain thoroughly in a colander set in the sink.
- In a big bowl, toss the basil and spinach together.
- In a skillet over medium heat, heat the olive oil; in the hot oil, cook and mix the garlic for a minute; mix in the prosciutto and cook 2 to 3 minutes more. Take off heat. Put to the bowl with the basil and spinach mixture; combine by tossing. Add in the drained pasta and toss once more. Put pepper and salt to season. Scatter the pine nuts and Parmesan cheese over, serve.

Nutrition Information

- Calories: 372 calories;
- Total Carbohydrate: 36.4 g
- Cholesterol: 15 mg
- Total Fat: 20.7 g
- Protein: 13.6 g
- Sodium: 329 mg

303. Spring Salad With Fennel And Orange

"The beautiful green, purple, light orange, white, and red colors make this lovely salad so tempting."
Serving: 8 | Prep: 25m | Ready in: 25m

Ingredients

- Dressing:
- 1/4 cup white sugar
- 1/4 cup red wine vinegar
- salt and pepper to taste
- 1 tbsp. chopped fresh basil
- 3 tbsps. olive oil
- Salad:
- 1 (10 oz.) bag mixed salad greens
- 1 small fennel bulb, thinly sliced
- 1 orange, peeled and segmented
- 1/2 red onion, thinly sliced
- 1/2 cup slivered almonds
- 1/2 cup dried cranberries

Direction

- In a small bowl, combine the salt, red wine vinegar, olive oil, basil, pepper, and sugar until the sugar dissolves completely; put aside. In a large bowl, toss the onion, cranberries, almonds, salad greens, orange, and sliced fennel. Pour the dressing all over the salad. Toss the mixture well before serving.

Nutrition Information

- Calories: 158 calories;
- Total Carbohydrate: 19.7 g
- Cholesterol: 0 mg
- Total Fat: 8.7 g
- Protein: 2.5 g
- Sodium: 19 mg

304. Stacked Tomato And Burrata Salad

"It's a little unfair comparing mozzarella and burrata, because burrata is significantly creamier and richer. It's not like comparing oranges and apples but more like comparing oranges with supermodels. In fact, burrata translated to English is "buttered", which is all you need to know"
Serving: 1 | Prep: 15m | Ready in: 15m

Ingredients

- 1 vine-ripened tomato, cored and cut into 1/2-inch slices
- flaked sea salt and freshly ground black pepper to taste
- 1/4 cup burrata cheese, or more to taste
- 1 tbsp. torn fresh basil leaves, or to taste

- 1 tbsp. extra-virgin olive oil

Direction

- In a plate, place bottom of tomato slice, add sea salt and black pepper to season. Scatter burrata cheese over tomato slice, add torn basil leaves on top. Pour olive oil over tomatoes. Put next tomato slice on top. Repeat the process of layering cheese and tomato with remaining slices. Finish with top tomato slice.

Nutrition Information

- Calories: 329 calories;
- Total Carbohydrate: 5.9 g
- Cholesterol: 45 mg
- Total Fat: 27.4 g
- Protein: 10.4 g
- Sodium: 486 mg

305. Steph's Summer Salsa

"This salsa is a crisp and chunky appetizer for summertime that is really a big hit for any BBQ parties."
Serving: 40 | Prep: 30m | Ready in: 30m

Ingredients

- 4 ears fresh corn kernels
- 4 tomatoes, chopped
- 1 hot yellow banana pepper, chopped
- 2 cloves garlic, minced
- 1 cup chopped green bell pepper
- 1 tbsp. chopped fresh basil
- 1 tbsp. chopped fresh sage
- 1 tbsp. chopped fresh thyme
- 1 lemon, juiced
- 2 tsps. olive oil

Direction

- Combine olive oil, lemon juice, thyme, sage, basil, green bell pepper, garlic, hot yellow banana pepper, tomatoes and corn kernels in a big bowl. Cover and refrigerate for a

minimum of 1 hour in the fridge before serving.

Nutrition Information

- Calories: 14 calories;
- Total Carbohydrate: 2.8 g
- Cholesterol: 0 mg
- Total Fat: 0.4 g
- Protein: 0.5 g
- Sodium: 2 mg

306. Strawberry Goat Cheese Pretzel Bites

"A combination of sweet strawberries, tangy goat cheese, and salty Pretzel Crisps topped with balsamic glaze and basil. Chill until serving."
Serving: 8 | Prep: 15m | Ready in: 15m

Ingredients

- 16 thin pretzel crackers (such as Snack Factory® Pretzel Crisps®)
- 1 (4 oz.) log goat cheese
- 2 tbsps. balsamic glaze, or to taste, divided
- 1/2 cup sliced fresh strawberries
- 4 leaves fresh basil, cut into strips

Direction

- On a serving platter, line pretzel crackers. Cover crackers with goat cheese. Sprinkle on top with half of the balsamic glaze. Set 3 sliced strawberries on each cracker; spread basil over strawberries. Drizzle on top with the balsamic glaze left.

Nutrition Information

- Calories: 320 calories;
- Total Carbohydrate: 50.2 g
- Cholesterol: 11 mg
- Total Fat: 10.3 g
- Protein: 9.1 g
- Sodium: 1593 mg

307. Strawberry Surprise Shake

"A quick breakfast drinks."
Serving: 1 | Prep: 5m | Ready in: 5m

Ingredients

- 8 fluid oz. almond milk
- 5 frozen strawberries, or more to taste
- 2 scoops vanilla protein powder
- 1 large lemon, juiced
- 1 tbsp. ground flax seed
- 6 basil leaves

Direction

- In a blender, blend basil, ground flax seed, lemon juice, protein powder, strawberries and almond milk till velvety.

Nutrition Information

- Calories: 489 calories;
- Total Carbohydrate: 28.6 g
- Cholesterol: 25 mg
- Total Fat: 8.3 g
- Protein: 78.2 g
- Sodium: 582 mg

308. Strawberry-gin Cocktail

"Make this delicious cocktail every strawberry season. You can also use raspberries if you wish."
Serving: 1 | Prep: 10m | Ready in: 10m

Ingredients

- 1 strawberry
- 2 fresh basil leaves
- 2 tsps. white sugar
- ice cubes
- 2 fluid oz. gin
- 1 fluid oz. fresh lemon juice
- 3 fluid oz. chilled club soda

Direction

- In a cocktail shaker, put in sugar, basil leaves, and strawberry. Use a cocktail muddler to crush the mixture well. Put 1/2 of the ice in the cocktail shaker, put the other half in a tall glass. Add lemon juice and gin in the shaker; cover and shake until the outside of shaker is frosted. Filter cocktail in the chilled glass with ice. Add club soda on top then stir. Serve.

309. Stuffed Leg Of Lamb With Balsamic-fig-basil Sauce

""A simple way to dress up lamb roast for the holidays using currants and dried plums tossed with crème de cassis, salted roasted almonds and mint as stuffing. The balsamic fig sauce sprinkled over the sliced lamb is the perfect finishing touch.""
Serving: 6 | Prep: 50m | Ready in: 2h

Ingredients

- 1/2 cup coarsely chopped prunes
- 1/4 cup currants
- 2 tbsps. creme de cassis liqueur
- 1 1/2 tbsps. minced fresh rosemary
- 1 1/2 tbsps. minced fresh thyme
- 1/2 tsp. ground coriander
- 1 1/4 tsps. salt
- 1 tsp. freshly ground black pepper
- 1 (4 lb.) boneless leg of lamb, rolled and tied
- 1/2 cup chopped roasted and salted almonds
- 2 tbsps. chopped fresh mint
- 3 cloves garlic, cut into thirds
- 2 tbsps. olive oil
- 1/2 cup balsamic vinegar
- 5 tbsps. butter
- 3 tbsps. honey
- 1/3 cup thinly sliced, stemmed Calimyrna figs
- 5 tsps. chopped fresh basil
- 6 leaves mint
- 6 leaves basil

Direction

- Warm up oven to 200°C or 400°F.
- In a small bowl, mix the chopped currants and prunes with the crème de cassis, and then set aside. Combine thyme, rosemary, salt, coriander, and pepper in another small bowl, and set aside.
- On a work surface, untie and unroll the lamb and lay it out flat. Make sure lamb is evenly thick and slightly rectangular in shape by trimming off excess fat and cutting out any thick parts open. Drizzle with half of the herb mixture. Combine the chopped mint and almonds into the prune mixture and spread evenly over the lamb. Roll it up starting with one of the short sides, and tie at 1-inch intervals with a kitchen twine. On the top of the lamb, cut nine slits about an inch deep and insert a slice of garlic in each slit. Rub lamb with olive oil and drizzle with the remaining herb mixture.
- On a rack set in a roasting pan, place lamb with seam-side up. Roast lamb in the preheated oven until desired doneness is achieved. To get a medium-rare result, roast until inserted thermometer at the center reads 140°F or 60°C. Remove from the oven and cover with a foil. Allow lamb to rest for about 15 minutes.
- In a small saucepan over high heat, bring balsamic vinegar to a boil while lamb is resting. Boil for about 4-5 minutes, or until vinegar has reduced by half. Once vinegar is reduced, mix in the sliced figs, butter, and honey. Mix until butter is melted, remove from heat, mix in chopped basil, and set aside.
- Remove twine from the cooked lamb and then cut into about 1/2-inch thick slices to serve. Arrange on a warm serving platter, sprinkle with fig sauce, and garnish with some mint and basil leaves.

Nutrition Information

- Calories: 631 calories;
- Total Carbohydrate: 29.2 g
- Cholesterol: 147 mg
- Total Fat: 39.7 g
- Protein: 38.2 g
- Sodium: 649 mg

310. Summer Garden Pork Chops

"A good way to make use of vegetables."
Serving: 4 | Prep: 35m | Ready in: 55m

Ingredients

- 2 tsps. salt
- 2 tsps. garlic powder
- 2 tsps. fresh rosemary
- 4 pork chops
- 2 carrots, chopped
- 1 onion, chopped
- 1 green bell pepper, chopped
- 2 leeks, chopped
- 1 large zucchini, chopped
- 2 tbsps. minced garlic
- 5 small tomatoes, coarsely chopped
- 1 cup vegetable broth
- 1 cinnamon stick
- 1/2 tsp. ground allspice
- 1/3 cup olive oil
- 4 fresh basil leaves

Direction

- Grind together rosemary, garlic powder and salt; rub onto chop. Slightly brown in minimum amount of oil; put aside.
- Sauté garlic, zucchini, leeks, green pepper, onion, and carrots. Mix very little till they burn lightly or start to caramelize. Layer half of vegetable (with tomatoes included) mixture over the bottom of a big saucepan or Dutch oven. Top with chops; pour the remaining vegetable mixture over the surface.
- In the sauté pan, heat vegetable stock; mix to loosen bits of food from the bottom. Pour over vegetable and pork chops.
- Put in basil, olive oil, allspice and cinnamon stick. Simmer 20 minutes.

Nutrition Information

- Calories: 374 calories;
- Total Carbohydrate: 23 g
- Cholesterol: 37 mg
- Total Fat: 24.9 g
- Protein: 17.4 g
- Sodium: 1798 mg

311.Summer Vegetable And Goat Cheese Galettes

"An easy to prepare vegetable tarts."
Serving: 8 | Prep: 20m | Ready in: 50m

Ingredients

- 2 tbsps. olive oil
- 1 cup chopped green onions
- 2 cloves garlic, minced
- 1 (5 oz.) creamy goat cheese log
- 1/2 cup grated Parmesan cheese
- 1 pinch cayenne pepper, or more to taste
- 2 sheets frozen puff pastry, thawed
- 1/2 lb. zucchini, thinly sliced
- 1/2 lb. roma tomatoes, thinly sliced
- salt and ground black pepper to taste
- 1 tsp. olive oil, or as needed
- 2 tbsps. thinly sliced basil leaves

Direction

- In a skillet over medium heat, heat 2 tbsps. of olive oil; in hot oil, cook and mix green onions for 3 minutes till softened. Put the garlic; cook for a minute till aromatic. Take off from heat.
- In a small bowl, mix cayenne pepper, Parmesan cheese and goat cheese; mix using a fork till incorporated.
- On a slightly floured surface, softly flatten every puff pastry sheet using a rolling pin. Into 4 squares, slice every sheet. From edges of every square, lightly slit a border approximately quarter-inch with a sharp knife, ensure not to go across the dough.
- Preheat an oven to 200 °C or 400 °F.

- On a baking sheet, lay puff pastry squares; on every square, scatter goat cheese mixture. Put onion mixture on top of every square. Put in refrigerator to chill for 5 to 10 minutes.
- In a pattern on every puff pastry square, set tomato slices and zucchini, overlapping the vegetables. Put black pepper and salt to season. Sprinkle with approximately a tsp. of olive oil.
- In the prepped oven, bake for 20 minutes till puff pastry is puffed and golden brown. Garnish with basil strips.

Nutrition Information

- Calories: 468 calories;
- Total Carbohydrate: 31.1 g
- Cholesterol: 18 mg
- Total Fat: 33.8 g
- Protein: 11 g
- Sodium: 324 mg

312. Sun-dried Tomato Dip

"You may serve this simple-to-make recipe with any type of cracker, pita chips (must-try) or fresh vegetables."
Serving: 16 | Ready in: 10m

Ingredients

- 1/4 cup oil-packed sun-dried tomatoes, drained and chopped
- 8 oz. cream cheese, room temperature
- 1/2 cup sour cream
- 1/4 cup mayonnaise
- 2 cloves garlic, minced
- hot pepper sauce to taste
- 3/4 tsp. salt
- 3/4 tsp. freshly ground black pepper
- 1/4 cup fresh basil

Direction

- Use a food processor to process the mayonnaise, pepper, sun-dried tomatoes, hot pepper sauce, sour cream, salt, cream cheese and garlic together until well-combined. Put in the basil and allow the food processor to continue running until the mixture is smooth in consistency. Keep it in the fridge for not less than 1 hour prior to serving time.

Nutrition Information

- Calories: 94 calories;
- Total Carbohydrate: 1.4 g
- Cholesterol: 20 mg
- Total Fat: 9.4 g
- Protein: 1.5 g
- Sodium: 180 mg

313. Sun-dried Tomato Hummus

"This is a creamy hummus made with pureed garbanzo beans and tahini (sesame seed paste), seasoned with garlic and lemon juice."
Serving: 16 | Prep: 15m | Ready in: 1h15m

Ingredients

- 4 cloves garlic
- 1 tsp. salt
- 3 tbsps. tahini paste
- 1/4 cup fresh lemon juice
- 2 (15.5 oz.) cans garbanzo beans, drained
- 1/2 cup olive oil
- 1/2 cup oil-packed sun-dried tomatoes, drained
- 1/4 cup finely shredded fresh basil
- 2 tbsps. olive oil
- 1/8 tsp. paprika (optional)

Direction

- In a food processor, process the lemon juice, tahini, salt and garlic until it becomes smooth. Stir in 1/2 cup of olive oil and garbanzo beans then blend until it becomes smooth again; occasionally scrape the bowl's side. Stir in the sun-dried tomatoes when the mixture is already smooth, then process until chopped to very fine pieces and combined well into the hummus. Lastly, put the basil and process several times until incorporated.

- In a shallow serving dish, spread the hummus and form several decorative grooves on the top. Let it chill in the fridge for a minimum of 1 hour, then trickle with 2 tbsps. of olive oil and sprinkle paprika on top prior to serving.

Nutrition Information

- Calories: 163 calories;
- Total Carbohydrate: 14.6 g
- Cholesterol: 0 mg
- Total Fat: 10.6 g
- Protein: 3.5 g
- Sodium: 349 mg

314. Sweet And Sour Christmas Fish Soup

"This recipe is the first thing that came to my mind when I was given a Lake Winnipeg walleye as a Christmas gift."
Serving: 4 | Prep: 30m | Ready in: 55m

Ingredients

- 4 cups chicken stock
- 1 cup water
- 1/2 lemon, juiced
- 1 onion, sliced
- 3 cloves garlic, minced
- 1 tsp. thinly sliced fresh ginger root
- 2 parsnips, peeled and thinly sliced
- 2 sprigs fresh thyme
- 1 tsp. crushed red pepper flakes
- 1 tsp. salt
- 1 tsp. ground black pepper
- 1 tbsp. honey, or to taste
- 1 lb. walleye fillets, cut into pieces
- 3/4 lb. bean sprouts
- 5 leaves fresh basil, chopped
- 2 green onions, chopped
- 1 sprig fresh mint leaves for garnish

Direction

- In a big pot, whisk lemon juice, water, and chicken stock with parsnips, ginger, garlic, and onion. Use pepper, salt, red pepper flakes, and thyme to taste. Simmer over medium-high heat and cook for about 10 minutes until onions are opaque and parsnips are soft.

- Take out and dispose the thyme sprigs. Mix in honey according to how sweet you want the soup to be. The broth shouldn't be too sweet. Reduce the heat to gently simmer and mix in bean sprouts and walleye. Gently cook for 5 minutes; add green onion and basil. Keep cooking for about another 5 minutes until the fish is translucent and flaky. Use pepper and salt to season. Use mint leaves to garnish and enjoy.

Nutrition Information

- Calories: 235 calories;
- Total Carbohydrate: 31 g
- Cholesterol: 97 mg
- Total Fat: 2 g
- Protein: 26.4 g
- Sodium: 658 mg

315. Sweet Pea Pesto Pasta

"To make this a main dish, add chicken or shrimp."
Serving: 6 | Prep: 5m | Ready in: 25m

Ingredients

- 1 lb. uncooked pasta
- 1 (15 oz.) can Del Monte® Sweet Peas, drained
- 1 cup packed fresh spinach leaves
- 1 cup packed fresh basil leaves
- 1/3 cup grated Parmesan cheese, plus more for optional topping
- 1/4 cup olive oil
- 1/4 cup chopped walnuts
- 2 cloves garlic, peeled
- 1/4 tsp. salt
- 1/4 tsp. ground black pepper
- Chopped fresh tomatoes (optional)

Direction

- Follow package instructions to cook pasta.

- At the same time, in a food processor or blender, place pepper, salt, garlic, walnuts, olive oil, Parmesan, basil, spinach, and peas.
- Ladle out 1/2 cup of hot pasta cooking water and add to the blender 2 minutes before finishing cooking pasta. Pulse until smooth, if necessary, scraping sides and putting in extra pasta water by the tbsp..
- Once pasta is done; slightly drain and bring back to the pot. Pour in sauce; toss to coat. Season with pepper and salt to taste. Serve immediately with tomatoes and extra Parmesan cheese if wanted.

Nutrition Information

- Calories: 454 calories;
- Total Carbohydrate: 66.4 g
- Cholesterol: 4 mg
- Total Fat: 14.7 g
- Protein: 14.7 g
- Sodium: 396 mg

316. Taiwanese Popcorn Chicken

"Popcorn chicken!"
Serving: 4 | Prep: 10m | Ready in: 27m

Ingredients

- 1/2 lb. skinless, boneless chicken thighs, cut into bite-sized pieces
- 1 tbsp. garlic powder
- 1 tbsp. freshly ground black pepper
- 1/2 tsp. curry powder
- 1/4 tsp. grated ginger
- 1 dash reduced-sodium soy sauce
- 1 pinch ground cinnamon
- 1 pinch Chinese five-spice powder
- 1 pinch salt
- 1/2 cup tempura batter mix, or as needed
- vegetable oil for frying
- 1 bunch Thai basil leaves

Direction

- Mix salt, five-spice powder, cinnamon, soy sauce, ginger, curry powder, black pepper, garlic powder and chicken pieces in big bowl; marinate for 10 minutes.
- Sprinkle tempura batter mix on chicken then toss to evenly and lightly coat.
- Heat oil to 175°C/350°F in big saucepan/deep fryer; fry chicken in batches in hot oil for 4 minutes till golden brown. Drain over paper towels.
- Raise oil temperature to 200°C/400°F; fry Thai basil leaves for 1 minute till crisp. Drain onto paper towels. Fry chicken for 2-3 minutes per batch a 2nd time; drain onto paper towels.
- Serve basil leaves and chicken together.

Nutrition Information

- Calories: 215 calories;
- Total Carbohydrate: 4.9 g
- Cholesterol: 37 mg
- Total Fat: 17 g
- Protein: 11.4 g
- Sodium: 83 mg

317. Thai Burgers

"A fun and unique recipe."
Serving: 6 | Prep: 30m | Ready in: 36m

Ingredients

- 1 3/4 lbs. lean ground beef
- 1/2 cup bread crumbs
- 2 tbsps. lemon grass, minced
- 2 tbsps. chopped fresh basil
- 2 tbsps. minced shallots
- 2 red chili peppers, seeded and minced
- 1/4 cup chopped peanuts
- salt and pepper to taste
- 2 limes

Direction

- Preheat a grill to high heat.

- Mix peanuts, chili peppers, shallot, lemon grass, breadcrumbs and ground round in a big bowl. Season with pepper and salt; shape to patties. Don't add peanuts till grilling time if making ahead of time.
- Oil the grate lightly; put burgers onto grill. Cook for 3-5 minutes for each side. Take off grill; sprinkle lime juice on burgers.

Nutrition Information

- Calories: 438 calories;
- Total Carbohydrate: 12.5 g
- Cholesterol: 99 mg
- Total Fat: 31 g
- Protein: 26.6 g
- Sodium: 160 mg

318. Thai Coconut Chicken Soup (noodle Bowl)

"You can make this Thai dish delicious, easy and quick."
Serving: 4 | Prep: 20m | Ready in: 45m

Ingredients

- 1 (8 oz.) package dried Thai rice noodles
- 6 cups chicken broth
- 2 stalks lemongrass
- 1 boneless, skinless chicken breast
- 1 cup sliced cremini mushrooms
- 1 fresh red chile pepper, minced, or more to taste
- 1 (14 oz.) can coconut milk
- 2 tbsps. grated ginger
- 2 tbsps. fish sauce (optional)
- 1 tbsp. minced garlic
- 2 tbsps. lime juice
- 1 pinch white sugar, or to taste (optional)
- 1 lime, cut into wedges
- 3 green onions, sliced
- 1 small bunch fresh basil leaves, chopped

Direction

- Boil a big pot of water. Take away from heat, place in noodles, and put cover.
- Remove skin and get rid of tough outer leaves from lemongrass. Coarsely chop pale inner stalk and put into a food processor; pulse for 1 to 2 minutes till minced.
- In a separate big pot, boil chicken broth. Put in red chile pepper, mushrooms, chicken and lemongrass. Let cook for 5 minutes, Lower heat to medium; mix in garlic, fish sauce, ginger and coconut milk. Allow the soup to simmer gently for 10 to 15 minutes till an inserted instant-read thermometer into the chicken registers a minimum of 74°C or 165 °F.
- Move chicken to a chopping board; chop thinly and put back to the pot. Mix in sugar and lime juice.
- Drain and distribute noodles into serving bowls. Scoop soup over. Top with basil, green onions, and a lime wedge.

Nutrition Information

- Calories: 484 calories;
- Total Carbohydrate: 58.5 g
- Cholesterol: 22 mg
- Total Fat: 22.9 g
- Protein: 13.1 g
- Sodium: 2120 mg

319. Thai Hot And Sour Soup

"Very quick and easy Thai sour cream soup."
Serving: 6 | Prep: 10m | Ready in: 25m

Ingredients

- 3 cups chicken stock
- 1 tbsp. tom yum paste
- 1/2 clove garlic, finely chopped
- 3 stalks lemon grass, chopped
- 2 kaffir lime leaves
- 2 skinless, boneless chicken breast halves - shredded

- 4 oz. fresh mushrooms, thinly sliced
- 1 tbsp. fish sauce
- 1 tbsp. lime juice
- 1 tsp. chopped green chile pepper
- 1 bunch fresh coriander, chopped
- 1 sprig fresh basil, chopped

Direction

- Boil the chicken stock in a big saucepan. Mix in the garlic and tom yum paste, cook for approximately 2 minutes. Mix in the kaffir lime leaves and lemon grass. In the saucepan, put the chicken, and cook for 5 minutes till juices run clear and the chicken is not pink anymore.
- Stir in the mushrooms. Put in the green chile pepper, lime juice and fish sauce. Keep on cooking till well incorporated. Take away from heat, put the basil and coriander, serve warm.

Nutrition Information

- Calories: 71 calories;
- Total Carbohydrate: 4.9 g
- Cholesterol: 21 mg
- Total Fat: 1.8 g
- Protein: 9.1 g
- Sodium: 639 mg

320. Thai Salmon Salad

"Spicy salmon salad that uses Southeastern Asian dressing."
Serving: 6 | Prep: 20m | Ready in: 55m

Ingredients

- 4 tbsps. fish sauce
- 4 tbsps. lime juice
- 2 tsps. brown sugar
- 4 Thai chiles, chopped
- 1 1/2 lbs. salmon fillet
- 1 tsp. olive oil
- 1 onion, thinly sliced
- 1 large tomato, chopped

- 1 cup chopped fresh basil
- 1 head lettuce

Direction

- Set oven to 400°F or 200°C to preheat.
- Start with preparing the dressing, combine lime juice, brown sugar, fish sauce and chopped chiles in a little bowl. Set the dressing on one side.
- Rub oil all over the salmon filet and arrange on a baking sheet. Bake in the oven for 20 or until salmon separates easily. Set aside and cool for 15 or more minutes.
- Transfer filet to a large bowl and break into big pieces using fork. Toss in basil, onion and tomato. Drizzle with dressing and toss lightly to mix well.
- When serving, place the mixture on lettuce leaves. Enjoy immediately.

Nutrition Information

- Calories: 249 calories;
- Total Carbohydrate: 11.3 g
- Cholesterol: 77 mg
- Total Fat: 10.8 g
- Protein: 26.8 g
- Sodium: 802 mg

---

321. Thai-style Rice Salad

"I accidentally came up with this spicy, flavorful recipe after studying and examining Thai's flavor. Sambal Oelek - a paste made of garlic-chili found in most Asian groceries section or Asian specialty stores is a wonderful condiment to Asian dishes, especially this dish."
Serving: 8 | Prep: 30m | Ready in: 3h

Ingredients

- 4 cups uncooked jasmine rice
- 2 tsps. unsalted butter
- 2 tsps. minced fresh ginger root
- 2 (14 oz.) cans coconut milk
- 2 cups water
- 1/2 tsp. salt

- 1 tbsp. peanut oil
- 2 cloves garlic, minced
- 1 shallot, minced
- 1 Thai chile pepper, seeded and minced
- 1 tsp. minced fresh ginger root
- 1 tsp. minced lemon grass
- 1/2 lb. peeled and deveined medium shrimp (30-40 per lb.)
- 1/2 red bell pepper, sliced
- 1 tbsp. chopped fresh basil
- 1 tbsp. fish sauce
- 1 tsp. soy sauce
- 1/2 lime, juiced
- 1 1/2 cups diced pineapple
- 2 tsps. white sugar, or to taste
- 1/4 cup chopped fresh cilantro

Direction

- Over high heat, boil salt, water, coconut milk, ginger, butter and rice in a saucepan. Lover the heat to medium low, and cover the saucepan, keep simmering for 20 minutes until the rice is tender and absorbs the liquid well. Remove from the heat, use a fork to fluff and put in the fridge until cold.
- Over medium high heat, in a large skillet, heat the peanut oil. Stir in the lemon grass, ginger, minced chile pepper, shallot and garlic and cook until shallot begins to go limp (for about 1 minute). Add shrimp to the mixture, keep cooking and stirring until the shrimp is pink, then add red bell pepper slices. Stir well. Keep cooking until shrimp is no longer opaque in the center. Use lime juice, soy sauce, fish sauce and basil to season.
- Stir pineapple, sugar, the shrimp mixture and the chilled rice together. Serve with cilantro sprinkled on top.

Nutrition Information

- Calories: 623 calories;
- Total Carbohydrate: 90.5 g
- Cholesterol: 46 mg
- Total Fat: 23.9 g
- Protein: 13.7 g
- Sodium: 386 mg

322. The Best Parmesan Chicken Bake

"A tempting mixture of savory sauce, cheesy and crunchy coating, and tender chicken in one dish."
Serving: 6 | Prep: 15m | Ready in: 50m

Ingredients

- 2 tbsps. olive oil
- 2 cloves garlic, crushed and finely chopped
- 1/4 tsp. crushed red pepper flakes, or to taste
- 6 skinless, boneless chicken breast halves
- 2 cups prepared marinara sauce
- 1/4 cup chopped fresh basil
- 1 (8 oz.) package shredded mozzarella cheese, divided
- 1/2 cup grated Parmesan cheese, divided
- 1 (5 oz.) package garlic croutons

Direction

- Set an oven to 175°C (350°F) and start preheating.
- Grease the bottom of a 9x13-inch casserole dish using olive oil and drizzle with hot red pepper flakes and garlic.
- In the bottom of the dish, place the chicken breasts and pour the marinara sauce on the chicken. Scatter on the marinara sauce with basil and place 1/2 of the mozzarella cheese on top first, then 1/2 of the Parmesan cheese. Scatter over the croutons, then place the rest of Parmesan cheese and the rest of mozzarella cheese on top.
- In the prepared oven, bake for 35 minutes to 1 hour (it depends on the thickness and shape of the chicken breasts), until the inside of the chicken is not pink anymore, and the croutons and cheese turn golden brown. An instant-read thermometer needs to register at a minimum of 70°C (160°F) when inserted in the thickest part of the chicken breast.

Nutrition Information

- Calories: 477 calories;
- Total Carbohydrate: 28 g
- Cholesterol: 100 mg
- Total Fat: 21.7 g
- Protein: 40.3 g
- Sodium: 1022 mg

323. The Deb (peach-basil Bourbon Smash) Cocktail

"This beverage is a great way to consume all ripe peaches and also a juice way to rest yourself a busy day. It can be stored in the fridge for maximum of 3 weeks."
Serving: 1 | Prep: 10m | Ready in: 1h25m

Ingredients

- Peach-Basil Syrup:
- 4 ripe unpeeled peaches, pitted and coarsely chopped
- 1 1/2 cups white sugar
- 1 cup water
- 3 sprigs basil, tied together with string
- Cocktail:
- ice cubes, divided
- 1 1/2 fluid oz. bourbon
- 3 dashes aromatic bitters (such as 18.21 Prohibition Aromatic Bitters)
- 2 fluid oz. lime-flavored sparkling water (such as La Croix®)
- 1 slice peach
- 1 leaf basil

Direction

- In a small pot, mix together 3 sprigs basil, water, sugar and chopped peaches in medium heat. Simmer while stirring sometimes for 5 minutes, until sugar has dissolved. Let the syrup cool to room temperature, 10 minutes. Get rid of basil sprigs.
- Pour the syrup into a Mason jar, close and chill in the fridge for an hour until thoroughly chilled.

- Put peaches and 3 fluid oz. of syrup into a cocktail shaker. Mess to break up peaches. Put in 4 ice cubes, bitters and bourbon. Cover and shake forcefully until ice is almost melted. Transfer into a cold 8-oz. glass. Place into leftover 4 ice cubes. Stir in sparking water gradually. Use a basil leaf and a peach piece to garnish.

Nutrition Information

- Calories: 1370 calories;
- Total Carbohydrate: 324.9 g
- Cholesterol: 0 mg
- Total Fat: 0.1 g
- Protein: 0.6 g
- Sodium: 42 mg

324. Three Pepper Pasta Salad

"This recipe has a lot of ingredients, but it's easy to make."
Serving: 8 | Prep: 15m | Ready in: 25m

Ingredients

- 1 (16 oz.) package tri-color pasta
- 2/3 cup olive oil
- 3 tbsps. white wine vinegar
- 1/4 cup fresh basil leaves
- 2 tbsps. grated Parmesan cheese
- 1 1/4 tsps. salt
- 1/4 tsp. ground black pepper
- 1 red bell pepper, julienned
- 1 yellow bell pepper, julienned
- 1 orange bell pepper, julienned
- 1 medium fresh tomato, chopped
- 1 (2.25 oz.) can black olives, drained
- 8 oz. mozzarella cheese, cubed

Direction

- Boil lightly salted water in a big pot. Add pasta to the pot, cook until al dente, about 8-10 minutes, and strain.

- In a food processor or a blender, process pepper, salt, Parmesan cheese, basil, white wine vinegar and olive oil until smooth.
- Combine olives, tomato, orange bell pepper, yellow bell pepper, red bell pepper, dressing mixture and cooked pasta in a big bowl. Put mozzarella cheese on top and enjoy.

Nutrition Information

- Calories: 483 calories;
- Total Carbohydrate: 48 g
- Cholesterol: 19 mg
- Total Fat: 25.2 g
- Protein: 16.2 g
- Sodium: 631 mg

325. Tofu Basil Dressing

"You can try this creamy dip or dressing in place of the usual oil-based vinaigrettes. It can also last for a week when chilled."
Serving: 4 | Prep: 10m | Ready in: 10m

Ingredients

- 1/2 (12 oz.) package firm silken tofu
- 2 tbsps. cider vinegar
- 2 tbsps. apple juice
- 2 tbsps. chopped fresh basil
- 1/2 tsp. Dijon mustard
- 1 clove garlic, minced
- 1 pinch salt

Direction

- In a blender, process salt, tofu, garlic, cider vinegar, Dijon mustard, apple juice and basil until smooth.

Nutrition Information

- Calories: 38 calories;
- Total Carbohydrate: 2.2 g
- Cholesterol: 0 mg
- Total Fat: 2 g
- Protein: 3.5 g

- Sodium: 59 mg

326. Tofu Pasta Salad

"Fresh and healthy vegetarian salad featuring veggies and tofu."

Serving: 6 | Prep: 20m | Ready in: 40m

Ingredients

- 1 1/2 (8 oz.) packages rigatoni pasta
- 2 tbsps. olive oil
- 2 cloves garlic, minced
- 1/2 (16 oz.) package tofu, drained and cubed
- 1/2 tsp. dried thyme
- 1 1/2 tsps. soy sauce
- 1 small onion, thinly sliced
- 1 large tomato, cubed
- 1 carrot, shredded
- 6 leaves fresh basil, thinly sliced
- 6 sprigs fresh cilantro, minced
- 1/4 cup olive oil

Direction

- Boil a big pot of lightly salted water; add rigatoni. Cook and stir for 13 mins until the rigatoni is cooked yet firm to chew; drain and cool pasta.
- On medium heat, heat 2 tbsps. of olive oil in a pan; add garlic. Cook and stir for 1-2 mins until aromatic; add in thyme and tofu. Cook for 5-10 mins until the tofu is light brown; pour in soy sauce. Take off heat and cool.
- In a big bowl, mix cilantro, rigatoni, basil, tofu mixture, carrot, onion, and tomato. Toss in a quarter cup of olive oil to coat.

Nutrition Information

- Calories: 387 calories;
- Total Carbohydrate: 47.8 g
- Cholesterol: 0 mg
- Total Fat: 16.7 g
- Protein: 11.9 g
- Sodium: 89 mg

327. Tomato Alfredo Sauce With Artichokes

"Delicious Alfredo sauce but less rich."
Serving: 5

Ingredients

- 1 (14 oz.) can artichoke hearts in water
- 2 tomatoes, chopped
- 1 onion, chopped
- 1 cup fresh sliced mushrooms
- 1/2 cup chopped fresh basil
- 1/2 cup whole milk
- 2 tbsps. all-purpose flour

Direction

- Chop artichoke hearts and put in a large skillet with juice. Add milk and flour to reach the preferred consistency of thickness.
- Put in basil, tomatoes, mushrooms and onion. Cook for a short time for the vegetables to become pretty, tasty and firm.
- Cook up a batch of your favorite spaghetti noodles (spaghettini or angel hair). Rinse well. Add artichoke sauce to cooked pasta to serve.

Nutrition Information

- Calories: 90 calories;
- Total Carbohydrate: 16.4 g
- Cholesterol: 2 mg
- Total Fat: 1 g
- Protein: 5.1 g
- Sodium: 490 mg

328. Tomato And Bacon Creamed Corn Casserole

"Shorter your cooking and cleaning time in the summer by cooking this side dish in a slow cooker.""
Serving: 16 | Prep: 20m | Ready in: 2h20m

Ingredients

- 1 Reynolds® Slow Cooker Liner
- 4 (10 oz.) packages frozen whole-kernel corn, thawed*
- 1 1/2 cups half and half, light cream, or whole milk
- 1 cup chopped onion
- 1/2 cup finely shredded Parmesan cheese
- 1/4 cup butter, cut up
- 1/2 tsp. salt
- 3/4 cup shredded Monterey Jack cheese
- 6 thick slices peppered bacon, crisp-cooked and chopped
- 1/2 cup chopped tomato
- 2 tbsps. snipped fresh basil

Direction

- Line Reynolds® Slow Cooker Liner over the bottom of a 5- to 6-quart slow cooker.
- In a blender, place 2 packages of corn and pour in milk or cream. Put the lid on and process until no lumps remain. Pour mixture into the prepared slow cooker.
- Mix salt, butter, Parmesan cheese, onion, and remaining corn into the corn mixture in the cooker. Mix carefully using a rubber spatula until incorporated.
- Cook, covered for 4 hours on low setting and 2 hours on high setting. Pour mixture into a serving dish to serve. Sprinkle with basil, tomato, bacon, and Monterey Jack cheese.

Nutrition Information

- Calories: 178 calories;
- Total Carbohydrate: 17.1 g
- Cholesterol: 28 mg
- Total Fat: 10.3 g
- Protein: 7 g
- Sodium: 284 mg

329. Tomato And Basil Quiche

"This quiche is the combination of some pre-made recipes. It's really simple to make but has sophisticate taste and look, as if it takes a whole day to make."
Serving: 6 | Prep: 20m | Ready in: 1h

Ingredients

- 1 tbsp. olive oil
- 1 onion, sliced
- 2 tomatoes, peeled and sliced
- 2 tbsps. all-purpose flour
- 2 tsps. dried basil
- 3 eggs, beaten
- 1/2 cup milk
- salt and pepper to taste
- 1 (9 inch) unbaked deep dish pie crust
- 1 1/2 cups shredded Colby-Monterey Jack cheese, divided

Direction

- Preheat the oven at 400°F or 200°C. Bake the pie crust for 8 minutes in preheated oven.
- Meanwhile, in a large skillet, heat the olive oil on medium heat. Sauté the onion until it softens; remove it from the skillet. Sprinkle basil and flour over the tomato slices, then sauté each side of these slices for one minute. Mix the eggs and the milk in a small bowl. Season it with salt and pepper.
- To the bottom of the pie crust, add one cup of shredded cheese and spread it evenly. Put onion on top of the cheese, then top it with the tomatoes. Pour in the egg mixture to cover. Sprinkle the remaining half cup of the shredded cheese on top.
- Bake the quiche for 10 minutes in the preheated oven. Lower the heat to 350°F (or 175°C) and continue baking for 15-20 minutes or until the filling puffs up and turns golden brown. Serve the quiche when they are still warm.

Nutrition Information

- Calories: 378 calories;
- Total Carbohydrate: 23 g
- Cholesterol: 127 mg
- Total Fat: 26.1 g
- Protein: 13.7 g
- Sodium: 698 mg

330. Tomato And Feta Galette

"This dish is so light and savory."
Serving: 6 | Prep: 15m | Ready in: 1h12m

Ingredients

- 1 tbsp. butter
- 1 tbsp. olive oil
- 1 large onion, diced
- 2 cloves garlic, minced
- 1 tbsp. fresh thyme
- salt and ground black pepper to taste
- 1 sheet frozen puff pastry, thawed
- 1 lb. tomatoes, sliced into 1/4-inch rounds
- 1/2 cup grated Parmesan cheese, or more to taste
- 1/2 cup panko bread crumbs
- 1/2 cup crumbled feta cheese
- 1 tbsp. fresh parsley
- 1 egg, beaten
- 2 tbsps. thinly sliced fresh basil

Direction

- Heat together the oil and butter on medium heat in the skillet; put in the onion. Cook and whisk for 10-15 minutes or till the onion turns translucent. Whisk the pepper, salt, thyme and garlic into the onion; cook and whisk for roughly 2 minutes or till becoming fragrant. Take the skillet out of the heat.
- Roll out the puff pastry onto the lightly floured surface. Use the parchment paper to line one baking sheet and add the puff pastry onto the parchment paper. Add the baking sheet into the freezer.

- Preheat the oven to 230 degrees C (450 degrees F).
- Arrange the slices of tomato onto the wire rack that is placed over the top of one baking sheet. Drizzle the salt on the slices of the tomato and put aside to drain the tomatoes, roughly 10 minutes.
- Combine together parsley, feta cheese, breadcrumbs, and Parmesan cheese in the bowl. Spread half of this cheese mixture on puff pastry, leaving one 1-in. border around edges. Layer onion mixture on the cheese mixture layer.
- Blot the tomatoes dry and arrange on the onion layer. Drizzle the rest of the cheese mixture on the tomato layer. Fold puff pastry border over edges of tomatoes and slightly brush the egg on pastry.
- Bake in preheated oven for roughly 20 minutes or till the crust becomes puffed and golden. Drizzle the fresh basil on the galette and let cool down for 15 minutes prior to slicing.

Nutrition Information

- Calories: 381 calories;
- Total Carbohydrate: 31 g
- Cholesterol: 53 mg
- Total Fat: 25.4 g
- Protein: 10.4 g
- Sodium: 442 mg

331. Tomato Basil Egg Salad Sandwich

"It's very quick and easy to make yet still very yummy."
Serving: 4 | Prep: 15m | Ready in: 15m

Ingredients

- 8 hard-boiled eggs, sliced
- 1/4 cup mayonnaise
- 1/2 tsp. Dijon mustard
- 1/4 tsp. onion powder
- 1/8 tsp. salt
- ground black pepper to taste

- 10 leaves basil, thinly sliced
- 1 tomato, sliced
- 4 leaves lettuce
- 4 English muffins, split and toasted

Direction

- In a bowl, combine black pepper, salt, onion powder, Dijon mustard, mayonnaise and eggs.
- Fold into egg mixture the basil.
- Lay out on top of toasted English muffins the lettuce and tomato slices.
- Scoop over vegetables the egg mixture to serve.

Nutrition Information

- Calories: 392 calories;
- Total Carbohydrate: 29.2 g
- Cholesterol: 429 mg
- Total Fat: 22.6 g
- Protein: 17.6 g
- Sodium: 486 mg

332. Tomato Basil Pasta Salad

"This pasta salad is a real time saver."
Serving: 8

Ingredients

- Reynolds Wrap® Aluminum Foil
- 1 (8 oz.) package bow tie pasta, cooked and drained
- 1 pint cherry or grape tomatoes, cut in half
- 1 medium yellow bell pepper, cut into cubes
- 1 (6 oz.) jar artichoke hearts, drained, coarsely chopped
- 4 large fresh basil leaves, cut into strips
- 2 tbsps. olive oil
- 2 tbsps. red wine vinegar or balsamic vinegar
- Salt and freshly ground pepper

Direction

- In a big bowl put together basil, artichoke hearts, yellow bell pepper, tomatoes and cooked pasta.
- In a small bowl, mix pepper, salt, vinegar and olive oil. Put dressing mixture atop pasta; mix by tossing.
- Cover using Reynolds Wrap Aluminum Foil. Chill for 2 hours or prior serving time.

Nutrition Information

- Calories: 172 calories;
- Total Carbohydrate: 26.8 g
- Cholesterol: 0 mg
- Total Fat: 5.3 g
- Protein: 5.3 g
- Sodium: 103 mg

333. Tomato Basil Soup

"A creamy dish that every member in my family loves. Tasting good on its own, but this soup goes better with a garlic bread."
Serving: 8 | Prep: 25m | Ready in: 55m

Ingredients

- 6 tbsps. butter
- 1 onion, thinly sliced
- 15 baby carrots, thinly sliced
- 2 stalks celery, thinly sliced
- 3 cloves garlic, chopped
- 1 (28 oz.) can tomato sauce (such as Hunt's®)
- 1 (8 oz.) can tomato sauce (such as Hunt's®)
- 1 1/4 cups chicken broth
- 2 tbsps. chopped fresh basil
- 1 tbsp. chopped fresh oregano
- salt and ground black pepper to taste
- 1 1/2 cups heavy whipping cream

Direction

- Add butter into a big pot, melt over medium-low heat, mix in garlic, celery, carrots and onion, cook for about 10 minutes until vegetables get tender. Mix in both amounts of oregano, basil, chicken broth and tomato sauce. Raise to medium heat and let it simmer for 10 to 20 minutes until soup is reduced.

- Pour the soup into a blender to fill no more than half full. Cover and hold down the lid, pulse several times then leave it blending. Add cream. Keep maintaining to puree in batches until smooth, pour the creamy soup into another pot.
- Heat the soup over medium-high heat for about 5 minutes longer until hot.

Nutrition Information

- Calories: 272 calories;
- Total Carbohydrate: 10.5 g
- Cholesterol: 84 mg
- Total Fat: 25.4 g
- Protein: 3 g
- Sodium: 752 mg

334. Tomato Basil Soup I

"A savory soup with basil and tomato will remind me of down home."
Serving: 4 | Prep: 20m | Ready in: 1h

Ingredients

- 1 tbsp. olive oil
- 2 tsps. minced garlic
- 1/4 cup minced onion
- 1/4 cup tomato paste
- 1 quart chicken broth
- 1 cup diced tomatoes
- 2 tsps. dried basil
- 1/2 tsp. dried marjoram
- 1/4 tsp. dried oregano
- 1/8 tsp. dried thyme
- 1/4 cup dry white wine
- 1 bay leaf

Direction

- Add onion and garlic to a big saucepan, cook in oil over medium heat until onion turns translucent. Mix in the tomato paste and cook until it gets rusty color. Mix in the chicken broth then wine, bay leaf, thyme, oregano, marjoram, basil and tomatoes. Boil them up then lower the heat and let simmer for half an hour.

Nutrition Information

- Calories: 73 calories;
- Total Carbohydrate: 7.2 g
- Cholesterol: 0 mg
- Total Fat: 3.6 g
- Protein: 1.5 g
- Sodium: 136 mg

335. Tomato Basil Spaghettini

"The strong taste of basil, garlic, and tomato combined with a fair amount of goat cheese will create an appetizing sauce to satisfy your senses."
Serving: 8 | Prep: 15m | Ready in: 25m

Ingredients

- 1 (16 oz.) package uncooked spaghettini
- 1 (14.5 oz.) can diced tomatoes with garlic
- 2 fresh tomatoes, chopped
- 1 cup fresh basil leaves
- 2 tbsps. minced garlic
- 2 tbsps. olive oil
- freshly ground black pepper to taste
- 1 lemon, juiced
- 4 oz. soft goat cheese

Direction

- Start boiling a large pot of lightly salted water. Add in pasta and cook until al dente, or for 8-10 minutes; then drain water.
- Mix pepper, olive oil, garlic, basil, fresh tomatoes, and the diced tomatoes in a food processor or a blender just until chunky.

- Carefully toss the mixture of tomato and cooked pasta in a bowl. Just before serving, dust the pasta with lemon juice and arrange goat cheese on top.

Nutrition Information

- Calories: 297 calories;
- Total Carbohydrate: 47.2 g
- Cholesterol: 7 mg
- Total Fat: 7.9 g
- Protein: 11 g
- Sodium: 306 mg

336. Tomato Brie Bow Tie Pasta

"It's a colorful, simple and tantalizing side dish used as a light main dish with fruit and green salad."
Serving: 8 | Prep: 10m | Ready in: 30m

Ingredients

- 1 (12 oz.) package bow tie pasta
- 2 (14.5 oz.) cans Italian-style diced tomatoes
- 1/2 lb. Brie cheese, cubed
- 2 tbsps. chopped fresh basil

Direction

- Bring lightly salted water in a big pot to a boil. Put in pasta and cook until al dente, or for about 8-10 minutes, then drain.
- At the same time, heat tomatoes in a big saucepan on moderately high heat. Bring to a slow boil and stir in cheese. Lower heat to moderately low and stir to melt the cheese.
- Toss together tomato sauce and pasta, then put chopped basil on top before serving.

Nutrition Information

- Calories: 266 calories;
- Total Carbohydrate: 34.1 g
- Cholesterol: 28 mg
- Total Fat: 8.8 g
- Protein: 12.3 g
- Sodium: 340 mg

337. Tomato Fennel Soup

"This would be an awesome, quick-cooking tomato soup that is suitable for the early days of the fall!"
Serving: 4 | Prep: 15m | Ready in: 50m

Ingredients

- 2 tbsps. olive oil
- 1 bulb fennel, chopped
- 1/2 onion, chopped
- 1 celery stalk, chopped
- 1 clove garlic, minced
- 1 (14.5 oz.) can diced tomatoes
- 1 cup low-sodium chicken broth
- 2 tbsps. chopped fresh basil
- 2 tbsps. chopped fresh parsley
- salt and ground black pepper to taste

Direction

- Put olive oil in a large saucepan and heat it over medium-high heat. Stir in celery, garlic, fennel, and onion and then cook in hot oil for approximately 10 minutes until tender.
- Pour chicken broth and tomatoes into the vegetable mixture. Simmer the mixture for 4 minutes. Take the saucepan away from the heat. Add the parsley and basil. Let the soup cool slightly.
- Fill a blender with the soup, no more than half-full. Cover the blender. Holding the lid down, pulse it a couple of times before blending it completely. Make sure to puree the soup in batches until smooth.

Nutrition Information

- Calories: 115 calories;
- Total Carbohydrate: 10.1 g
- Cholesterol: 1 mg
- Total Fat: 7 g
- Protein: 2.8 g
- Sodium: 275 mg

338. Tomato Spinach And Basil Soup

"Dried basil can replace for fresh basil in this recipe."
Serving: 4 | Prep: 5m | Ready in: 15m

Ingredients

- 2 tbsps. butter
- 1 large yellow onion, chopped
- 1 tsp. minced garlic
- 1 1/2 cups milk
- 1 (28 oz.) can tomato puree
- 1 tbsp. white sugar
- 2 cups fresh spinach, torn
- 1/4 cup chopped fresh basil
- 1/2 tsp. salt
- 1/4 tsp. freshly ground black pepper
- 1 tbsp. grated Parmesan cheese

Direction

- In a big saucepan on medium heat, melt butter. Sauté garlic and onion 3 minutes. Mix in milk and cook, mixing occasionally, about 2 minutes. Mix in sugar and tomato puree. Combine well; put on cover and heat to a boil on high heat. Decrease to low heat and simmer 5 minutes with cover. Put in pepper, salt, basil and spinach; simmer without cover, mixing occasionally, about 2 minutes. If wished, sprinkle parmesan cheese over top.

Nutrition Information

- Calories: 208 calories;
- Total Carbohydrate: 29.3 g
- Cholesterol: 24 mg
- Total Fat: 8.5 g
- Protein: 7.8 g
- Sodium: 1218 mg

339. Tomato, Cucumber & White-bean Salad With Basil Vinaigrette

"This is a light dinner or lunch bean salad recipe that needs no cooking and made with summer's juicy cucumbers and cherry or grape tomatoes. This simple salad is extraordinary because of the fresh basil that upgrades a simple vinaigrette recipe."
Serving: 4 | Prep: 25m | Ready in: 25m

Ingredients

- ½ cup packed fresh basil leaves
- ¼ cup extra-virgin olive oil
- 3 tbsps. red-wine vinegar
- 1 tbsp. finely chopped shallot
- 2 tsps. Dijon mustard
- 1 tsp. honey
- ¼ tsp. salt
- ¼ tsp. ground pepper
- 10 cups mixed salad greens
- 1 (15 oz.) can low-sodium cannellini beans, rinsed
- 1 cup halved cherry or grape tomatoes
- ½ cucumber, halved lengthwise and sliced (1 cup)

Direction

- In a mini food processor, place honey, pepper, salt, oil, basil, shallot, mustard, and vinegar and then process until the contents are mostly smooth. Pour into a large bowl. Add cucumber, tomatoes, greens, and beans. Stir to coat.

Nutrition Information

- Calories: 246 calories;
- Total Carbohydrate: 22 g
- Cholesterol: 0 mg
- Total Fat: 15 g
- Fiber: 8 g
- Protein: 8 g
- Sodium: 271 mg
- Sugar: 5 g
- Saturated Fat: 2 g

340. Tomato-bread Salad With Basil And Capers

"Capers make this salad special."
Serving: 10 | Prep: 30m | Ready in: 1h30m

Ingredients

- 5 cups 1/2-inch cubed French or Italian bread
- 1 1/2 lbs. tomatoes, stemmed and cut into medium dice
- 2 medium garlic cloves, minced
- 1/2 large red onion, cut into small dice
- 1/2 cup torn fresh basil leaves
- 1/4 cup drained capers
- 1/4 cup olive oil
- 2 tbsps. red wine vinegar
- 1 pinch ground black pepper, to taste

Direction

- Position rack to the center of oven; preheat oven to 250°.
- On a cookie sheet with a rim, place bread cubes. Bake 30 minutes till bread is dried out; put aside to cool.
- At the same time, in a medium bowl, dice and salt the tomatoes. Mix in garlic; allow to sit 30 minutes until juicy.
- Prepare the rest of ingredients; put into tomatoes; toss together. Put in bread cubes; toss. Modify seasonings, adding pepper to taste. Allow to sit 10 minutes; serve.

Nutrition Information

- Calories: 218 calories;
- Total Carbohydrate: 33.7 g
- Cholesterol: 0 mg
- Total Fat: 6.6 g
- Protein: 7 g
- Sodium: 447 mg

341. Tomato-herb Vinaigrette

"This sauce is versatile and easy to make. You can use it with pasta salads, vegetables, grilled fish, or grilled meats."
Serving: 8 | Prep: 25m | Ready in: 25m

Ingredients

- 1/4 cup red wine vinegar
- 2 tbsps. Burgundy wine (optional)
- 1/2 tsp. salt
- 1/2 tsp. white sugar
- 1/2 tsp. black pepper
- 1 cup olive oil
- 2 tsps. minced garlic
- 1 tbsp. chopped fresh thyme
- 1 tbsp. chopped fresh marjoram
- 1 tbsp. chopped fresh basil
- 1 tbsp. chopped fresh tarragon
- 3 shallots, minced
- 1 cup diced tomatoes

Direction

- In a glass bowl, put wine and vinegar. Mix in pepper, sugar and salt until the sugar dissolves. Gradually add olive oil to the bowl while stirring rapidly to combine. Mix in tarragon, basil, marjoram, thyme and garlic; fold in tomatoes and shallots. Put in the fridge to store until eating.

Nutrition Information

- Calories: 265 calories;
- Total Carbohydrate: 5.5 g
- Cholesterol: 0 mg
- Total Fat: 27.1 g
- Protein: 0.8 g
- Sodium: 150 mg

342. Tony's Summer Pasta

"This recipe is from my husband's workplace."
Serving: 6 | Prep: 10m | Ready in: 15m

Ingredients

- 1 (16 oz.) package linguini pasta
- 6 roma (plum) tomatoes, chopped
- 1 lb. shredded mozzarella cheese
- 1/3 cup chopped fresh basil
- 6 cloves garlic, minced
- 1/2 cup olive oil
- 1/2 tsp. garlic salt
- ground black pepper to taste

Direction

- In a medium-sized bowl, mix black pepper, garlic salt, olive oil, garlic, basil, cheese and tomatoes. Put aside.
- At the same time, based on the instruction on package, cook pasta.
- Drain pasta and move to 1 serving bowl. Use tomato mixture to toss in. Serve.

Nutrition Information

- Calories: 635 calories;
- Total Carbohydrate: 60 g
- Cholesterol: 48 mg
- Total Fat: 31.9 g
- Protein: 29.1 g
- Sodium: 627 mg

343. Tuscan Tomato Soup (pappa Al Pomodoro)

"You need day-old bread, Parmesan, and tomatoes to make this soup. You can also make a gourmet dish with this soup as a base, adding to the top with prawns and fish."
Serving: 4 | Prep: 15m | Ready in: 55m

Ingredients

- Tomato Sauce:
- 3 tbsps. extra-virgin olive oil
- 1 onion, finely chopped
- 1 carrot, finely chopped
- 1 rib celery, finely chopped
- 4 cups passata (crushed tomatoes)
- 2 tbsps. milk
- salt
- Stock:
- 1 onion, peeled
- 1 carrot
- 1 stalk celery
- 4 cups water
- 8 cups stale Italian bread, crumbled
- 1 1/4 cups grated Parmesan cheese
- 1 tbsp. extra-virgin olive oil, divided
- 2 tbsps. Parmesan cheese, shaved
- 5 leaves chopped fresh basil

Direction

- In a big saucepan, heat 3 tbsps. of olive oil over medium heat; add chopped celery, chopped carrot, and chopped onion. Cook for 15 minutes until tender, tossing frequently. Mix in milk and tomato pasta. Use salt to season, put a cover on and simmer the tomato sauce for 20 minutes until the flavors have blended well.
- In a stockpot, mix together whole celery stalk, whole carrot, and whole onion; add water to cover and boil. Simmer about 15 minutes. Drain the vegetables and keep the stock warm.
- Mix into the tomato sauce with 1 1/2 cups of stock. Put in stale bread, toss and put aside for 15-20 minutes so the bread can get tender.
- In a blender, mix together 1 tsp. of olive oil in, 1 1/4 cups grated Parmesan cheese, and the tomato-bread mixture; process until the mixture has a mousse-like consistency.
- Pour the soup into bowls and enjoy with shaved Parmesan cheese. Sprinkle with left olive oil. Use basil leaves to garnish.

Nutrition Information

- Calories: 567 calories;
- Total Carbohydrate: 67 g
- Cholesterol: 25 mg
- Total Fat: 24.8 g

- Protein: 22.6 g
- Sodium: 1235 mg

344. Tuscan White Bean Soup

"A great Italian soup that you'll love!"
Serving: 6 | Prep: 55m | Ready in: 55m

Ingredients

- 4 slices bacon, finely chopped
- 1 medium yellow onion, quartered lengthwise
- 1 medium stalk celery, quartered crosswise
- 1 medium carrots, quartered crosswise
- 2 cloves garlic, lightly crushed
- 3 (19 oz.) cans Progresso® cannellini beans, drained
- 1 dried bay leaf
- 1/2 cup white wine
- 1 (32 oz.) carton Progresso® reduced sodium chicken broth
- 2 tbsps. olive oil
- 1 tbsp. finely chopped garlic
- 1/4 tsp. crushed red pepper flakes, or to taste
- 1/4 cup lightly packed fresh basil leaves, sliced
- 1/2 tsp. gray sea salt
- 1/8 tsp. freshly ground pepper

Direction

- In a Dutch oven/4-qt. saucepan, cook 2 garlic cloves, carrot, celery, onion and bacon for 5 minutes, occasionally mixing on medium high heat. Reduce heat to medium. Add broth, wine, bay leaf and beans. Cover. Cook, occasionally mixing, for 20-25 minutes till veggies are tender. Take off heat. Cool for 15 minutes.
- Meanwhile, heat olive oil in 8-in. skillet for 1 minute on medium high heat. Put 1 tbsp. chopped garlic. Cook, frequently stirring, for 3-5 minutes till garlic starts to brown. Mix red pepper flakes in. Cook for several seconds. Mix basil in. Cook till basil wilts.

- Discard bay leaf from the bean mixture. Put mixture into food processor. Puree, covered. Put back into saucepan. Mix pepper and salt in. Simmer for 5-10 minutes, frequently mixing, on medium heat till heated thoroughly.
- Put soup into solo soup bowls. Put basil mixture on top of each.

Nutrition Information

- Calories: 324 calories;
- Total Carbohydrate: 42.6 g
- Cholesterol: 7 mg
- Total Fat: 8.1 g
- Protein: 15 g
- Sodium: 1226 mg

345. Vegan Pasta And Lentil Casserole

"You can make it for lunches."
Serving: 8 | Prep: 30m | Ready in: 1h5m

Ingredients

- 2 tbsps. extra-virgin olive oil
- 1 onion, diced
- 1 head garlic, sliced
- 1 (8 oz.) package sliced mushrooms
- 1 Japanese eggplant, halved and sliced
- 6 cups diced buttercup squash
- 1 (28 oz.) can diced tomatoes
- 1 cup red lentils
- 4 cups small pasta shells
- 6 cups vegetable stock
- 1/4 cup rice vinegar
- 1/4 cup soy sauce
- 1 tbsp. tomato paste
- 1 cup nutritional yeast
- 1 (.75 oz.) package basil leaves, cut into thin strips
- 1/2 tsp. hot paprika (optional)
- 1 pinch ground black pepper to taste

Direction

- In a Dutch oven, combine oil, garlic, and onion over medium heat. Cook and stir for 3-5 minutes, until the onion softens. Sequentially add buttercup squash, Japanese eggplant, and mushrooms, stirring well after each addition.
- Add tomatoes into the Dutch oven and stir. Place in red lentils, continue to stir, then add pasta shells. Next, pour in the stock; lower the heat to medium-low; cover and simmer for half an hour, until the pasta is almost thoroughly cooked. Occasionally stir to make sure that the pasta doesn't adhere to the bottom of the Dutch oven.
- In a small bowl, mix tomato paste, soy sauce, and rice vinegar. Pour into the Dutch oven and stir to blend. Then put in nutritional yeast and continue to stir. Add black pepper, paprika, and basil; stir 1 more time.

Nutrition Information

- Calories: 475 calories;
- Total Carbohydrate: 82.7 g
- Cholesterol: 0 mg
- Total Fat: 6.5 g
- Protein: 26.5 g
- Sodium: 844 mg

346. Vegan Squash Pesto

"A vegan pesto recipe."
Serving: 6 | Prep: 10m | Ready in: 10m

Ingredients

- 1 cup diced yellow squash
- 1 cup walnuts
- 1/2 cup fresh basil
- 1/2 cup fresh spinach
- 4 cloves peeled garlic
- 1/2 tsp. pink salt
- 1/2 tsp. cayenne pepper

Direction

- Blend cayenne pepper, salt, garlic, spinach, basil, walnuts and yellow squash till smooth in a blender.

Nutrition Information

- Calories: 118 calories;
- Total Carbohydrate: 4.1 g
- Cholesterol: 0 mg
- Total Fat: 11 g
- Protein: 3.1 g
- Sodium: 197 mg

347. Vegan Sun-dried Tomato Pesto

"Mix with tofu, margarine and soy cream cheese to make a spread."
Serving: 3 | Prep: 30m | Ready in: 30m

Ingredients

- 2 cups fresh basil leaves
- 5 sun-dried tomatoes, softened
- 3 cloves garlic, crushed
- 1/4 tsp. salt
- 3 tbsps. toasted pine nuts
- 1/4 cup olive oil

Direction

- In a blender/electric food processor, puree nuts, salt, garlic, tomatoes and basil. Slowly add olive oil, slowly blending until mixture reaches your preferred texture.

Nutrition Information

- Calories: 227 calories;
- Total Carbohydrate: 4.8 g
- Cholesterol: 0 mg
- Total Fat: 22.7 g
- Protein: 3.6 g
- Sodium: 266 mg

348. Vegan Tomato, Cucumber, And Lentil Salad

"A satisfying vegan fresh salad recipe with spicy onion, sweet balsamic vinegar, basil and lentils."
Serving: 4 | Prep: 20m | Ready in: 45m

Ingredients

- 8 cups water
- 1 lb. dried lentils
- 1 English cucumber, peeled and cut into bite-size pieces
- 2 tomatoes, cut into bite-size pieces
- 1/2 red onion, finely chopped
- 1/2 cup finely chopped fresh basil
- 1/4 cup balsamic vinegar

Direction

- In a big pot, mix together the lentils and water, then boil. Lower the heat and gently simmer for about 20 minutes, until the lentils become soft yet not mushy. Drain the extra liquid and move to a big bowl.
- Stir the basil, red onion, tomatoes and cucumber into the lentils, then dress it with balsamic vinegar.

Nutrition Information

- Calories: 439 calories;
- Total Carbohydrate: 76.9 g
- Cholesterol: 0 mg
- Total Fat: 1.5 g
- Protein: 30.7 g
- Sodium: 30 mg

349. Vegetarian Italian Pasta Salad With Arugula

"This Italian pasta salad is made with arugula, artichoke hearts, basil, tomatoes, mozzarella, and Caprese ingredients. You can enjoy this salad with a barbeque."
Serving: 8 | Prep: 15m | Ready in: 3h30m

Ingredients

- 1 (16 oz.) box penne pasta
- Dressing:
- 4 tbsps. olive oil
- 4 tbsps. balsamic vinegar
- 3 tbsps. maple syrup
- 2 cloves garlic, grated
- 2 tsps. Dijon mustard
- sea salt and freshly ground black pepper to taste
- 5 tomatoes, chopped
- 1 (15 oz.) can artichoke hearts, well drained and quartered
- 1 (8 oz.) package fresh mozzarella cheese, cubed
- 1/2 bunch basil, chopped
- 4 cups arugula

Direction

- Boil lightly salted water in a big pot. Put in penne and cook for 11 minutes until soft yet firm to the bite, tossing sometimes.
- As the penne cooks, make the dressing. In a small bowl, combine maple syrup, balsamic vinegar and olive oil until fully blended. Mix in the grated garlic. Stir in mustard and use pepper and salt to season.
- Strain the penne and remove into a big bowl. Stir in half of the dressing. Let it cool for 60 minutes.
- Stir basil, mozzarella cheese, artichoke hearts and tomatoes into the penne. Put a cover on and put in the fridge to chill for a minimum of 2 hours.
- Stir in arugula and the leftover dressing right before eating.

Nutrition Information

- Calories: 407 calories;
- Total Carbohydrate: 58.1 g
- Cholesterol: 18 mg
- Total Fat: 12.8 g
- Protein: 17.5 g
- Sodium: 580 mg

---

350. Veggie And Goat Cheese Quinoa Burgers

"A lovely veggie burger recipe."
Serving: 4 | Prep: 20m | Ready in: 1h2m

Ingredients

- 1 cup cooked quinoa
- 1 cup canned pumpkin
- 3/4 cup fresh basil, chopped
- 1 medium beet, peeled and shredded
- 1/2 cup quick-cooking oats
- 1/2 cup soft, spreadable goat cheese, divided
- 2 cloves garlic, minced
- 1/2 tsp. salt
- 1/2 tsp. ground ginger
- 2 tbsps. vegetable oil
- 4 slices Nature's Own® Perfectly Crafted Multigrain Bread, toasted
- Fresh basil (optional)
- Diced tomato (optional)
- Sliced red onion (optional)

Direction

- Mix ginger, salt, garlic, 1/4 cup goat cheese, oats, beet, 3/4 cup basil, pumpkin and quinoa till combined well in big bowl; cover. Chill till easy to work with or for 30 minutes.
- Heat oil in very big skillet on medium heat. Meanwhile, divide mixture to 4 portions; press every portion to 4-in. patty.
- In hot oil, cook patties on medium heat till lightly browned and firm, flipping once halfway through cooking, for 12-15 minutes.

- Spread leftover 1/4 cup goat cheese on toasted bread slices; put quinoa burgers on top. Garnish with sliced red onion, diced tomato and/or extra fresh basil if desired.

Nutrition Information

- Calories: 304 calories;
- Total Carbohydrate: 45.7 g
- Cholesterol: 2 mg
- Total Fat: 10.9 g
- Protein: 8.6 g
- Sodium: 683 mg

---

351. Venison Mostaccioli Casserole

"A great way to use venison!"
Serving: 8 | Prep: 20m | Ready in: 1h23m

Ingredients

- 1 (16 oz.) package mostaccioli or medium tube pasta
- 1 tbsp. olive oil
- 1 yellow onion, chopped
- 1 lb. ground venison
- 1 (15 oz.) can tomato sauce
- 1/4 tsp. dried basil
- 1/8 tsp. garlic powder
- salt and pepper to taste
- 1/4 cup grated Parmesan cheese
- 3 cups grated Mozzarella cheese

Direction

- Preheat an oven to 190°C/375°F. Grease 9x13-in. baking dish lightly.
- Boil a big pot of lightly salted water; add pasta. Cook for 8-10 minutes till al dente; drain. Reserve pasta.
- Meanwhile, put olive oil in skillet on medium high heat. Mix onions in. Cook for 5 minutes till translucent and soft. Add venison. Cook for 10 minutes till not pink and crumbled. Drain if needed. Mix garlic powder, basil and

tomato sauce in. Season with pepper and salt to taste. Turn heat off.

- Casserole: Put a layer of venison sauce on bottom of prepped baking dish. Sprinkle parmesan cheese on sauce; layer with cooked pasta. Put sauce on top, layer using pasta, and 1/2 mozzarella. Repeat layers with leftover ingredients, finishing with layer of mozzarella cheese. Use aluminum foil to cover dish.
- In preheated oven, bake for 20 minutes. Remove foil cover. Bake for 10 more minutes till cheese topping is light gold.

Nutrition Information

- Calories: 417 calories;
- Total Carbohydrate: 47.6 g
- Cholesterol: 70 mg
- Total Fat: 11.9 g
- Protein: 30.7 g
- Sodium: 608 mg

352. Vietnamese Fresh Spring Rolls

"Refreshing spring rolls. You can dip it in both or one of the sauces."
Serving: 8 | Prep: 45m | Ready in: 50m

Ingredients

- 2 oz. rice vermicelli
- 8 rice wrappers (8.5 inch diameter)
- 8 large cooked shrimp - peeled, deveined and cut in half
- 1 1/3 tbsps. chopped fresh Thai basil
- 3 tbsps. chopped fresh mint leaves
- 3 tbsps. chopped fresh cilantro
- 2 leaves lettuce, chopped
- 4 tsps. fish sauce
- 1/4 cup water
- 2 tbsps. fresh lime juice
- 1 clove garlic, minced
- 2 tbsps. white sugar
- 1/2 tsp. garlic chili sauce
- 3 tbsps. hoisin sauce

- 1 tsp. finely chopped peanuts

Direction

- Boil water in a medium saucepan. Boil the rice vermicelli for 3-5 minutes or until al dente. Drain.
- In a big bowl, fill with warm water. Dip a wrapper in hot water to soften for a second. Lay the wrapper flat. Put lettuce, cilantro, mint, basil, a handful of vermicelli, and 2 shrimp halves into a row across the middle. Leave about 2 inches on each side uncovered. Fold the uncovered sides going in, then roll wrapper tightly, starting at the end with lettuce. Repeat process with the rest of the ingredients.
- Mix chili sauce, sugar, garlic, lime juice, water, and fish sauce in a small bowl.
- Mix peanuts and hoisin sauce in a separate small bowl.
- Serve the spring rolls with hoisin sauce mixtures and fish sauce mixtures.

Nutrition Information

- Calories: 82 calories;
- Total Carbohydrate: 15.8 g
- Cholesterol: 11 mg
- Total Fat: 0.7 g
- Protein: 3.3 g
- Sodium: 305 mg

353. Walnut Pesto

"You can use toasted or raw walnuts. You may add parmesan cheese, too."
Serving: 2 | Prep: 10m | Ready in: 10m

Ingredients

- 2 cups basil leaves
- 1/2 cup walnuts
- 1/4 cup olive oil
- 2 cloves garlic
- 1 tbsp. lemon juice

Direction

- In a food processor, blend lemon juice, garlic, olive oil, walnuts and basil until it looks like a paste.

Nutrition Information

- Calories: 455 calories;
- Total Carbohydrate: 6.9 g
- Cholesterol: 0 mg
- Total Fat: 47.3 g
- Protein: 6.1 g
- Sodium: 3 mg

---

354. Warm Heart Stew

"I felt like making a soup had all ingredients that my family loves. This warm heart stew has all of the robust bratwurst of the season and best beans."

Serving: 8 | Prep: 15m | Ready in: 4h15m

Ingredients

- 6 bratwursts, chopped
- 4 carrots, chopped
- 1 onion, chopped
- 2 (14 oz.) cans chicken stock
- 1 (14 oz.) can beef broth
- 1 1/2 cups sauerkraut
- 1 (15 oz.) can pinto beans, drained
- 1 (15 oz.) can kidney beans, drained
- 1 (15 oz.) can navy beans, drained
- 1/4 cup chopped fresh basil leaves
- 1 tbsp. parsley
- salt to taste

Direction

- Place the onion, carrots, and bratwursts in a slow cooker. Pour in beef broth and chicken stock. Mix in kidney beans, sauerkraut, basil, parsley, pinto beans, navy beans, and salt.
- Cover and cook on high for about 4 hours.

Nutrition Information

- Calories: 382 calories;

- Total Carbohydrate: 32.2 g
- Cholesterol: 50 mg
- Total Fat: 19.8 g
- Protein: 19.1 g
- Sodium: 1826 mg

---

355. Watermelon And Basil Martini

"This chic and fashionable summer martini is best enjoyed while wearing flip-flops."

Serving: 2 | Prep: 10m | Ready in: 10m

Ingredients

- 2 slices peeled and thinly-sliced cucumber
- 2 leaves fresh basil
- 1 tbsp. white sugar
- 4 fluid oz. watermelon vodka
- 1 cup crushed ice
- 1 tsp. fresh lime juice
- 1 tsp. simple syrup (equal parts water and sugar)
- 2 slices peeled and thinly-sliced cucumber

Direction

- In a bowl, add 2 thin slices of cucumber with sugar and basil leaves. Use a fork to smash till softened. Loosen the mixture by adding in a tsp of watermelon vodka. Fill a cocktail shaker with crushed ice and put in the cucumber-basil mixture. Top with simple syrup, lime juice and the leftover watermelon vodka then shake. Into 2 chilled martini glasses, strain the drink and use 1 slice of peeled cucumber to garnish each cocktail. Enjoyed best wearing flip-flops.

Nutrition Information

- Calories: 172 calories;
- Total Carbohydrate: 8.4 g
- Cholesterol: 0 mg
- Total Fat: 0 g
- Protein: 0.1 g
- Sodium: 3 mg

356. White Bean Dip With Pine Nuts

"The ingredients amount I uses makes a cup, but you can easily double/triple the amounts."
Serving: 8 | Prep: 10m | Ready in: 2h10m

Ingredients

- 2 tbsps. pine nuts
- 2 tsps. chopped fresh basil
- 1 tsp. chopped fresh oregano
- 1 cup cooked Great Northern beans
- 2 cloves garlic, cut in half
- 1 tsp. lime juice
- 1 roma (plum) tomato, roughly chopped
- sea salt to taste
- black pepper to taste
- 1 tbsp. olive oil

Direction

- Process oregano, basil and pine nuts 2-3 times to ground the nuts finely in a food processor, covered. Add garlic and beans; process for 30-60 seconds till smooth. Put pepper, salt, tomato and lime juice in; pulse 2-3 times till mixture is spreadable and smooth. Drizzle oil into the dip as food processor runs. Add 1 tbsp. of water at a time in till dip is at the preferred consistency if the mixture is too thick.
- Refrigerate for at least 2 hours – overnight to blend flavors; serve.

Nutrition Information

- Calories: 56 calories;
- Total Carbohydrate: 5.7 g
- Cholesterol: 0 mg
- Total Fat: 2.9 g
- Protein: 2.5 g
- Sodium: 41 mg

357. Whole Fish Fried With Basil And Chiles

"Use 10-14-oz. lean, flaky and mild fish. Use big pot and lots of room to deep-fry fish."
Serving: 4 | Prep: 15m | Ready in: 30m

Ingredients

- 1 whole (10 oz.) tilapia, or more as desired
- oil for deep frying
- Sauce:
- 1 tbsp. vegetable oil, or as desired
- 1 yellow onion, chopped
- 5 large red chile peppers, sliced
- 5 cloves garlic, chopped
- 2 tbsps. fish sauce
- 2 tbsps. light soy sauce
- 1/4 cup Thai basil leaves, or to taste
- 1/4 cup chopped fresh cilantro, or to taste

Direction

- Cut a few angled slits along fish body, cutting down to rib bones. Cut 2 lateral slits along back of fish, from heat to tail on any side of dorsal fin to guarantee maximum crispiness and quickly cooking.
- Heat oil to 175°C/350°F in big saucepan/deep fryer for frying.
- Put fish into hot oil gently; fry for 2-3 minutes per side till crispy. Remove fish from oil gently; drain on paper towel-lined plate.
- Heat 1 tbsp. vegetable oil in big skillet/wok on medium heat; mix and cook garlic, red chile peppers and onions for 5-10 minutes till lightly brown. Add soy sauce and fish sauce; take wok off heat. Mix cilantro and basil immediately into sauce.
- Put fish on big serving platter; put sauce on top of fish.

Nutrition Information

- Calories: 338 calories;
- Total Carbohydrate: 9.2 g
- Cholesterol: 26 mg
- Total Fat: 26.7 g

- Protein: 16.6 g
- Sodium: 1033 mg

358. Whole Wheat Vegan Couscous Salad

"You can add many kinds of vegetables into this dish."
Serving: 4 | Prep: 25m | Ready in: 40m

Ingredients

- 1 cup water
- 1 cup whole wheat couscous
- 1 small red onion
- 1 carrot, chopped
- 1/2 cup finely chopped celery
- 1/2 cup dried cranberries
- 1/2 cup finely chopped green onions
- 1/2 cup alfalfa sprouts
- 1/2 cup chopped fresh parsley
- 1/4 cup finely chopped toasted walnuts
- 1 tbsp. garlic paste
- 2 tbsps. extra-virgin olive oil
- 1 tbsp. apple cider vinegar
- 1 small bunch chopped fresh basil, or to taste
- 1 lemon, juiced
- salt and ground black pepper to taste

Direction

- In a saucepan, boil water; take away from heat, mix in couscous. Put on cover, let sit about 10 minutes till water is fully absorbed. Use a fork to fluff couscous.
- Stir walnuts, parsley, alfalfa sprouts, green onions, cranberries, celery, carrot, and red onion into the couscous.
- In a bowl, mix together lemon juice, basil, apple cider vinegar, and olive oil. Spread over couscous mixture. Mix in black pepper and salt.

Nutrition Information

- Calories: 406 calories;
- Total Carbohydrate: 66.5 g

- Cholesterol: 0 mg
- Total Fat: 13 g
- Protein: 11.3 g
- Sodium: 195 mg

359. Yummy Pesto Mashed Potatoes

"A tasty mashed potato with pesto for vibrant color that every kid will love. A little black pepper and grated cheese with sun-dried tomatoes would make this more amazing."
Serving: 4 | Prep: 5m | Ready in: 30m

Ingredients

- 4 medium potatoes, peeled and cubed
- 1 tbsp. butter
- 1/4 cup milk, or as needed
- 1 tbsp. basil pesto

Direction

- In a saucepan, add the potatoes with enough of water to cover. Boil, cook for about 10 minutes until they get tender. Drain, add milk and butter, mashing until the mixture reaches your preferred texture. Blend in pesto then serve.

Nutrition Information

- Calories: 216 calories;
- Total Carbohydrate: 38.2 g
- Cholesterol: 10 mg
- Total Fat: 5.1 g
- Protein: 5.5 g
- Sodium: 69 mg

360. Yummy Vegan Pesto Classico

"You can switch dairy for nutritional yeast. Freeze very well. Add sun-dried tomato slices for extra flavor."
Serving: 16 | Prep: 15m | Ready in: 15m

Ingredients

- 1/3 cup pine nuts
- 2/3 cup olive oil
- 5 cloves garlic
- 1/3 cup nutritional yeast
- 1 bunch fresh basil leaves
- salt and pepper to taste

Direction

- In a skillet, cook pine nuts on medium heat until lightly toasted, constantly stirring.
- In a food processor, slowly mix basil, nutritional yeast, olive oil, garlic and pine nuts, processing until smooth. Season with pepper and salt.

Nutrition Information

- Calories: 106 calories;
- Total Carbohydrate: 1.7 g
- Cholesterol: 0 mg
- Total Fat: 10.6 g
- Protein: 2.2 g
- Sodium: 1 mg

361. Zoodle Vegetable Bake

"This veggie casserole is made with zoodles, peppers, broccoli mixed with mushrooms, and other veggies. It is topped with mozzarella cheese and baked. It is a little runny; so, I use a slotted spoon to serve."
Serving: 8 | Prep: 30m | Ready in: 1h7m

Ingredients

- 1/4 cup avocado oil
- 1/2 cup butter
- 3 cloves garlic, minced, or more to taste
- 2 zucchini
- 1 large head broccoli, broken into florets
- 10 mushrooms, stemmed and sliced, or more to taste
- 6 mini bell peppers, sliced
- 15 leaves basil, or to taste, divided
- 1 large tomato, diced
- 1/4 cup tomato sauce
- 1/2 tsp. oregano, or to taste
- salt and ground black pepper to taste
- 10 slices fresh mozzarella cheese, or to taste

Direction

- Start preheating oven to 400 deg F or 200 deg C. Use avocado oil to grease a 9x13-in. pan.
- In a frying pan, melt butter on medium heat, 2 minutes. Mix in garlic.
- Use a spiralizer to slice zucchini into noodles.
- In a big bowl, mix broccoli, half the basil leaves, mushrooms, zucchini noodles, and bell peppers. Mix in the butter mixture until well blended.
- Put the veggie mixture in the greased pan; layer with tomatoes. Put pepper, tomato sauce, salt, and oregano on top. Put the remaining basil leaves in pan; layer with mozzarella cheese. Use aluminum foil to cover.
- Put in oven and bake for 20-30 minutes or until cheese melts. Use heatproof gloves or an oven mitt to take the aluminum foil off. Continue baking until cheese is bubbling and vegetables are tender, 15-30 minutes.

Nutrition Information

- Calories: 301 calories;
- Total Carbohydrate: 8.3 g
- Cholesterol: 58 mg
- Total Fat: 26.3 g
- Protein: 9.3 g
- Sodium: 211 mg

362. Zucchini Cucumber Gazpacho

*""There is nothing perfect rather than enjoying this cool
and healthy soup in the summer.""*
Serving: 4 | Prep: 15m | Ready in: 45m

Ingredients

- 2 cucumbers - peeled, seeded, and cubed
- 2 zucchini, cubed
- 3 tbsps. lemon juice
- 8 basil leaves
- salt and ground black pepper to taste
- 1/4 cup yogurt

Direction

- In the food processor, combine pepper, salt, basil leaves, lemon juice, zucchini and cucumbers together; whisk until smooth. Transfer into a bowl; mix in yogurt.
- Keep it in a refrigerator for at least 30 minutes. Serve.

Nutrition Information

- Calories: 37 calories;
- Total Carbohydrate: 7.7 g
- Cholesterol: < 1 mg
- Total Fat: 0.5 g
- Protein: 2.2 g
- Sodium: 58 mg

363. Zucchini Foil Packets

"A healthy and yummy dish!"
Serving: 4 | Prep: 10m | Ready in: 25m

Ingredients

- 1/4 cup unsalted butter, melted
- 1/4 cup freshly grated Parmesan cheese
- 1 tsp. dried basil
- 1 tsp. dried oregano
- Kosher salt and freshly ground black pepper, to taste
- 4 zucchini, cut into 1/4-inch rounds

- 2 tbsps. chopped fresh parsley leaves
- Reynolds Wrap® Heavy Duty Aluminum Foil

Direction

- Preheat charcoal or gas grill to high heat.
- Whisk oregano, basil, parmesan and butter together. Add pepper and salt to taste.
- Distribute the zucchini on 3-4 sheets of Reynolds rap heavy-duty aluminum foil. Put butter mixture on zucchini. Bring the side of the foil up; fold the ends and top of the foil twice, sealing the packet. Leave room for heat circulation inside.
- On the grill, put foil packets. Cook for 15-20 minutes till just cooked through.
- Immediately serve. If desired, garnish with parsley.

Nutrition Information

- Calories: 145 calories;
- Total Carbohydrate: 4.7 g
- Cholesterol: 35 mg
- Total Fat: 13.2 g
- Protein: 3.6 g
- Sodium: 191 mg

364. Zucchini Lasagna

*""I am so delighted of this remarkable concoction because
everyone loves its wonderful taste. You can't go wrong
with the mixture of cream cheese, zucchini and noodles.""*
Serving: 12 | Prep: 30m | Ready in: 1h40m

Ingredients

- 9 lasagna noodles
- 3 cubes chicken bouillon
- 2 cups boiling water
- 1/2 cup butter
- 1 large onion, finely chopped
- 2 tsps. minced garlic
- 1/2 cup all-purpose flour
- 1 tsp. salt
- 1 1/2 cups milk

- 6 oz. cream cheese, cubed
- 2 large carrots, finely chopped
- 1/2 cup chopped fresh basil
- 1/2 tsp. ground black pepper
- 2 cups small curd cottage cheese, divided
- 1 large zucchini, cut into 1/8-inch thick rounds
- 1 cup grated Parmesan cheese, divided
- 2 cups shredded mozzarella cheese, divided

Direction

- Let oven warm up to 350°F or to 175°C. Prepare a 9x13-inch baking sheet and coat with grease.
- Let a pot of salted water boil then cook lasagna noodles one by one. Over medium heat, slowly stir noodles to restrain from sticking to each other. Let it boil for 8 to 9 minutes until al dente. Use strainer to drain and let it set in the sink.
- In the boiling water, melt bouillon cube and put aside.
- Dissolve butter in a big skillet over medium fire then stir onion and garlic until brown for ten minutes. Lower down heat if needed to refrain burning the vegetables. In the same skillet, mix in flour and then add chicken bouillon mixture then add milk little by little while stirring to make the sauce smooth. Mix in cream cheese then stir until it melts and combines into the sauce. Mix in black pepper, basil and carrots; lower heat and let it simmer until just under a boil. Take off from the heat.
- Even out one cup of sauce into the bottom of the baking dish. On top, arrange 3 lasagna noodles. Even out one cup of cottage cheese and then pour one more cup of the sauce. Halve the sliced zucchini and then spread on top of the sauce. Dash it with 1/3 cup of parmesan cheese. Dash 2/3 cup of mozzarella cheese. Create two more layers and finish it off with 3 lasagna noodles, a cup of sauce and remaining 1/3 Parmesan cheese and 2/3 cup mozzarella cheese. Then wrap dish with a foil.
- Let bake in a warmed up oven until it becomes hot and forms bubbles for about 35 minutes. Take off foil and put it back inside the oven.

Allow it to bake for another 15 minutes until cheese becomes golden brown. Wait for 10 minutes to cool and then serve.

Nutrition Information

- Calories: 349 calories;
- Total Carbohydrate: 24.4 g
- Cholesterol: 62 mg
- Total Fat: 20.4 g
- Protein: 17.7 g
- Sodium: 975 mg

365. Zucchini Ribbon And Spinach Saute

"A dish made with zucchini that's perfect to serve with fresh grilled fish."
Serving: 4 | Prep: 15m | Ready in: 25m

Ingredients

- 2 tbsps. olive oil, or more as needed
- 1 zucchini, sliced into long ribbons with vegetable peeler or knife
- 2 cloves garlic, minced
- 2 cups baby spinach, or more to taste
- 1/2 cup thinly sliced basil leaves
- 2 tbsps. sunflower seeds
- 1 tsp. salt
- 1/2 tsp. ground black pepper
- 1 tsp. extra-virgin olive oil, or more as needed

Direction

- In a big skillet, heat the olive oil on medium heat, then add garlic and zucchini into the hot oil. Turn the garlic and zucchini using tongs to coat it with oil for about 30 seconds. Mix in spinach and let it cook for 2 minutes. Add pepper, salt, sunflower seeds and basil and let it cook for about 2 minutes until it becomes soft. Place onto a big platter and drizzle extra-virgin olive oil on top prior to serving.

Nutrition Information

- Calories: 112 calories;
- Total Carbohydrate: 3.9 g
- Cholesterol: 0 mg
- Total Fat: 10.4 g
- Protein: 2.2 g
- Sodium: 599 mg

Index

A

Alfalfa sprouts, 202

Allspice, 178

Almond, 23, 46, 63, 93–94, 166, 175–177

Almond milk, 176

Anchovies, 72

Anise, 32–33, 129

Apple, 3–4, 26, 77, 99, 175, 186, 202

Apple juice, 186

Arborio rice, 81

Artichoke, 3–4, 6–7, 15–16, 32, 66, 68, 76, 124–126, 135, 187, 189–190, 198

Asparagus, 3–6, 18, 23, 32, 88–89, 105–106, 109–111, 113, 122, 138

Avocado, 3, 5–6, 17, 20–21, 46, 77–78, 100–101, 121, 142, 168–169, 203–204

B

Bacon, 3–7, 13, 20–22, 24, 30, 63, 80, 83, 95, 110, 141, 169–170, 187, 195

Bagel, 6, 42, 146

Baguette, 3, 12, 27, 119, 152

Baking, 11–12, 18–19, 23–25, 27, 34–35, 38, 40, 43, 51, 56–57, 63–64, 66, 68–70,
74–75, 79, 84–85, 89–90, 96, 98, 103–104, 108–110, 113, 116, 118–119, 121, 123, 127–128, 130–131, 134, 142–146, 151–153, 156–165, 169, 179, 183, 188–189, 199, 204–205

Baking powder, 63, 68–69

Balsamic vinegar, 11, 25, 32, 38, 41–42, 45–46, 63–64, 69–70, 78, 91, 93, 112–113, 119, 125, 127–128, 133, 135, 137, 140, 142, 146–148, 158–159, 162, 165, 172, 177, 189, 197–198

Banana, 3, 26, 175

Basil, 1, 3–9, 11–206

Basmati rice, 109–110

Bay leaf, 12–13, 26, 190–191, 195–196

Beans, 3, 5, 12–13, 17, 19–20, 32–33, 36, 39, 53, 81–82, 90–91, 96, 99, 106–107, 109, 126–127, 147, 152, 172–173, 179, 193, 195, 200–201

Beef, 3, 6, 32–33, 36, 43, 48, 60, 90, 117–118, 123, 129, 150, 156, 164, 167–168, 172–173, 181, 200

Beer, 5, 40, 97–98

Black beans, 172

Black pepper, 11–12, 15–26, 29–30, 32–34, 36–38, 40–43, 45, 49–57, 60–63, 65–73, 77, 80–82, 85, 87, 89–94, 96,

W

Y

Z

Conclusion

Thank you again for downloading this book!

I hope you enjoyed reading about my book!

If you enjoyed this book, please take the time to share your thoughts and post a review on Amazon. It'd be greatly appreciated!

Write me an honest review about the book – I truly value your opinion and thoughts and I will incorporate them into my next book, which is already underway.

Thank you!

If you have any questions, **feel free to contact at:** _msingredient@mrandmscooking.com_

Ms. Ingredient

www.MrandMsCooking.com

Printed in Great Britain
by Amazon

14168139R00127